ENGLAND SINCE THE INDUSTRIAL REVOLUTION
1815–1935

ENGLAND SINCE THE INDUSTRIAL REVOLUTION
1815 – 1935

A SIMPLE HISTORY

J. HAMPDEN JACKSON
Author of
Europe Since the War · *The Post-War World*

LONDON
VICTOR GOLLANCZ LTD
1936

Printed in Great Britain by
The Camelot Press Ltd., London and Southampton

CONTENTS

I. THE COMING OF THE MACHINE   p. 13
The New Farms—Machines for Spinning and Weaving—Coal and Iron—Roads and Canals—The Plight of the Workers—The Abuse of Child Labour.

II. YEARS OF DISTRESS, 1815–30   p. 28
Results of the War—The Romantics—William Cobbett—Robert Owen—The Evangelicals—The Regency—Riots and Repression—Co-operatives and Trade Unions.

III. THE VIENNA SETTLEMENT AND AFTER, 1815–30   p. 45
The Peace Settlement—England's Foreign Policy—Castlereagh and the Congress System—Canning's Commercial Policy—The New World—The Eastern Question—Revolutions of 1830.

IV. THE WHIG REFORMS, 1830–41   p. 64
Parliamentary Reform—Humanitarian Reforms—The New Poor Law—Municipal Reform—The Consolidated Trades Union—The People's Charter.

V. THE EARLY VICTORIAN AGE, 1837–50   p. 78
The Tractarians—The Political Economists—The Two Nations—Irish Immigration—Peel's Financial Reforms—The Repeal of the Corn Laws—The End of Chartism—The Railway Age.

VI. AN EMPIRE IN THE MAKING, 1815–70   p. 98
The Empire in 1815—Wakefield and the Colonial Reformers—The Durham Report—India: annexations and reforms—Mutiny—Trade with the Far East—Trade with the White Colonies.

CONTENTS

VII. REVOLUTION IN EUROPE, 1830–71   *p.* 115
Palmerston—The Revolutions of 1848—The Russo-Turkish War, 1853–56—The Crimea—Italian Unity—The American Civil War—German Unity—The Paris Commune.

VIII. THE MID-VICTORIAN AGE, 1850–74   *p.* 131
The Bases of Prosperity—Gladstone and Finance—Disraeli and the Second Reform Bill—Gladstone's First Ministry—Mid-Victorian Comfort—Mid-Victorian Culture—The First "Great Depression."

IX. EMPIRES OR NATIONS ? 1874–86   *p.* 149
Disraeli's Social Reforms—The Route to India—Eastern Question again—Discovery of Africa—The Zulu War—Gladstone's Second Ministry—Egypt and the Sudan—Failure of Gladstone's Policy.

X. THE LIBERATION OF IRELAND, 1815–1935   *p.* 166
The Grievances of the Irish—O'Connell and Catholic Emancipation—Young Ireland and the Famine—The Fenians and the Land League—Gladstone and Home Rule—Ulster and the Irish Nationalists—The Irish Free State.

XI. THE LATE VICTORIAN AGE, 1886–1906   *p.* 182
Rhodes in Africa—The South African War—The Grab for Africa—Joseph Chamberlain—Free-Trade *versus* Tariff Reform—The Passing of Victorianism—The Emancipation of Women.

XII. THE WORKING-CLASS MOVEMENT, 1880–1913   *p.* 199
Co-operation and Trade Unionism—English Socialism—The New Unions—The I.L.P.—The Fabian Society—Conservative Reforms for the Workers—Liberals' Social Reforms—The Parliament Act—Strikes of 1911–12.

CONTENTS

XIII. THE CAUSES OF THE GREAT WAR *p. 217*
Competing Empires—Germany's Industrial Revolution—Germany's Needs: Colonies and a Navy—*Pièces de Résistance*: Morocco and the Near East—Preparation for War—The Balkan Crisis.

XIV. THE GREAT WAR, 1914–18 *p. 232*
War in the Open—The War of Blockade—Jutland and the Somme—The Submarine Campaign and Nivelle's Offensive—The Russian Revolution—Germany *Contra Mundum*—The Cost.

XV. THE VERSAILLES SETTLEMENT AND AFTER, 1919–35 *p. 250*
The Peace Treaties—The League of Nations—The Mandate System—The New Europe—The Years of Plenty—The World Depression—The Versailles Settlement Fails.

XVI. YEARS OF TRANSFORMATION, 1918–35 *p. 267*
The Post-War Slump — The Gold Standard — The "General" Strike—The Crisis of 1931—The End of *Laisser-faire*—The New British Empire—Conclusion: the Second Industrial Revolution.

APPENDICES:
I. The Social Services	288
II. Local Government	289
III. Overseas Investment	293

LIST OF MAPS AND DIAGRAMS

MAPS

Europe in 1815	*page* 47
The Eastern Question	58
Industrial Britain	96
Europe in 1878	153
South Africa	157
Europe in Africa	189
Europe in Asia	219
The Western Front	234
The Great War	238
Post-War Europe	254

DIAGRAMS

Growth of Population of England and Wales	*page* 17
Exports from the United Kingdom, 1850–75	133
British Industrial Output and Shipping, 1850–73	135
Real Wages, 1790–1904	143
British Overseas Trade, 1913–34	277
Nature of British Imports and Exports	285

PREFACE

THIS BOOK is intended for people knowing little or nothing of English history who want to find out something of the causes of present discontents, and something of the immediate past, apart from which the present must remain incomprehensible.

Rather more than a century ago the people of England embarked on a new stage in their development. They adopted the Machine, and rapidly and painfully readjusted their whole way of life in accordance with it. To-day we are beginning to see that these methods of readjustment are inadequate; we are overthrowing the policy of *laisser-faire* which has been our gospel for a hundred years. This is not the time to predict what the next gospel will be, but perhaps it is the right time to survey the age which fathered it—the first machine-age which, for good or for evil, is passed.

The author is indebted to many people for help with this book. Particularly he would like to thank Mr. C. E. Carrington, Mr. K. C. Boswell and Mr. P. D. Whitting who read the manuscript and made most useful suggestions, Mr. E. R. Roper Power and Mr. A. R. B. Fuller who read the proofs, and Mary Nicholson who drew the maps and diagrams.

Chapter I: THE COMING OF THE MACHINE

The New Farms – Machines for Spinning and Weaving – Coal and Iron – Roads and Canals – The Plight of the Workers – The Abuse of Child Labour.

WHEN THE LAST GREAT WAR but one came to an end, in 1815, Englishmen found to their surprise that they were living in a new world. It seemed that in the twenty-two years during which they had been at war with revolutionary France the whole face of the country had changed.

Actually the change had begun far back in the eighteenth century—all changes come slowly, it is only the realisation of them that is sudden. The typical Englishman, when the long reign of George III (1760–1820) began, was an independent villager, working his small holding to raise enough food to keep his family. Often he had common rights—the right of grazing his animals on the common land. Sometimes he had a strip or two of land on the open fields which were cultivated according to the ancient custom of the manor, one year under winter wheat, one year under spring oats or barley, the third year fallow. The typical villager worked hard and long, with little thought of profit and none of progress; he was content to live the life which his ancestors had lived for generations. For his womenfolk, when the elaborate house-work was done, there was often enough a little money to be earned in cottage industries—spinning the wool, perhaps, which the merchants brought round on their pack-horses. For his sons, if he had more than his holding could support, there were openings as craftsmen in the village—as smith, wheelwright, thatcher, carpenter, miller, or the like; or else if they had no calling for a craft they might go as labourers to one of the bigger farms where they were lodged and fed, at the board of the farmer. His family was largely self-supporting: they still baked their own bread, brewed their own ale, made their own clothes, milked their own cow, killed and cured their own meat, grew their own vegetables, cut their own fuel. And for the other things he wanted he rarely went outside his own village.

The New Farms. Now all that was disappearing. Three thousand Acts of Parliament, passed during the reign of George III by the aristocracy of landowners who ruled Great Britain, had allowed landowners to enclose strip after strip in the open fields and acre after acre of the poor man's common. One-fifth of the land of England was enclosed in this way until by 1815 the independent small-holder had almost vanished. Nothing remained now of the open fields, and little of the commons except a few blasted heaths. The typical villager was independent no longer. Deprived of his grazing rights for cow and horse and pig, deprived of his right to cut turf and gather wood on the common, he was obliged to go and work as a hind (agricultural labourer is the modern phrase) for the landowner or his tenant farmer. The farmers no longer fed and lodged their labourers; they built tiny cottages which they rented to them, with perhaps a patch of vegetable garden. " Why do not farmers *feed* and *lodge* their workpeople as they did formerly ? " asked William Cobbett. " Because they cannot keep them upon so little as they give them in wages. That is the real cause of the change." The typical countryman was dependent now on the wages he received for his labour on the big farms. These wages amounted in most cases to no more than a shilling a day. And prices were rising fast: the price of bread was doubled during the war years. This was not the end of the countryman's misfortunes. There was no longer any spinning-work for his womenfolk—that, as we shall see later, was now being done in mills; and the village craftsmen were being driven out of work by machine-made goods sent down from the towns.

THE COMING OF THE MACHINE

Meanwhile the landowners had prospered exceedingly; a few thousand of them now owned all the good agricultural land in England. They had learned new methods of agriculture. They had learned how to plant turnips, swedes and mangels, to rest the land between crops of corn; these root-crops provided food for the cattle during the winter months so that the farmers were able to keep their herds alive instead of killing off all but a few head every autumn, as had been the custom from time immemorial. They adopted machines to do much of the work which had before been done by hand: a drill-machine for sowing, a horse-drawn hoe, a threshing machine worked first by oxen and later by water-mill. The small-holder, who could not raise the capital necessary for these improved methods, and who would probably have been too conservative to adopt them anyway, had in many cases to sell his holding. Swollen by Enclosures and by purchase, the landowners' farms became large units: a hundred to three hundred acres was considered a medium-sized farm in England at a time when twelve to fifty acres passed as a medium-sized farm in Germany. Thanks to the new methods they became efficient units: Thomas Coke (1752–1842), a Norfolk landowner, increased the rent of his land by lavish expenditure and bold experiment from £2,200 to £20,000 a year, and William Bakewell, a Leicestershire farmer, raised flocks and herds which made his name a household word wherever stock was bred.

These improvements, together with the high prices which every war sets upon agricultural produce, made the farmers a newly rich class. They bought pink coats and rode to hounds with the gentry. They stocked their covers with pheasants and joined the landowners in pressing for more stringent Game Laws and in setting spring-guns to trap poachers. The spring-guns, which often proved fatal to game-keepers as well as to poachers, were made illegal in 1824, but the Game Laws stayed. Poaching remained punishable by seven years' transportation to the Antipodes, and villagers, being deprived of land and beasts, sometimes starved on one side of a hedge while, on the other, food enough for them all was preserved for the sport of landowner and farmer.

At the beginning of the nineteenth century England was the first agricultural country in the world. It was well for her that she was, for she had now many more mouths to feed. The most startling fact of all to the post-war generation was the increase in the population. It had been imagined that the population of Great Britain was stable at a figure somewhere around 7 millions; but in 1801 when the first census was taken it was discovered that there were over 10 millions, and the census of 1811 showed this figure to have increased by another 2 millions, and that of 1821 by 2 millions more.

Agriculture had become a most prosperous industry, prosperous for all except the labourer. He, in many cases, found himself a pauper. If he were in work, his wages were often inadequate to support his family. If he were out of work, there was nothing for him but to apply to the parish for relief. He might not leave his parish to seek work elsewhere—that was barred by a series of Settlement Acts. His parish might offer him one of two forms of solace. One was the workhouse, which in those days was a form of prison for the aged, the infirm and the young.

> *Theirs is yon House that holds the Parish-Poor,*
> *Whose walls of mud scarce bear the broken door;*
> *There, where the putrid vapours, flagging, play,*
> *And the dull wheel hums doleful through the day;*
> *There Children dwell who know no Parents' care;*
> *Parents, who know no Children's love, dwell there ...*
> *The Lame, the Blind, and, far the happiest they!*
> *The moping Idiot and the Madman gay.*[1]

The other form of relief was the Speenhamland scale. In 1795 the Berkshire magistrates had met at the Pelican Inn at Speen (now part of Newbury) and had drawn up a scale of allowances for the needy to make a man's earnings up to 3s. a week for himself and 1s. 6d. for his wife and each

[1] Crabbe.

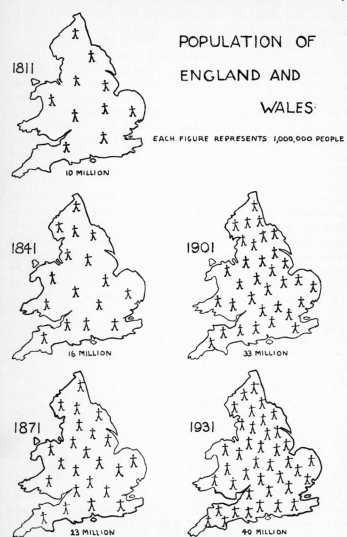

additional member of his family. This scale, drastically reduced, was adopted in most parts of the country, until by 1815 one-tenth of the population was receiving gifts of money " from the rates." It had the advantage of saving the villagers from starvation and the propertied-classes from revolution. But it demoralized the labourer by making him dependent on charity instead of a decent wage, it pandered to the farmer by encouraging him to pay less than a living wage to his labourers on the understanding that their wages would be made up out of public money, and it ruined the struggling small-holder by making necessary an increase in the rates which he could not afford to pay.

Machines for Spinning and Weaving. The character of the countryside was changing, but that was nothing to the transformation which was coming over the towns. In 1801 there was only one big town, London, with its 900,000 inhabitants. No other had a tenth that number and only six had more than 50,000.[1] The rest were little country towns existing as markets for the produce of the villages and as centres of manufacture, in the literal sense of handicrafts. There were no exporting industries worth the name when George III's reign began, except the woollen industry. In those days the only English products known the world over were the fine cloths of the West Country and East Anglia and the coarser cloths of Yorkshire. Lancashire was making fustians—mixtures of cotton and linen—and Birmingham metal goods, the first Wedgwood works had just been built at Burslem, but there was still no considerable export of cotton, metalwork or crockery, nor yet of iron and coal. Nor was England importing any of the necessities of life except sugar, which came from the plantations of the West Indies. In essentials England was still a self-sufficient nation.

[1] Manchester–Salford (counted as one), Liverpool, Birmingham, Southwark, Bristol and Leeds. In 1931 London had 8,000,000, Birmingham over a million and there were 110 English towns with over 50,000.

THE COMING OF THE MACHINE

Almost imperceptibly a change was coming which was to revolutionize industry and turn England from a country of villagers to a country of townsmen. That change was the invention of new machines. As might have been expected, the first improved machines were for spinning. In 1764 Richard Hargreaves, a poor and illiterate Lancashire weaver, invented a machine called the Spinning Jenny (gin means engine) by which eight, and later a hundred, spindles, could be worked by one person. Four years later Arkwright, a travelling barber, invented a water-frame for spinning on rollers. In 1779 Crompton, a working weaver like Hargreaves, produced a machine called the Mule (because it was a cross between jenny and water-frame) which made possible the spinning of a finer and more uniform thread.

Soon the spinning machines were turning out more yarn than the weavers could deal with and inventors began to turn their minds to applying machinery to weaving. As early as 1733 John Kay had invented an appliance called the Flying Shuttle for throwing the shuttle over the loom. In 1789 Edmund Cartwright, a scholarly parson, patented a loom that could be driven by machinery. It was many years before the power-loom replaced the hand-loom in the wool industry, but by the seventeen-eighties Arkwright, now a prosperous capitalist, had set up a mill where the new inventions were to turn out cotton cloth by water-power.

The first effect of the coming of the machine was to revolutionize the cloth industry in a number of ways. Machinery made possible for the first time in England the manufacture of pure cotton cloth. The cotton industry thus created became mechanized much more rapidly than the woollen industry which had its old traditions and plant to hamper it.

Secondly, the use of water- instead of man-power meant that industry had to move to parts of England where water-power was available. Cotton-mills were set up in Lancashire where there were streams running down from the Pennines to drive the machinery and where the climate was wet enough to keep the cotton-yarn moist. Woollen-mills were set up in Yorkshire beside the East Pennine streams and near the sheep-grazing districts of the Wolds.

Thirdly, machines involved the growth of a new class of capitalist-manufacturer, that is of men who bought raw materials and machines and hired workers to manufacture them into finished goods. The clothier of the old days of the West Country cloth industry had owned the raw material, yet the spindles and looms were the property of the workers themselves. But the workers could not afford to buy the new machines. Only men with spare capital could do that. Country gentlemen, rich farmers and shopkeepers, anyone who had a little money put by or who could borrow some bought gins and looms, built mills and factories and set up as manufacturers. Under this capitalist system expansion and improvement were possible in a way they had never been before, but the workers became dependent on the capitalists. They were no longer craftsmen owning their own tools; they had nothing now but their hands. In the countryside wage-labourers had already replaced the smallholders; now in the towns wage-earning factory " hands " were beginning to replace the craftsmen.

The next stage in the Industrial Revolution was the discovery of a new source of power. For thousands of years mankind had used four sources of power and four only: man-power, horse-power, wind-power and water-power. Steam-power had been known since the days of classical Greece but no use had been made of it, unless one counts the steam-engines which pumped the water out of mines in the seventeenth century. But now that machines were in existence which seemed to cry out for a new power to drive them, a number of Englishmen bent their minds to the problem of applying steam to industry. The most successful of these inventors was James Watt who produced a steam-engine which drove a piston attached to a crank: the crank turned a wheel and power from the wheel was transmitted by belts to the machine. Watt went into partnership with a capitalist called Matthew Boulton and in 1775 the firm of

Watt and Boulton began to manufacture steam-engines in Birmingham. Ten years later the first steam-engines were driving spinning machines.

Coal and Iron.
The new machines were made of iron and steel and the new engines were fuelled with coal. If iron-ore and coal had not been available in England the Industrial Revolution would have ended when it began, with a few ingenious inventions. Iron had been mined in England from prehistoric times. Whenever it was found near an oak-forest it was smelted with charcoal derived from the oak, worked into pigs of soft metal and wrought with the hammer into shape. The great iron district was the Weald of Sussex, but by the eighteenth century the oak-woods of the Weald were giving out, and iron-masters, casting about for new ways of melting iron now that the demand for their material was increasing so rapidly, hit upon the method of melting the ore with coal. They moved from the forests to the coal-fields of the Midlands and the North, taking with them many of the Weald ironworkers and their families, as the prevalence of Sussex names and phrases in Northern England to-day can prove. Here they wrought iron for the new industrial purposes, making pistons and cranks instead of the fire-irons and gates of olden days, and cast huge pieces of iron into moulds for girders for factories and the first iron bridges, and later for rails for locomotives and plates for ships. A new " Black Country " came into existence in Staffordshire and Worcestershire, and whole districts of Lanarkshire, Northumberland, Durham and Yorkshire became black in everything except name.

This new use of coal which brought the ironworkers from the forests to the mines also brought the factory-workers from the rivers to the growing towns round the coal-fields. Cotton and woollen manufacturers moved their mills from the rivers into new works where coal was cheap. Some Wiltshire weavers migrated to a group of mills in the North and called the place after their home-town, which was

Bradford-on-Avon. Bradford, Huddersfield and Leeds in the woollen industry, Liverpool and Manchester in the cotton grew into great industrial cities. Cotton was now the first of English industries: between 1748 and 1824 imports of raw cotton increased by 445 per cent. Wool was not far behind; the demand for raw wool was now far more than English sheep could provide, and between those same dates the wool imports increased by 280 per cent. Meanwhile the production of iron in England was increasing out of all reckoning—from a paltry 17,350 tons in 1740 to 400,000 tons in 1820 and to 1,348,000 in 1839.

Roads and Canals. This development of industry would have been impossible if there had not been taking place at the same time a development in the means of communication. In a country like England where the rivers are not navigable the simplest form of communication is by road. Yet the highways of England were deplorable. In theory it was the business of the parish to keep open every traditional right-of-way, and there was a parish officer responsible for seeing that the parishioners carried out the work. In fact the officer neglected his duties and the work was not done. In 1660 the Government hit upon a plan for farming out the business of roadmaking to private companies who thereby gained the right of setting turnpikes to levy a toll on the users of the road. The Turnpike Trusts, of which there were over a thousand in 1820, sometimes made good roads and occasionally made good money, but on the whole the roads were disgraceful and travel slow, dangerous and costly.

When the French wars ended improvements began under two engineers of genius. The General Post Office, anxious to speed up the mail-service between London and Dublin, set James Telford to build a highway from Chester to Holyhead. Through the hills which flank the north coast of Wales Telford blasted a way for his road and over the Conway River and the Menai Straits he built great iron suspension bridges. About the same time a Scottish engineer, John Macadam, was experimenting with a new method of road-surfacing which consisted of rolled and crushed granite, a process which came to be called "macadamizing." The new roads brought in a golden age of coaching. Coaches now could keep up an average of six to eight miles an hour over long distances. Every day some eighty coaches started from the White Horse Tavern in Piccadilly, and every night wayside inns received the travellers. Whole armies of grooms and ostlers, drivers, stable-boys and waiters sprang to life on the English roads.

Roads, though excellent for travellers and for mail, were of little use for heavy goods. Coal, for instance, could not be carried by road. How was coal to be brought cheaply between Liverpool and Manchester? It cost 12s. a ton to carry it by river along the Mersey and the Irwell. To solve this problem a rich coal-owner, the Duke of Bridgewater, employed an illiterate millwright called Brindley to build a canal. In 1773 Brindley had finished his canal. The aqueduct by which he carried it over the River Irwell was one of the wonders of the time. An age of feverish activity in canal-construction followed. Gangs of "navigators" (navvies) laboured with pick and shovel till by 1830 almost the whole canal system as it exists to-day had been completed. The Grand Junction Canal linked London with the industrial Midlands and the North. Three separate canals, rising by a system of locks to 500 and 650 feet over the Pennine passes, linked Lancashire and Yorkshire towns. Canal-transport cost a third of transport by road, and the speed—a steady 2½ m.p.h. by day and night—was not contemptible.

The great age of coaching and canals lasted from about 1780 to 1840. It was the first age of English industrialism. Then came the invention of the locomotive engine, and traffic left the roads and waterways for the railways. Gradually the bustling life of the roads, so well loved by Dickens and Borrow and Surtees, languished, not to rise again until the twentieth century and then in an unrecognizable form. Gradually the canals languished too; they have never been revived.

The Plight of the Workers. The invention of new machines and the development of steam-power came so suddenly that men were intoxicated by them. It seemed that God had put a new talent into the hands of whomever had money to invest and that he would be an unfaithful servant who did not make full use of his gift. There was no time to think of consequences; every moment was filled by making use of the new machines, building factories to house them and the men who tended them, and constructing roads and wagons, canals and barges to transport their products. The capitalists on the eve of this Industrial Revolution forgot one thing, the same thing that their successors forgot a century later when the great development of deadly gases and high explosives came: they forgot the work-people. And so it came about that the people became the servants of the new machines, instead of the machines the servants of the people.

Distress began in the country, where enclosures and the new methods of farming had reduced the villager to the status of a labourer dependent on his wages. His womenfolk had lost their earning power now that the spinning industry had been taken to the towns. William Cobbett, riding through England between 1821 and 1830, is the best reporter of rural conditions. In Leicestershire he saw cottages reduced to " hovels made of mud and straw, bits of glass or old cast-off windows, without frames or hinges frequently, and merely stuck in the mud wall. Enter them and look at the bits of chairs or stools, the wretched boards tacked together to serve for a table, the floor of pebble broken or of the bare ground, look at the thing called a bed and survey the rags on the backs of the inhabitants." In Hampshire, " I asked a man who was hedging on the side of the road how much he got a day. He said, 1s. 6d.: and he told me that the *allowed* wage was 7d. a day for the man and *a gallon loaf a week for the rest of his family*; that is to say, one pound and a quarter ounces of bread for each of them; and nothing more ! And this, observe, is one-third short of the bread allowance of gaols, to say nothing of the meat and clothing and lodging of the inhabitants of gaols." In Lincolnshire " I saw three poor fellows digging stone for the roads, who told me that they never had anything but bread to eat and water to wash it down. One of them was a widower with three children; and his pay was eighteenpence a day; that is to say, about three pounds of bread a day each for six days in the week; nothing for Sunday, nothing for lodging, washing, clothing, candlelight, or fuel ! Just such was the state of things in France on the eve of the Revolution ! "

In the new towns that sprung up round the centres of coal and iron the state of things was no better. They were slums from the day they were built. Writing of the new quarters of Manchester, Professor Nassau Senior wrote: " These towns have been created with the utmost disregard of everything except the immediate advantage of the speculative builder. A carpenter and builder unite to buy a series of building-sites and cover them with so-called houses. In one place we found a whole street following the course of a ditch, because in this way deeper cellars could be secured without the cost of digging, cellars not for storing wares or rubbish, but for dwellings for human beings. Not one house of this street escaped the cholera. In general the streets of these suburbs were unpaved, with a dung-heap or ditch in the middle; the houses are built back to back, without ventilation or drainage, and whole families are limited to the cover of a cellar or garret."

The hours of work in the new mines, mills and factories were dictated by the machines. To ensure the biggest profits furnaces must never be let out and machines must be kept running day and night; and so it came to pass that the usual working-shift was one of twelve hours—a day shift and a night shift. When the machinery was not run continuously, longer shifts were the rule: a thirteen- to sixteen-hour day was not uncommon, and this went on for six days a week for fifty-two weeks in the year. (The Bank Holidays Act was not passed until 1871.) Long hours had not been unknown in the eighteenth-century workshops, but in them there had been a friendly, family atmosphere, with smoking and singing, and breaks for parties and sports, and with holidays for feasts and slack times. In the new factories the atmosphere was very different: rigid discipline was the rule, with no talking and no whistling, and the doors of the shops shut —and often the windows too, for heating purposes—and fines for unpunctuality and untidiness and a dozen other misdemeanours. The word " work " began to take on a new sense of drudgery which it has never lost since.

The Abuse of Child Labour.

The greatest difficulty of the employers at the beginning of the century was to get enough people to do the work. At first employers found a cheap form of labour in children from the workhouses. These apprentice-children, as they were called, were consigned to their employers from the time they reached the age of about seven until they were twenty-one. During this period they were given no pay; often they were put up in a " prentice-house " near the factory and were set to work for as long as they could be kept awake every working day —with cleaning duties, as like as not, on Sundays. To all intents and purposes they were slaves.

By 1816 this abuse of apprentice-labour was restricted by Act of Parliament, but by that time employers had found a new source of child labour. The change from water- to steam-power meant a change from the country to the towns, and in the towns there were plenty of parents needy enough to be glad to put their children to work for a few extra pence. Paid labour was more satisfactory than prentice-labour. (One of the workhouses had refused to send apprentices unless one idiot was taken with every score of normal children supplied.) In the mines boys were set to draw the trucks of coal along the low galleries, harnessed to the truck by a girdle round the waist and a chain, and girls were used for opening and shutting the trap-doors which ventilated the mine. In the factories children worked as long and as hard as the adults. Parliamentary Commissioners collected abundant evidence on this point in

1833. "I was seven years of age," one witness said, "when I began to work at Bradley Mill near Huddersfield. The hours of labour were from five in the morning until eight at night, with an interval for rest and refreshment of thirty minutes, at noon.... There were about fifty children, of about the same age as I was. Strapping was the means by which the children were kept at work. It was the main business of one of the overlookers to strap the children up to this excessive labour." And Bradley Mill was no exception.

Even on these conditions parents were glad to put their children to work. There used to be a market in Bethnal Green every Monday and Tuesday morning where children were to be obtained on hire for 1s. 8d. a week for their parents and 2d. for "themselves and tea." It was common, too, to use children as chimney-sweeps, sending them like human brushes to clean chimneys too tortuous for stiffer tools. Parents used to sell their children outright to sweeps for two or three guineas and be glad of the money to save themselves from starvation.

From all this it must seem that the capitalists and employers of the age were monsters of callousness and iniquity. They were not. They were simply enterprising men who found themselves in control of machines for creating wealth the like of which the world had never seen. And they used the machines blindly and instinctively for their own profit. They were no more, and no less, to be blamed than the motorists of the early 1930's who drove their high-powered machines in such a way that 6,000 people were killed and 250,000 hurt every year on the open roads of England.

Chapter II: YEARS OF DISTRESS, 1815–30

Results of the War – The Romantics – William Cobbett – Robert Owen – The Evangelicals – The Regency – Riots and Repression – Co-operatives and Trade Unions.

In the old days when nations were self-contained and had little trade beyond their own borders, victory in war brought prosperity: there was loot and tribute to be wrung from the vanquished. But in modern times when nation trades with nation, victory, like defeat, must bring distress. There is no loot worth the taking; and tribute wrung by a commercial Power from its customers means loss of trade. The soldiers have to be found immediate civilian employment. The money borrowed in wartime has to be paid back by heavy taxation. The farmers who have been accustomed to high prices for wartime food have to get used to low prices again. The thousands of providers of the stores of war have to face the loss of public demand for their goods.

The Results of the War. This was the position of England after Waterloo. Peace brought the very opposite of prosperity. There was unemployment because 200,000 soldiers and sailors were looking for jobs at home. There was heavy taxation because of the National Debt—and this needs some explanation. The Government meets an emergency like war by calling for money. The money is not given, as one might suppose, out of the fullness of the people's hearts to tide the nation over a crisis: it is lent on the Government's guarantee to pay interest and is called the National Debt, though it is not the nation's debt to another nation but the Government's debt to the investors. These investors naturally belong to the richer classes. To pay their interest the Government has to tax the whole nation, and these taxes always prove most burdensome to the poor. During the war years the National Debt had increased from £247,000,000 to £880,000,000. In the Budget of 1814 over £37,500,000 were set aside as interest to be paid to investors in Government funds. " More than half the income of the nation," as the French historian Halévy has remarked, " was taken from the working classes and given to idle fundholders and civil and military officials." Later Budgets increased the burden of the working classes. The Income Tax, which is paid by the rich alone, was abolished in 1816. Indirect taxes, which are paid by rich and poor alike were increased. Sydney Smith, writing in 1820, complained that there were " taxes upon every article which enters into the mouth or covers the back or is placed under the foot. Taxes upon everything which is pleasant to see, hear, feel, smell, or taste. Taxes upon warmth, light and locomotion. Taxes upon everything on earth or under the earth, on everything that comes from abroad or is grown at home. . . . Taxes on the sauce which pampers the rich man's appetite, and the drug which restores him to health, on the ermine which decorates the judge, and the rope which hangs the criminal; on the poor man's salt and the rich man's spice; on the brass nails of the coffin and the ribands of the bride; at bed and board, couchant and levant we must pay. The schoolboy whips his taxed top; the beardless youth manages his taxed horse with a taxed bridle on a taxed road; and the dying Englishman, pouring his medicine which has paid 7 per cent into a spoon which has paid 15 per cent, flings himself back upon his chintz bed which has paid 22 per cent and expires in the arms of an apothecary who has paid £100 for the privilege of putting him to death. . . . His virtues are handed down to posterity on taxed marble, and he will then be gathered to his fathers to be taxed no more."

Heavy taxation was not the worst consequence of the war. During the war years business men and farmers had prospered, though the working classes, in the throes of the Industrial Revolution, had been wretchedly poor; after the war even business men and farmers knew bad times.

One cause of their distress was the failure of the British banking system. There were three types of bank at the beginning of the nineteenth century. First came the Bank of England. It was then, as it is now, a joint-stock company making a profit for its stockholders by carrying on the banking business of the Government as well as the business of an ordinary banker; but at that time it did not hold the reserves of the other banks as it does to-day. Then came the London banks which had developed out of goldsmiths' and other shops and which made their profit by guarding customers' deposits which they lent out at high rates of interest. Finally there were the country banks. These were not so much banks in our modern sense as rich private individuals (in many cases brewers, such as Tollemache) who lent their own bank-notes in return for interest in cash. They felt safe in issuing notes for much greater sums than they actually possessed, because it was reasonable to suppose that everyone would not demand cash for their notes at the same time. But when war ended nearly everyone did want cash, with the result that between 1814 and 1816 no less than 240 country banks stopped payment and 89 went into bankruptcy.

The farmers were in trouble for another reason. While Napoleon had been preventing the English from buying wheat on the continent the farmers at home had made their fortunes by getting famine prices for their wheat: the 4lb. loaf which cost 7*d.* or 8*d.* just before the war was fetching over 1*s.* 3*d.* by the end. But now that Napoleon was gone there was every prospect of the price being reduced by the arrival of cheap wheat from abroad. Instead of rejoicing at this prospect of plenty, Parliament, which was composed largely of landowners, hastened to pass measures which would keep out foreign wheat in the interest of the English farmer. In 1815 a Corn Law was passed forbidding the import of wheat unless the price was over 80*s.* a quarter. This is a very high price and it was rarely reached during the whole generation (1815–46) in which the Corn Laws were in force. Yet because of these laws and of a succession of bad harvests, bread remained scarce and dear, and the working classes had a new misfortune to add to those inflicted by the coming of the Machine.

It was precisely in the years which followed Waterloo that the Machine spread fastest and the misfortunes were felt most. It may well be asked if there was no one to tell the rulers of England what was happening, no one to call attention to the grinding misery of the poor. There was indeed: a number of men spent their lives in protesting, from every angle, against the abuses of the age. They were ignored or persecuted for their pains.

The Romantics. First the poets. Oliver Goldsmith had described the evils of enclosure as early as 1770 in *The Deserted Village*. No one minded because the village was in Ireland. John Clare, an English peasant, described similar evils in 1820 in a poem on the village of Helpstone; no one minded because Clare was insane. William Blake, a prophet as well as a poet, had seen the death of the soul of England in the Machine and the " dark, Satanic mills," and had called upon his generation " to build a new Jerusalem in England's green and pleasant land "; no one minded because Blake was a " mystic," which was considered not far different from being insane. Shelley protested in poem after poem against the materialism of the age[1]; no one minded because he was an " atheist "—he had been sent down from Oxford for expressing unorthodox religious opinions—and anyhow he was suspected of being a Jacobin. It was enough to call a person a Jacobin in those days to put him outside the pale of society; that word, like the word Bolshevik in our own time, was loaded with all the sins that revolutionaries had ever committed.

But poets are not to be judged by their effect upon politics; any political effect their work may have is felt not in their own age but in the next. The early nineteenth

[1] *Men of England, wherefore plough*
For the lords who lay ye low?
Wherefore weave with toil and care
The rich robes your tyrants wear?

century was a great age of English poetry. It was an age of literary *Romanticism*, which means an assertion of one's own intuitive convictions against the forms and conventions of the time. Typical of this Romantic attitude was John Keats (he died in 1828 when in his twenty-seventh year). Typical, too, were William Wordsworth and Samuel Taylor Coleridge who turned their backs on both the stale gossip of the London drawing-rooms and the whirr of the new machinery and retired to the Lake District, whence they published poems urging a new simplicity and a return of man to his natural sources of inspiration. Typical in another way was George Gordon, Lord Byron, who in 1824 went to fight for the liberty of Greece and lost his life of fever at Missolonghi.

Byron was the most popular poet of the age. He was alive to most of the abuses of the time but he was scarcely the man to remedy them; he preferred to shock Europe by his promiscuous love-affairs and his scathing attacks on the public figures of the time. His attacks on conventions and reputations carried no weight because they were so obviously intended to be startling. Englishmen read Byron and were shocked but not moved.

The most popular novelist of the age was Walter Scott, a Border landowner, whose long romantic stories of old times exactly suited the public taste. In the wild scenery and adventure of the Waverley novels the reading public could forget the disturbing circumstances of their own time. They took Scott's books as an antidote to the evils of the age.

William Cobbett. Meanwhile a more homely writer was doing yeoman service in the cause of reform. William Cobbett was a Surrey farmer's son, a vigorous country-bred Englishman who might, if he had had less intelligence, have posed as the model for John Bull. After a stormy career as a soldier he left the army in order to expose a financial scandal in his regiment and fled to France and to America. When he returned to England in 1802 he found that the country he had known as a lad was being changed by the Machine. There was no shadow of doubt for him that the change was for the worse. He set to work to attack the Machine and the regiment of profiteering ministers, capitalists, stockbrokers, fund-holders and manufacturers ("lords of the loom") which it had brought with it. These, which he called collectively "the *Thing*," he spent the rest of his days in damning. In 1809 he started to produce his weekly *Political Register* and continued it till his death in 1835. Working people clubbed together to buy the paper though it cost a shilling and a halfpenny, and in 1816, when the price was reduced to 2*d*., they bought it by the tens of thousands. Cobbett was the begetter of popular journalism but he was far more than a journalist. Often unfair and self-contradictory, he none the less wrote with the directness which is the essence of style and with a passion which makes him readable to-day. He loved the English country and the good workmanship and good living that it fostered, and he upheld those values to a generation which was denying them. More clearly than any of his contemporaries except the poets he saw the evil inherent in the capitalist *Thing*. "A national debt, and all the taxation and gambling belonging to it, have a natural tendency to draw wealth into great masses. These masses produce a power of *congregating* manufactures, and of making many work at them, for the *gain of a few*. The taxing government finds great convenience in these congregations. It can lay its hand easily upon a part of the produce; as ours does with so much effect. But the land suffers greatly from this, and the country must finally feel the effects of it. The country people lose part of their natural employment. The women and children, who ought to provide a great part of the raiment, have nothing to do. The field *must* have men and boys; but where there are men and boys there will be *women* and *girls*; and as the lords of the loom have now a set of real slaves, by the means of whom they take away a great part of the employment of the country-women and girls, these must be kept by the poor rates in whatever degree they lose employment through the lords of the loom. One would think that nothing could be much plainer than this; and yet you hear the *jolterheads* congratulating themselves upon the growth of Manchester, and such places!"

Robert Owen. Even more useful than Cobbett's exposures was the work done by another poor man's son, Robert Owen. Cobbett wanted to put the clock back to the old agricultural way of life; Owen wanted to put it forward and to use the Machines for providing a new standard of well-being for all classes. " I can make manufacturing pay," he said, " without reducing those whom I employ to misery and moral degradation." This sounded a wild paradox, for most employers assumed that they could make no adequate profits without sweating their workers.

After working as a shop-assistant from his tenth to his eighteenth year (during which time he often thought himself lucky to get five hours' sleep a night), Owen was fortunate to get a manager's job, and when he was twenty-nine he became a partner in the great cotton mill at New Lanark. From 1800 to 1825 Owen worked at making this mill the model for the world. When he came it was a typical sweatshop. There were nearly 500 apprentice-children, of five years old and upwards, who worked thirteen hours a day like the rest of the 1,600 inhabitants of the filthy village which the owners had thrown up round the mill. Robert Owen refused to employ any child under ten, he opened playgrounds and schools, he added a storey to the workers' houses so as to give every family a minimum of two rooms, he laid down streets and had the refuse collected regularly, he opened stores and sold provisions at cost price, thus saving the working people threepence in every shilling they spent. Instead of going bankrupt, as everyone had prophesied, New Lanark made handsome profits. Visitors flocked from all over Europe to see it; between 1815 and 1825 twenty thousand names were inscribed in the visitors' book, including that of the future Tsar Nicholas I of Russia. Robert Owen had given a triumphant demonstration of the possibilities of machine industry to benefit every class.

Yet no one imitated Robert Owen's example. Perhaps it

was that he went too far. He put forward a scheme known as " Mr. Owen's Plan " for Villages of Co-operation (which we to-day might call garden cities) proposing that communities of 500 to 1,500 people should build blocks of flats arranged on three sides of a square with the fourth side open to the sun, and with a green belt of park-land round the blocks, and beyond that factories and workshops. He sketched a plan by which each community was to produce its own food by working the land and to exchange the products of their community-factories for other necessities and for money to pay off the interest on the capital that had been borrowed to found the community. This was altogether too advanced for the times. Owen went to America and started a village called New Harmony, and though he returned to England and took a prominent part—as we shall see—in the working-class struggles of 1832–34, he had gone too far now to hope that his ideas would ever be taken up by the ruling class.

The Evangelicals. One of the main reasons for which their contemporaries distrusted Owen and Cobbett and the other men who wanted a *radical* reform of the system of Government was that these Radicals did not believe in Churches. While the Industrial Revolution was in its infancy Churches—or Chapels—had won a new hold on the hearts of the English and Welsh people. In those troubled times men needed forms of organized religion which would interpret the ways of God to man in a new way. They found what they wanted within the Established Church in Evangelicalism and outside it in Methodism. Each laid stress on the moral virtues and on the authority of the Bible rather than on sacramental grace and the authority of a Catholic Church. Between them the two parallel movements swept the country, so that not to belong to either involved a social stigma in the respectable middle and working classes. The most *influential* reformers of the time were the Evangelicals, particularly the little group known as the *Saints* or the *Clapham Sect*, who centred round William Wilberforce and his friends Thomas Clarkson, James Stephen and Zachary Macaulay. They believed that the working class should be taught to suffer their misfortunes with Christian fortitude. Wilberforce wrote: " that their more lowly path has been allotted to them by the hand of God; that it is their part faithfully to discharge its duties, and contentedly to bear its inconveniences; that the present state of things is very short; that the objects about which worldly men conflict so eagerly are not worth the contest; that the peace of mind, which Religion offers indiscriminately to all ranks, affords more true satisfaction than all the expensive pleasures that are beyond the poor man's reach; that in this view the poor have the advantage; that, if their Superiors enjoy more abundant comforts, they are also exposed to many temptations from which the poor are happily exempted." This clashed directly with Owen's view that the character of the poor could be transformed by bringing them up in decent conditions.

It was Wilberforce's view that prevailed: he gained the ear of the politicians and Owen lost it. He had devoted a lifetime to the art of arousing public opinion and bringing its pressure to bear upon the unrepresentative Governments of those days. Many lasting reforms owe their inception to Wilberforce: missions sent to the heathen, money devoted to teaching English children to read the Bible in Church-schools and Sunday-schools and, most famous of all, the abolition of slavery. The Anti-Slavery Society, formed by him and Thomas Clarkson in 1823, bore fruit ten years later —it was the year of Wilberforce's death—in the Act which made the employing of slaves illegal throughout the British Empire and devoted £200,000,000 to compensating the slave-owners for their loss. Planters were forbidden to work negroes for more than 45 hours a week. It is odd that Wilberforce and his friends were unconcerned by the fact that in their own country the whole working class were in what amounted to slavery, working 78 hours a week for the barest pittance.

The Regency Government. The suffering people of England could expect no sympathy from their rulers. Gone

YEARS OF DISTRESS

were the days when Tudor monarchs forced through Parliament Bills forbidding the enclosure of common land and ordering magistrates to fix a minimum wage for labourers in their districts. The Sovereign had now lost all contact with his people. King George III lived in retirement at Windsor, suffering from blindness, deafness and what the *Annual Register* for 1815 called "the alienation of his rational faculty." His place was taken by his eldest son George, first as Prince Regent (1811–20) and later as King George IV (1820–30). This Prince had better taste and a more amiable disposition than any ruler that the House of Hanover had so far given to England. Under his patronage John Nash built Waterloo Place, the Duke of York's Steps, Old Regent Street and the stately crescents of Regent's Park, and lesser architects transformed Windsor Castle and Buckingham Palace into their present forms. He suggested that Jane Austen should dedicate her novel *Emma* to him and he was pleased to confer a knighthood upon Walter Scott. Yet it was he who dragged the Crown of England into greater disrepute than it has known within modern times. Leigh Hunt wrote of him when he became Regent that he " was a violator of his word, a libertine over head and ears in debt and disgrace, a despiser of domestic ties, the companion of gamblers and demireps, a man who has just closed half a century without one single claim on the gratitude of his country or the respect of posterity." And Charles Lamb, another gentle critic, wrote verses describing him as " the Prince of Whales."[1] As a young man he had married a respectable Roman Catholic widow called Mrs. Fitzherbert —a union which was illegal under the Royal Marriage Act. Ten years later he repudiated the virtuous Mrs. Fitzherbert

---

[1] *No fatter fish than he*
Flounders round the polar sea.
See his blubbers—at his gills
What a world of drink he swills. . . .

Every fish of generous kind
Scuds aside or sinks behind;
But about his presence keep
All the Monsters of the Deep.

in order to contract a legitimate marriage with Caroline of Brunswick, an ill-washed and foul-mouthed German princess. He did not, however, give the Princess any reason to be faithful to him and she ran away to Italy with some disreputable friends. There she might have stayed in oblivion had not the Prince become King and she, by consequence, Queen of England. George was now faced with the alternative of acknowledging this creature as Queen or of getting Parliament to pass a Bill dissolving his marriage on the grounds of Caroline's infidelity. He chose the latter course, but the public was so indignant at the idea of the profligate George's posing as an injured husband, and the House was so much moved by Brougham's speech in the Queen's defence, that the Bill had to be dropped. Caroline would have continued to enjoy a tremendous popularity had she not returned to England and made a scene outside Westminster Abbey when the coronation ceremony was being performed within. This was too much for the British public. Opinion turned against her[1] and no one was sorry when she died in the following month (August 1821). By this time there was little or no respect left in England for the Royal Family.

George IV died nine years later and was succeeded by his brother, the Duke of Clarence, as King William IV (1830–37). William was the third son of George III (who had no less than fifteen children). The second son, Frederick Duke of York, had died in 1827 to the regret of no one except the soldiers, for whom he had done good work at the War Office. William IV had done no good work anywhere. He had filled the post of Lord High Admiral, and that was all. By the time he came to the throne the " Sailor-King " was a confirmed drunkard.

The Kings' ministers were almost as far out of contact with the people as the Kings themselves. Lord Liverpool was Prime Minister for fourteen long years and was remarkable

[1] *Gracious Queen, we thee implore*
To go away and sin no more,
And if that effort be too great,
To go away at any rate.

for nothing so much as his inability to understand the needs of the country. From 1815 to 1822 the only man of ability in his ill-famed Tory ministry was Lord Castlereagh, and he—the " cold-blooded, smooth-faced pallid miscreant " of Byron's poem—was too busy with making the Peace Treaties and conducting foreign policy to attend to the state of affairs at home. That business was left largely to Lord Eldon, the Chancellor, a self-made man who was unable to believe that anything could need reform in a world in which he had been able to rise from the ranks.

Riots and Repression.

It is not surprising that the working classes, despairing of reform, began to turn to rioting. During the war there had been attempts by workers to smash the machines which were taking honest men's jobs. The riots were reputed to have been started by Ned Ludd, a Leicester worker, who broke two stocking-frames in a fit of rage. Historians have laughed at Ned Ludd for being a village idiot but he did at least see the root of the evil; no one to this day has discovered how to introduce machinery without putting some workers out of a job. In his own day machine workers adopted his name, calling themselves Luddites and pretending that they were acting under orders of "General Ludd." There was an outburst of wrecking among the knitting-frame workers of Nottingham in 1812 which spread to Lancashire, Cheshire and Yorkshire. The culprits were treated with terrible severity, eight men being hanged after the assizes at Manchester and fourteen men at York.

In the distress which followed the war a new outbreak of Luddite risings occurred in the Midlands.[1] Rioting was spreading now to London itself.

[1] *The guilty may fear but no vengeance he aims*
At the honest man's life or estate.
His wrath is entirely confined to wide frames
And to those that old prices abate . . .
Let the wise and the great lend their aid and advice
Nor e'er their assistance withdraw
Till full fashioned work at the old-fashion price
Is established by Custom and Law.
       (From the song, *General Ludd's Triumph*.)

In December 1816 a crowd, fired by the teaching of Thomas Spence, a Radical bookseller, gathered in the Spa Fields outside London and marched in procession to the City, raiding gunsmiths' shops as they went, and getting as far as the Royal Exchange before they were dispersed by Matthew Wood, the Lord Mayor of London. Another incident occurred in the new year when a crowd mobbed the Regent on his return from opening Parliament and smashed the windows of his carriage.

The Government jumped to the conclusion that the country was on the verge of revolution. They took action, not by trying to redress the grievances of the people, but by repression and espionage. The *Habeas Corpus Act* was suspended in March 1817 to enable authorities to imprison suspects without charge or trial. In the same month a number of poor cotton workers from Lancashire, whose wages had been no more than three or four shillings a week, planned to walk to London to present a petition to the Regent. The March of the Blanketeers, as they were called from the rugs they took with them to sleep in, got no further than Macclesfield.

The Government still believed that treason was being plotted in the North and Midlands. They employed a spy, Mr. Oliver by name, to ferret it out. Oliver's methods took the form of preaching sedition and sending to the authorities the names of anyone who listened to him. In Nottingham he found a genial public-house braggart, Captain Brandreth, who talked of leading an insurrection. With encouragement from Oliver, Captain Brandreth led a party of rioters over the county border to Derbyshire where they were arrested. At the subsequent trials Brandreth and two others were sentenced to death and fourteen men to transportation. So ended the Derbyshire insurrection.

Naturally enough, discontent continued. In August 1819 a great crowd gathered in St. Peter's Fields, Manchester, to listen to Orator Hunt, a famous Radical leader. The magistrates were foolish enough to send a body of yeomanry to arrest Hunt, and then, seeing the yeomanry in danger of a buffeting, sent four troops of Hussars to disperse the crowd. In the mêlée that ensued five or six men were killed and seventy injured; the incident became known as the Manchester Massacre, or Peterloo.

It was at this point that Castlereagh and Sidmouth passed the notorious Six Acts for which they have gone to history as the destroyers of the liberties of Englishmen. The effect of these Acts was (1) to deprive defendants of the right of objecting to the framing of their accusation, (2) to render publishers of seditious libels liable to transportation, (3) to make drilling of civilians illegal, (4) to authorize magistrates to search houses and seize arms, (5) to suppress undesirable newspapers, and (6) to make it illegal to hold a public meeting without a magistrate's consent.

Co-operatives and Trade Unions.

The working class was thus deprived of most means of working legally for their own betterment. It is not surprising that a few extremists should have resorted to terrorism. A certain Arthur Thistlewood formed a plot to assassinate the Cabinet Ministers while at a dinner party; his plans were revealed by Edwards, a government spy, and the authorities raided the conspirators in a stable in Cato Street.

But the majority of the workers found honest and peaceful means of combining for their own good. Three great forms of working-class organisation date their origin from these years of distress. The first was the Friendly Societies or Benefit Clubs to which poor men contributed a few pence a week to funds out of which they would be paid relief in times of sickness or unemployment; there were said to be nearly 700,000 members of such societies in 1816. The second was the Co-operative Societies which began with the clubbing together of workers in certain districts to buy their provisions wholesale and to retail them themselves, thus cutting out shop-keepers' profits. This movement is often dated from 1844 when the Rochdale Pioneers founded their Society (as will be described in a later chapter on the Working-Class Movement) but as early as 1832 there were

500 Co-operative Societies in existence and they had a powerful champion in Robert Owen. It was in connection with these societies that the word Socialism first came into use.

The third and most effective form of working-class organization was the Trade Union. In the old days wages and conditions of work had been regulated by the magistrates. Any conspiracy on the part of either workers or masters to overthrow the magistrates' decision was made illegal under the Combination Acts. But early in the nineteenth century Parliament deprived the magistrates of their power over wages and apprentice-labour, thus leaving the employers with a free hand to dictate conditions of work. Instead of repealing the Combination Acts at the same time, Parliament let them be strictly enforced against employees—so that any protest on the part of the workers against low wages was treated as a crime—yet made no attempt to enforce them against employers who were in practice allowed to make agreements among themselves to keep wages low and hours long. Not only strikes but even petition for higher wages on the part of a few workers became an offence punishable by imprisonment. This did not prevent the growth of all manner of unions among the workers in various trades—the weavers and spinners of Dewsbury, for instance, had a union 5,000 strong in 1819— but they were secret and unlawful associations.

The revolutionary tendencies of these secret societies were obvious to everybody, and it was skilfully pointed out by Francis Place that they arose from the iniquities of the Combination Acts and that to repeal those Acts would be the way to end the danger. Francis Place was a tailor who had built up a successful business in the Charing Cross Road. After 1818 he left the conduct of the business to his son and devoted his energies to working for Radicalism. Many were the social reforms that had their origin in the little library behind Place's shop. After years of untiring agitation in collecting and arranging evidence and in getting it laid before the House of Commons, Place induced

YEARS OF DISTRESS

Parliament to repeal the Combination Acts in 1824. Trade Unions and strikes were henceforth legal.

Repeal was followed by disturbances which shocked Place as much as they frightened the Government. The Port of London was paralysed by a shipwrights' strike and in Glasgow and in Dublin " black-legs " (employees who went on working while their fellows were on strike) were actually murdered by trade-unionists. Place's work was now to persuade the Government not to make these outbreaks an excuse for going back on their reform of 1824. He was moderately successful: in 1825 a new Act was passed allowing unions and other combinations of workmen but forbidding " molestation or obstruction," in other words forbidding any attempt to induce a man to give up his job. So Trade Unions were legal but picketing, the only method by which a strike could hope to succeed, was not.

The industrial workers now had an instrument which they might in time learn to use to their own advantage, but for the present they were no better off. Conditions in the 1820's were actually worse than ever before and the agricultural workers turned to rioting for a way out of their sufferings. " Captain Swing " was their leader as " General Ludd " had been the leader of the industrial machine-wreckers (it is touching that both movements should have had to invent a mythical hero in their lack of a real leader). The " Swing " movement began in Kent and Sussex in the late summer of 1830 and spread to Berkshire and Buckinghamshire, to Hampshire and to Wiltshire, where it reached its height in November. The villagers demanded, in most cases, a wage of 2s. a day. Sometimes they burned ricks: sometimes they carried an unpopular official over the parish boundaries in a dung-cart: sometimes they set fire to a workhouse: more usually they broke up the new threshing machines. At first the farmers were in agreement with the labourers and promised higher wages, but Lord Melbourne, then Home Secretary, ordered stern treatment. And stern treatment there was: at the Winchester Assizes, though not one single life had been taken by the rioters, 101 prisoners were condemned to death, of whom 2 were actually executed and 95 transported for life. Altogether 457 men and boys were transported to Van Diemen's Land (Tasmania) and New South Wales for their part in the peasants' revolt of 1830.

Yet the working-class agitations during these years of distress were not in vain. They were sufficient to teach the aristocrats who ruled England that repression was not enough.

Chapter III: THE VIENNA SETTLEMENT AND AFTER, 1815–30

The Peace Settlement – England's Foreign Policy – Castlereagh and the Congress System – Canning's Commercial Policy – The New World – The Eastern Question – Revolutions of 1830.

THE ATTEMPTS of the ruling classes to put the clock back to the eighteenth century were more successful on the continent than in England. The men who came to Vienna for the Congress in 1814 had learned nothing by twenty years of war against revolutionary France. They met in an eighteenth-century atmosphere of powdered hair and high-heeled shoes, and were so dilatory that the octogenarian Prince de Ligne felt bound to remark " Le Congrès danse mais ne marche pas." The revolutionary slogan of Liberty, Equality, Fraternity was anathema to them; they looked on the countries of Europe as a series of gentlemen's estates and their main pre-occupation was to restore each estate to the family which had owned it before the Revolution—provided that such a restoration was not too repugnant to the four royal and noble gentlemen who were the actual authors of the treaties.

The Peace Settlement. Like the Versailles Settlement of a century later, the Vienna Settlement was the work of a small committee. Unlike the men at Versailles members of this committee were not responsible to a popular electorate. Two of them, Tsar Alexander I of Russia and King Frederick William III of Prussia, were autocratic monarchs; another, Metternich, was the minister of an autocratic monarch; and the fourth, Castlereagh, though responsible to the British Parliament, was not hampered by having to consider public opinion in England. They were divided by mutual jealousy but were united by mutual fear of the revolutionary ideals. Liberty, Equality, Fraternity had led to the Terror and the Grande Armée; therefore Liberty, Equality, Fraternity were to be suppressed.

So France was restored to the Bourbons in the enormous person of Louis XVIII, though he had spent the best part of his life fighting for the enemies of France. Germany was repartitioned among thirty-nine dynasties, though the German people had fought as a single nation in the War of Liberation. Italy was reduced once more to what Metternich delighted to call " a mere geographical expression " (though Napoleon had showed that there was such a thing as Italian nationalism): Lombardy and Venetia went to Austria, Parma and Piacenza to Napoleon's Austrian wife, Marie Louise, Genoa was given to Sardinia and the kingdom of the Two Sicilies to the Bourbon Ferdinand IV.

The victors recompensed themselves amply—Russia took most of Poland and Prussia took half of Saxony and a state of 2,000,000 inhabitants in the Rhineland—but they were not vindictive. The French emissary, Talleyrand, shared their councils and indeed played a considerable part in redrawing the map of Europe. They did not annex an acre of French soil, and though after Napoleon's amazing Hundred Days return they imposed an indemnity and an army of occupation upon France, the money was paid and the army withdrawn within a couple of years. France was left intact; even her overseas Empire was not seriously dismembered, for she retained her Indian stations, her fishing rights off Newfoundland and most of her West Indian islands. At the same time precautions were taken against the possibility of French aggression in the future by bolstering her eastern frontiers with a number of buffer states. On the north-east a composite kingdom was created by the amalgamation—it can hardly be called a union—of the provinces which to-day are Holland and Belgium; further south the Rhineland was put in Prussian hands; the Confederation of Switzerland was recognized as

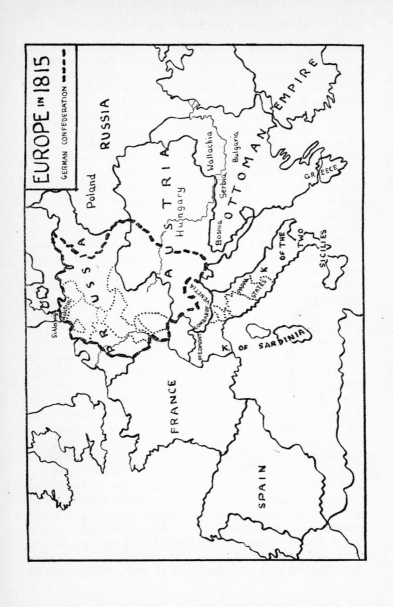

independent by the Great Powers; and in the south-east Piedmont was combined with Savoy in the kingdom of Sardinia.

Besides their anxiety to restore as far as possible pre-war conditions the makers of the Vienna Settlement were genuinely anxious to preserve peace in the future. For this Alexander had a most ambitious project. He planned what he called a Holy Alliance between Russia, Austria and Prussia, promising that " as a result, the only principle in operation, either between the said governments or between their subjects, will be that of rendering reciprocal service: to display to one another, by an unalterable good-will, the mutual affection with which each should be animated, to regard one another without exception as members of one and the same Christian nationality." This might have been all very well if Alexander had meant what he said, but as Castlereagh remarked, " the Emperor's mind was not completely sound." Certainly in subsequent negotiations Alexander showed himself as rapacious and as unchristian as anyone.

The Holy Alliance remained an aspiration. The actual arrangement for safeguarding the peace of Europe which emerged from the Congress of Vienna was an alliance of a less holy nature. At the Vienna Treaty of March 1815 " the High Contracting Parties "—Russia, Austria, Prussia and Great Britain—" agreed to renew at fixed intervals meetings devoted to the great interests they have in common and to the discussion of measures which shall be judged most salutary for the repose and prosperity of the nations and for the maintenance of the Peace of Europe." This Congress System was the great contribution of the men of Vienna to the prevention of war. It remained in operation for about fifteen years, and thanks partly to it, there was no international war in Europe for a whole generation. But the Congress System aimed at prevention rather than cure. It prevented the outbreak of war but did nothing to remove the causes, which were the demand of subject peoples for their liberty. And so, although there was no international war in the generation that followed 1815, there were revolutions in almost every continental country.

England's Foreign Policy.   England had done very well, in a quiet way, out of the Peace Treaties. She had kept Ceylon, the Cape of Good Hope, Trinidad, St. Lucia, Tobago, Malta, Heligoland and the Ionian Islands—in other words a number of important Dutch colonies and a number of still more important naval bases. England's foreign policy for the future was to be a simple one: to keep her mastery of the seas, especially of the Narrow Seas and of the Mediterranean, so that the coast would be clear for her ever-growing export trade. There were two potential dangers here: one was that France and Spain might attempt to shut the Western ports to British shipping, the other that Russia might expand through the Black Sea and the Aegean and put a fleet on the Mediterranean in rivalry to the British. We shall see how these dangers haunted British ministers in varying degrees throughout the nineteenth century.

Castlereagh and the Congress System.   The means which England took to secure her aim during the years 1815–30 depended on the different attitudes of two successive Foreign Ministers. From 1815 to 1822 foreign policy was directed by the suave Castlereagh. He believed in the Congress System, but the Powers were too suspicious of one another for the method of co-operation to have much positive success. The nature of this suspicion showed itself clearly at the first Congress which was held at Aix-la-Chapelle in 1818. The five Powers—France had now been admitted to the Alliance—were distressed by the trade in slaves. They agreed that it could be put down only by allowing allied ships the right to search suspicious vessels, but they refused to confer any such right because the mainland states were frightened of the additional influence which the British fleet might thereby gain. The same distrust showed itself over the question of the Barbary pirates. The mainland Powers wanted an international fleet to be sent to the Mediterranean to exterminate these pests which were preying on Mediterranean shipping from the hidden harbours of North Africa, but Castlereagh would not agree. He preferred pirates to Russian men-o'-war in the Mediterranean.

A more serious question arose at the second Congress, which was held at Troppau in 1820. All over Europe the middle classes had caught the infection of Revolutionary France to the extent that they wanted Liberalism and Nationalism. Liberalism was the new form of the old ideals of Liberty and Equality; Liberals wanted freedom to express opinions, freedom to elect a parliament which would make the laws of their country and limit the powers of the monarchs. Nationalism was the new form of Fraternity; nationalists insisted that peoples of similar race, language and traditions should be under independent governments. Now the Vienna Settlement had denied these ideals, and the great continental Powers wanted to use the Congress System as an instrument for repressing them. When in 1820 the Spaniards rose in revolt against their monarch and demanded that he should grant a Constitution—or guarantee of liberty—to his subjects, Alexander proposed to send an army of 100,000 from Russia to suppress them. But Castlereagh refused to be a party to this: " With the internal affairs of other countries," he said at Troppau, " we have nothing to do." It was one of the most important statements of policy ever made by a Foreign Secretary. The rulers of Russia, Austria and France were determined to use the Alliance to crush the hydra of Liberalism and Nationalism whenever it should raise a head: not otherwise, in their opinion, could the peace of Europe be preserved. Castlereagh, though he had a reputation as a persecutor of Liberalism at home, refused to commit England to a policy of persecution abroad.

This difference of attitude split the next two Congresses. The Powers met at Laibach in 1821 to discuss a revolt that had broken out against the Bourbons in Naples. Austria sent an army to suppress it, but Castlereagh would not allow

England to intervene. In the following year there was a Congress at Verona to discuss the Spanish question again. Ferdinand VII had been forced to proclaim a Constitution, and France had sent an army to help Ferdinand. The Constitution was nothing more or less than that which the French revolutionaries had proclaimed in 1791. Russia, Austria and Prussia—Alexander I, Francis II and Frederick William III, or " the three gentlemen of Verona " as Brougham called them—supported France. The Powers were still fighting the ideas of Revolutionary France. But Castlereagh held firmly to his policy and the Congresses broke up in disagreement.

Canning's Commercial Policy. In that year (1822) Castlereagh committed suicide and England's foreign policy came under the direction of George Canning. He was a brilliant, far-sighted man, the only really talented statesman the Tory party had produced since Pitt. As member of Parliament for the merchant constituency of Liverpool he was determined to follow a more active policy in support of England's foreign trade.

Since the time of Henry VII the commercial policy of England had been Mercantilism. The idea behind the mercantile system was that each country should aim at producing at home all the necessities of life, so that it should be independent of other nations in the event of war. In England this had led to three sets of restrictions. First, foreign importers were restricted by heavy taxes on foreign food and materials. Secondly, the Navigation Acts insisted that all goods brought into English or colonial ports should be carried either in British ships or in the ships of the country which sent them. Thirdly, the British colonists were restricted by laws forcing them to trade with England rather than with foreign countries which might offer better terms: the colonies were regarded as plantations whose function was to grow commodities for the exclusive use and benefit of the Mother Country.

The most effective early attack on the mercantile system

was made by the Scottish philosopher Adam Smith who wrote *The Wealth of Nations* (1776) to prove that wealth increases most rapidly when each country produces what it is best fitted by its national resources and genius to produce. " If a foreign country can supply us with a commodity cheaper than we can make it, better buy it of them with some part of our own industry employed in a way in which we have some advantage." Thus England, with her new machines and increasing capacity for mass-production should abolish restrictions on trade and live by exchanging industrial goods for the food and materials of overseas countries. Adam Smith's ideas were taken up by the young Pitt until the French Revolutionary wars cut short his efforts for reform. Now, in the eighteen-twenties, they were adopted by George Canning and by his colleague William Huskisson, another Liverpool M.P. These men did not convert England to Free Trade—that battle was not to be fought out till the forties—but they did make serious inroads into these three sets of mercantile restrictions.

First Huskisson succeeded in reducing the taxes on foreign food and raw materials. Thanks to this, sugar, coffee, wines and spirits became cheaper, and the Macclesfield silk industry (with duties on raw silk reduced from $5s.\ 7\frac{1}{2}d.$ to $4d.$ a pound) and the Yorkshire woollen industry (with duties on raw wool reduced from $6d.$ to $1d.$ a pound) were able to forge ahead. He also abolished the hearth tax and the tax on windows and generally simplified the cumbrous system of which Sydney Smith had complained so bitterly in 1820.

Secondly Huskisson moderated in 1823 the old Navigation Acts so as to remove restrictions from the shipping of any nation which would consent to remove its restrictions from British shipping. There was a great outcry that this would ruin our merchant service but Canning and Huskisson were amply vindicated by results, for in the next twenty-one years our shipping increased by 45 per cent. Most European Powers accepted Huskisson's invitation to abolish their restrictions on British ships, but Holland, our old rival on the high seas, refused. Canning's reply to this, made in a despatch to the ambassador at The Hague in 1826, ran:

In matters of commerce the fault of the Dutch
Is offering too little and asking too much.
The French are with equal advantage content
So we clap on Dutch bottoms just twenty per cent.

Thirdly Huskisson mitigated many of the restrictions on the trade of the colonies. He allowed foreign countries to send their goods to colonial ports. His policy here was not Free Trade but Imperial Preference. He insisted that the colonies should tax foreign goods more highly than goods from the mother-country and in return he gave the colonies preference over foreigners in British markets by seeing that foreign goods paid higher import duties than goods from the colonies. Thus Canadian timber paid less than Baltic timber—so much less that some Baltic merchants used to send their cargoes to Canada to be re-shipped from there under the guise of Canadian timber. Canadian corn, too, had a preference. In 1828 he revised the Corn Laws so that overseas corn paid duties on a Sliding Scale—high duties when the price of English corn was low and low duties when it was high—and the duties paid by Canadians were always less than half those paid by foreigners. In silk, India had a preference. In wool, Australia was in 1825 allowed freedom from duty, while other importers had to pay a $1d.$ a pound.

In foreign policy, Canning had no use for Congresses. He agreed with Castlereagh's policy of refusing to help in suppressing Liberal movements abroad but he went further than Castlereagh in that he saw that England's foreign trade might be advanced by actually encouraging Liberal revolts in certain countries. His opportunity was not long in coming.

The New World. The Spanish and Portuguese colonists in South America were in revolt against their mother-countries. Spain and Portugal, who since the sixteenth century had ruled the continent from the Rio Grande to Tierra del Fuego, were now decadent. Napoleon had wrecked what power they had of holding Empires together, and since Waterloo the Powers at the Congresses had done their best to keep them weak. Opinion in England favoured the colonists. Sentimental Englishmen, seeing in their revolt not the attempt of a handful of unscrupulous settlers to seize the wealth of a continent for themselves but the vindication of the Rights of Man against the rule of Tyrants, took their high-falutin proclamations literally and applauded their successes. Bankers kept the fire of revolt burning by raising loans on the London market. Disbanded soldiers and sailors, sick of the corruption and repression at home, set sail across the Atlantic to strike a blow in the cause of liberty. Six thousand British soldiers fought for the independence of Bolivia and Venezuela in 1818. Lord Cochrane (later Lord Dundonald), the most brilliant British sailor of all time, with the possible exception of Nelson, commanded in turn the so-called navies of Chile and Brazil and in the years 1820 to 1823 drove the Spanish fleet from the Pacific and the Portuguese fleet from the Atlantic sea-board of South America. But the official attitude of England under Castlereagh was to refuse to assist the rebels; any other course would have wrecked the Congress System in Europe.

Canning on the other hand put English interests first and the Congress System last. He was determined to open up English trade with South America, and to do that it was necessary to prevent France from winning what Spain and Portugal had lost. France, he knew, was on the point of intervening: Chateaubriand had a scheme for appointing French princes to rule in South America. So Canning invited President Monroe of the United States to collaborate with him in opposing French aggression. Monroe was as anxious as Canning to keep the French out of America, but he was also anxious to keep out the English. In December 1823 he issued in a message to Congress the famous Monroe Doctrine: " With the existing colonies or dependencies of any European Power we have not interfered and shall not interfere. But with the governments who have declared their independence and maintained it, and whose independence we have, on great consideration and just principles acknowledged, we could not view any interposition for the purpose of oppressing them, or controlling in any other manner their destiny, by any European Power, in any other light than as a manifestation of an unfriendly disposition towards the United States." In other words, the United States reserved the right to do what she liked with the rest of America but warned the European Powers that any interference from them would mean war with the United States.

Thus Canning had lost the chance of collaborating with the United States. But he did not lose the chance of posing as the champion of the new republics in Europe. " I determined," he announced to the House of Commons, " that if France held Spain, it should be Spain without the Indies; I called the New World into existence to redress the balance of the Old." It was his way of saying that Great Britain recognized the independence of Colombia, Buenos Aires and Mexico and had sent Consuls to open up British trade with the new republics.

At first enthusiasm over the commercial possibilities of the South American republics was disastrous. English manufacturers dumped their surplus products across the Atlantic without asking themselves how their new clients could afford to pay. English financiers, such as Rothschild, Goldschmidt and Baring, made huge loans to new republics —over £150 millions between 1818 and 1825—before they discovered that the Republics were insolvent.[1] Some people

[1] The Barings had come from Germany in the eighteenth century and had settled down as capitalists in the West-Country wool trade. The Rothschilds were international bankers with a representative in every European capital. Byron, appalled by their power, attacked them savagely in *Don Juan*:
> Who hold the balance of the world? Who reign
> O'er congress, whether royalist or liberal?
> Who rouse the shirtless patriots of Spain?
> (That make old Europe's journals squeak and gibber all.)
> Who keep the world, both old and new, in pain
> Or pleasure? Who make politics run glibber all?
> The shade of Buonaparte's noble daring?—
> Jew Rothschild, and his fellow-Christian, Baring.

even made a loan to a "Kingdom of Poyais" which did not exist outside the fertile brain of an ingenious Scotsman. Bubble companies were formed for all manner of fantastic purposes—one for sending Scottish milkmaids to milk the savage cattle of Buenos Aires, another for exporting warming pans and skates to the American tropics. The result was a financial crisis. The bubble burst in the first week of December 1825 when twenty-six English banks stopped payment. Panic was averted only by a prompt coining of gold to enable the Bank of England to redeem its notes.

When Parliament met in February 1826 it was urged that trade with South America should be curtailed to prevent a recurrence of the crisis. But Brougham replied: " As well it might be argued that we ought not to open a new market, or discover a new colony with which to trade, as that we were not to adopt sound and wise and enlightened principles of commerce, because the one as well as the other might give rise to overtrading on the part of certain individuals." Brougham's argument won and the Government set about a reform of the English banking system. The Government considered that the fault lay not in trade with new markets but in the condition of the English private banks which had proved too weak to stand the strain in 1825. Consequently in 1826 an Act was passed allowing banks consisting of more than six members—that is, joint-stock banks—to be established anywhere outside a sixty-five mile radius of London. Hitherto the only bank of this nature had been the Bank of England. Henceforth joint-stock banks were to be allowed in the provinces. In 1833 an Act was passed allowing them in London. This was the beginning of the end of the private banking system: within six years after the passing of the Act of 1826 the number of private banks in England had dropped from 554 to 311 and no less than 86 joint-stock banks had been established. The latter included banks which were later to become known as the Midland, Lloyds, the National Provincial (with head office in Gloucester) and Barclays Bank (in the Eastern Counties). The process of crowding out the private banker and of binding the joint-stock banks into ever larger units continued until 1918, when the five banks we have named, together with the Westminster Bank (1835), controlled between them practically all the joint-stock banking business in England.

South American trade survived the crisis of 1825 and a huge trade sprang up between the continent and England. The railroads and rolling stock of the new republics were all made in English foundries and with English capital. In 1914 some $135,000,000 worth of goods were exported from the United Kingdom to the Argentine Republic alone, and our capital invested there amounted to over $1,000,000,000. By that time the United States too had a huge surplus of wealth to send to South American markets and by 1920 their exports and investments were heavier than ours. The policy of Canning and Monroe had succeeded beyond their wildest imaginings.

The Eastern Question. The attention of Canning, and indeed of every politician in Europe, was next turned towards the East. The Empire of the Ottoman Turks spread over all the countries known as the Balkans—which word itself is Turkish and means the Mountains. At the beginning of the nineteenth century the revolutionary spirit of Nationalism had spread to these European colonies of Turkey: the Serbs had rebelled to win their freedom in 1804, there were risings in Montenegro and Roumania, and now in 1821 the Greeks rose in insurrection against their Turkish rulers. It seemed inevitable that sooner or later the whole rotten structure of the Ottoman Empire would crumble away. And then what would happen? Presumably Russia would seize Constantinople and England's worst fear—that of a Russian fleet in the Mediterranean—would be realized. This was the redoubtable Eastern Question which was to worry English statesmen until the Russian Empire itself fell in 1917.

There were two lines of policy open to England. She might either protect the unspeakable Turk against the

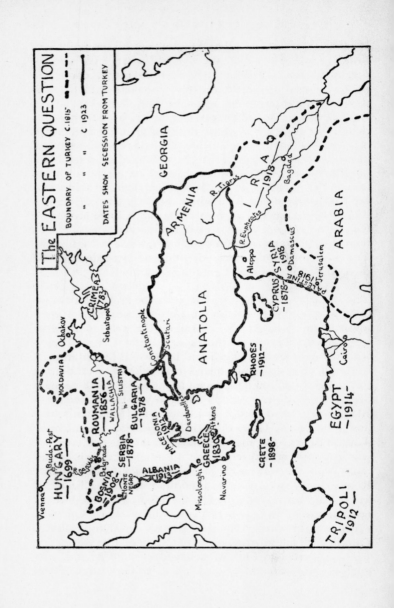

Russian, or else she might compete with Russia for the privilege of helping the Ottoman colonies in their revolt against Turkey. Canning chose the latter alternative and determined to support the Greeks. Russia was anxious to help the Greeks because she had her eye on the Aegean ports, and Canning saw that the best way of depriving Russia of winning the credit, and consequently the rewards, of making Greece free was for England to share the rôle of liberator. Public opinion in England was strongly in favour of intervention in Greece for other reasons. The Greeks like the South American colonists were rebelling against an imperial overlord; like the South Americans they had called in Cochrane to command their " navy "; like the South Americans they had found ready lenders in the London money market. Educated Englishmen had been brought up to regard Greece as the seat of the greatest civilization the world has ever known. Not thinking how much two thousand years of bondage would have altered the Greek character, they let themselves be stirred to enthusiasm by the declamations of Byron and to indignation by the news that in Constantinople the Turks had hanged the Venerable Patriarch of the Greek Church together with three archbishops on their way from Mass.

This indignation soon turned to fury. In 1824 the Sultan of Turkey called upon his vassal the Pasha of Egypt to assist him against the Greeks. This remarkable man, Mehemet Ali by name, had begun his career as an Albanian tobacconist. By a series of incredible exploits he had made himself master of Cairo and had actually turned Egypt into a modern state, nationalizing the land, establishing industries and organizing—with French help—a formidable army and fleet. Now at the age of fifty-five he was at the height of his powers and only too ready for a campaign against the Greeks, for he dreamed of expanding his influence over Constantinople itself. He sent his son Ibrahim Pasha to Greece and Ibrahim seized Crete, overran the Morea and proceeded to deport all the Greeks he could lay hands on to Egypt as slaves. This was enough to provoke England and

France to send a fleet to Navarino Bay with orders to support the Greeks, but to avoid fighting. The orders were not carried out. On October 20, 1827, Ibrahim fired on an English boat; the French flagship fired back; and before anyone quite realized what was happening a general engagement had taken place and the Egyptian and Turkish fleets lay shattered in Navarino Bay.

It was left to the French to drive the Turkish and Egyptian forces out of the Morea while the Russians carried the war as far as Adrianople. The independence of Greece was acknowledged by Turkey at the Treaty of Adrianople in 1829 and three years later the new state formally recognized England, France and Russia as her joint protectors. Greece was free, and England and France had gained a valuable share in the Levant trade; but the Eastern Question was anything but settled. Russia was bearing down upon Turkey from the north and it would not be long before England's intervention would again be advisable, if not precisely necessary, in the Near East.

A few weeks before Navarino Canning had died and his place as Prime Minister and Foreign Secretary was taken by the Duke of Wellington. The old soldier had before him the most difficult of all his campaigns. He stood for the old order at home and abroad, at a time when public opinion everywhere was clamouring for radical reform. Huskisson and Palmerston and the rest of Canning's progressive friends resigned, outraged by the reactionary policy of the Prime Minister who could describe Navarino as an "untoward event." The mob clamoured for his resignation.

The Irish Catholics were in arms for emancipation from the laws restricting their liberty (see Chapter X) and the Duke, though he hated the idea of liberty for Catholics, gave way and with Peel's help forced the Bill for Catholic Emancipation through Parliament, thereby averting civil war in Ireland. He must have regretted ever having taken office. At home he was fighting a hopeless rearguard action. And he had to stand by while on the continent the

THE VIENNA SETTLEMENT AND AFTER 61

system which had been established as a result of his victories over Napoleon was being everywhere threatened by revolution.

The Revolutions of 1830. For fifteen years the conquerors of Revolutionary France had suppressed every sign of revolutionary tendencies in Europe. They began by setting themselves against any trace of liberalism or nationalism and they ended by opposing everything that remotely resembled progress towards social justice. In France the vacillating Louis was succeeded by his rabidly reactionary brother Charles X. In Russia Alexander, who had at least been nominally enlightened, was succeeded by that savage Imperialist Nicholas. In Rome the Popes opposed any form of educational progress and continued to ban books that hinted that the world was round. In Austria, Metternich ruled supreme and spread the methods and notions of the eighteenth century over Germany and North Italy. All over Europe the intellectual leaders of the middle classes were secretly plotting revolution. At last, in 1830, the revolutions broke out.

The first occurred, as one might expect, in France. One July day the citizens of Paris awoke to find their pavements ripped up for barricades and the rattle of musketry sounding down the narrow streets. By the end of the month Charles X and his clerical ministers had fled and the Chamber had elected the Duke of Orleans, Louis Philippe, to the new title of King of the French. He was an uninspiring ruler, but he made an end of priest-ridden politics and a beginning of sound middle-class reforms in France.

In August the revolutionary movement spread to Belgium. The Belgians had always hated their unnatural union with Holland. They differed from the Dutch in race, language and religion and resented being ruled from Amsterdam by Protestant Dutchmen. France supported the Belgian rising—hoping to annex the Belgian provinces for herself. This was too much for the British Foreign Secretary, Palmerston. It had always been a prime consideration of England's foreign policy that the Low Countries should not be under the control of any great Power: our trade with them was too valuable for us to let it be at the mercy of any influential foreigner. So Palmerston, like a good Canningite, took up the cause of Belgian independence, which was duly recognized in 1831 and ratified in 1839 when a young Queen of England had to sign as one of her first important official acts a " scrap of paper " by which the Powers guaranteed the liberty of Belgium. It was an unsatisfactory little nation that was thus called into being, for the people of the various Belgian provinces had little in common except the fact that they had been under foreign rule of one sort or another throughout their history, but it suited the English book to have a grateful client on the other side of the Narrow Seas. Palmerston found a German who had long been resident in England, Leopold of Saxe-Coburg, to be the first King of the Belgians.

The other revolutions of 1830 were less successful than the French and the Belgian. In Germany there were risings against the reactionary princes of Hesse, of Brunswick, of Hanover and of Saxony. The movement never assumed the dimensions of a national rising; it came to nothing. In Italy there were similar risings, against the Duke of Modena and, above all, against the Pope in his capacity as temporal ruler of the Papal States. Here Metternich took a hand: Austrian soldiers soon had the Duke of Modena restored and the Papal States reduced to subservience to the Holy See. In Poland the Nationalist revolt was more violent: in November, Polish soldiers in Warsaw murdered their Russian officers and then, instead of organizing against the inevitable Russian reprisal, turned aside to a terrible pogrom of Jews. Two hundred thousand Russians marched into Poland in the New Year and a new reign of terror began for the Poles. All over the continent of Europe the liberal and nationalist revolutionaries failed in 1830. They would rise again.

Meanwhile in England, too, discontent was swelling

THE VIENNA SETTLEMENT AND AFTER

towards revolt. The working classes were on the verge of insurrection, striking in the industrial North, rickburning in the agricultural South. The middle classes were clamouring for the vote which would give them seats in Parliament and a say in the government of the kingdom. The old Duke bowed before the storm. He threw a contemptuous sop to the reformers by passing a Beer Bill abolishing the whole of the duty on beer.[1] Then, in November 1830, he resigned and made way for Lord Grey, the first Whig Prime Minister for forty-eight years.

[1] Sydney Smith wrote a few weeks later: "Everybody is drunk. Those who are not singing are sprawling. The sovereign people are in a beastly state."

Chapter IV: THE WHIG REFORMS, 1830–41

Parliamentary Reform – Humanitarian Reforms – The New Poor Law – Municipal Reform – The Consolidated Trades Union – The People's Charter.

THE EUROPEAN REVOLUTIONS of 1830 had been risings of the middle classes. To avert a similar disaster in England, Lord Grey proposed to give the middle classes representation in Parliament.

To most of the ruling families this seemed a revolutionary proposal which would destroy the very constitution of England. In reality it was nothing of the sort. The old House of Commons consisted of landed gentry and of rich merchants and financiers; together with the peers of the House of Lords they and their families formed an aristocracy which had ruled England for hundreds of years. The principle behind the old House of Commons was that it should represent Property. The more property a man had, the more votes he should be able to command at Parliamentary elections. Thus in the county constituencies the vote was held by freeholders whose land was worth forty shillings or more a year. In the boroughs (towns) conditions differed: in some the Mayor and Corporation nominated the members, in others the tenants of certain areas were allowed to vote, but in a few (notably Westminster) the right to vote was held by every inhabitant.

In the old days this system had worked well enough; the richest men had in fact controlled the votes and secured representation in the Commons. But by 1830 it had ceased to work, for the Commons no longer represented the wealth of England. The boroughs and county of Cornwall, for instance, were poverty-stricken, yet they still returned almost as many members as the whole of Scotland. The town of Old Sarum was empty and the town of Dunwich had been swallowed up by the sea, yet a member for each sat in the House. The Industrial Revolution had brought riches to the Midlands and the North, yet towns like Birmingham and Manchester had no members at all. Besides this all manner of corrupt practices had become common. Urban landowners brought strangers into the town, providing lodging in return for their votes. Boroughs were advertised for sale in the papers and were bought up by war-profiteers and by rich planters from the West Indies. Reform, in a word, was overdue.

Parliamentary Reform. The Bill which Grey and his Cabinet—all but two of whom were peers—put before the House of Commons in March 1831 proposed (i) to abolish about 50 " rotten " boroughs, (ii) to take away the second member from 90 other small towns, (iii) to redistribute these 140 seats among large towns and large counties, (iv) to give the vote in the counties to rich tenant farmers as well as to freeholders and (v) to give the vote in the towns to every householder who paid more than £10 a year in rent.

This Reform Bill was moderate in the extreme. For years Cobbett, Place, Hunt and the Radicals in general had been urging universal suffrage—the right of every man to have a vote. The Bill confined the vote to the well-to-do. Further, the Radicals had been urging secret ballot. The Bill retained the old system of public vote on the hustings— by which each voter mounted a platform and cast his vote out loud in public. Thus the rich could still influence the voting and secure representation in the Commons: landowners could secure the votes of tenant farmers by threatening to turn them out, and capitalists could secure the votes of employees and tradespeople by threatening to dismiss the former and to withdraw their custom from the latter.

Moderate as it was, the Bill was received with execration by the borough-mongering families who saw in it the end of their political power, and with delight by the working classes who, rather surprisingly, saw in it the beginning of the end of their misfortunes.

It needed something like an insurrection to pass the Bill. The first round of the fight took place in the Commons in the spring of 1831. The Second Reading was passed by a majority of one, but in Committee the Commons rejected the Bill; the Whigs had lost the first round. Grey promptly dissolved Parliament and the second round was fought out in the constituencies at the summer elections. Feeling was now running high all over the country (a mob smashed the Duke of Wellington's windows in Piccadilly). A new Parliament was returned with a large reforming majority and in September a slightly re-cast Reform Bill passed the House of Commons; the second round had been won by the Whigs. But the fight was not yet over. When the Bill went up to the Lords it was thrown out, and William IV, who had just celebrated his coronation, refused to create new peers to turn a minority into a majority. Instead, he prorogued Parliament and left the third round to be fought out in the country during the recess.

England narrowly escaped revolution during those autumn months. There were riots all over the country. In London Lord Londonderry was knocked off his horse, and shops displayed placards, "No taxes paid here until the Reform Bill is passed." In Derby the mob stormed the county gaol and set the prisoners free; in Nottingham they burned down the Castle, which belonged to the Duke of Newcastle; in Bristol the whole city was seized by rioters who burned the Mansion House, the Customs House and the Bishop's Palace. When Parliament met again in December the members had learned their lesson. The Commons passed the Bill and in the new year the Lords docilely let it through—the King had at last promised to create new peers for the purpose.

The result of the Reform Bill of 1832 was this: the government of England continued to be carried on by aristocrats, but instead of depending for their support on fifteen thousand buyable voters these men had to appeal to an electorate of some hundreds of thousands who were for the most part manufacturers and business-men and shopkeepers. Consequently the new Parliaments were being constantly pressed by the middle class to pass reforming measures. The manufacturers wanted reforms which would abolish the restrictions on trade, the middle class as a whole wanted lower rates and taxes.

Humanitarian Reforms. It was some years before the members of the middle class got what they wanted. The first reforms after 1832 were none of their choosing. The Parliament of 1833 was humanitarian rather than economic in outlook. It passed Wilberforce's daring Bill for the Abolition of Slavery, which was to wreck the British West Indian sugar trade in spite of the £20,000,000 paid in compensation to the slave-owners who well knew that white men cannot and black men will not work in that climate except under compulsion. More important still, it passed a Factory Act sponsored by Lord Shaftesbury. This was to be the first effective Act of an enormous code of laws which have been passed since 1833 to protect the workers from oppression. The Act of 1833 did not go far. Employers were forbidden to employ children under nine years of age and were not allowed to work women and young persons for more than ten hours a day. No restriction was placed on the hours worked by men. But Shaftesbury's Act was a great advance on the earlier Factory Acts of 1802 and 1819, for unlike them it provided for the appointment of inspectors to see that its terms were carried out.

The Evangelicals were successful in 1833 in turning the attention of Parliament to a third cause, one in which reform was almost equally necessary. England was one of the last great nations to organize a system of national education. Frederick the Great had established national schools in Prussia, Maria Theresa in Austria, Napoleon in France, yet England had nothing but a few private schools. Only one English child in eleven was receiving any sort of schooling in 1833. Of these some learnt to read at Dames' schools where their parents paid perhaps fourpence a week to a Dame who usually kept a shop of some sort at the same time as her school. Others attended establishments kept by private schoolmasters—such as the one in Liverpool where the school consisted of a garret measuring 10 feet by 9 and containing one cock, two hens, three terriers, as well as the master and a class of forty children. But most of the childrem who managed to learn the three R's (reading, writing and arithmetic), did so at the schools which had been founded and endowed by two private religious societies: the *British and Foreign Schools Society*, which was Whig and Nonconformist, and the *National Society for the Education of the Poor in the Principles of the Established Church*, which was Tory and Church of England. These societies, which were inordinately jealous of each other, practised the principles of education which had been discovered by Joseph Lancaster, the Quaker, and Dr. Bell, the Church of England parson. These inestimable men had arrived by separate routes at the conclusion that children could be taught by children: once a master had taught a child a lesson he could leave him as a monitor to repeat the lesson to his juniors. By this system a thousand children were being taught to read by one single master in one single hall in Manchester. It was to these two societies that the Government made the first grant of public money to education, in 1833. Seven years later a Board of Education was established at Whitehall to supervise the spending of the money.

At the same time reformers outside Parliament were busy providing for the educational needs of the day. After primary education to teach an illiterate nation to read, the main needs were first to provide young mechanics with technical instruction to fit them to handle the new and increasingly complex machinery, and secondly to provide sons of the newly rich capitalist class with higher education to fit them for the positions which their fathers had made for them as leaders of men. Something was done to satisfy the first need by George Birkbeck's foundation in 1823 of a Mechanics' Institute in London. Within a few months this model had been copied by nearly every town in the kingdom. But it was to be many years before public money would be voted for the establishment of Technical Schools and Evening Classes. The second need was more effectively satisfied. Dr. Arnold transformed Rugby into a school where rich men's sons could obtain, together with a thorough grounding in the classics, an education destined to turn them into what Dr. Arnold called " Christian Gentlemen." The older Public Schools followed Arnold's example and transformed themselves from lordly and disorderly establishments into models of efficient and evangelical teaching. The country Grammar Schools increased their fees and their numbers. New Public Schools were founded for the newly rich classes. The Universities underwent a similar transformation. Oxford and Cambridge shook off the drunken drowsiness which had characterized them in the eighteenth century and began to insist on a modicum of intellectual activity on the part of students and teachers. But Oxford and Cambridge were devoted largely to classical and theological studies; besides, their doors were shut to all who were not members of the Church of England. To meet the need for a University teaching modern subjects and open to non-Churchmen, Lord Brougham founded University College—" the godless institution in Gower Street." The Churchmen followed with the foundation of King's College in the Strand and in 1836 these two institutions became part of the new University of London.

The New Poor Law. By the year 1834 the humanitarian ardour of the Government had cooled; the time had come to listen to the financial demands of the middle class. The most pressing of these was the demand for a new Poor Law. There was nothing much to be said in favour of the existing system of poor-relief and every sort of objection could be raised against it. In the first place it made each parish responsible for its own poor; this was all very well while population was stable but now that it was increasing fast some parishes found themselves deluged with paupers while others had none at all; also, by confining paupers to their own parishes, it annoyed the industrialists of the North who were wanting fresh supplies of cheap labour for their factories. Secondly the Speenhamland system of giving allowances to the unemployed had become, in Carlyle's phrase, " a bounty on unthrift, idleness, bastardy and beer drinking." Thirdly many parishes had got into the habit of hiring the unemployed to farmers and paying two-thirds of their wages out of the rates on condition that the farmer paid the other third: this tempted farmers to refuse to employ men who were not technically paupers getting parish relief. But the main objection raised at the time to the existing system was that it was too heavy on the rates, too expensive, and it was primarily with a view to cutting down expense that the Poor Law Amendment Act was passed in 1834. Under the new law the parish system was abolished. Parishes were grouped for purposes of poor-relief into a few large Unions which were managed by Boards of Guardians elected from the combined parishes and were under the supervision of a central Poor Law Commission in London. The Speenhamland system of allowances was abolished and with it the system of hiring paupers out as labourers; in its place a workhouse was built in every Union and to the workhouse applicants for relief were sent.

The new law achieved its main object: it cut down expense. Within five years the rates were reduced by £3,000,000. But it had almost as many disadvantages as the old system. In the first place it made no distinction between the man who would not work and the man who could not; both were treated as wicked idlers and sent to the workhouse. Secondly the workhouses were little better than prisons. The Secretary of the Poor Law Commission himself explained: " By the Workhouse System is meant having all relief through the workhouse, making this workhouse an uninviting place of wholesome restraint, preventing any of its inmates from going out or receiving visitors, without a written order to that effect from the overseer; disallowing beer and tobacco and finding them work according to their ability." (And he might have added that they disallowed cards and talking over meals.) Thirdly the workhouses separated husbands and wives, parents and children; the old parish workhouses had at least allowed families to live together within their bleak walls. Fourthly the Union officials were not properly supervised and fell into all manner of corrupt practices. The picture drawn by Dickens in *Oliver Twist* can hardly have been exaggerated; we know that in the Andover Workhouse the inmates were so starved that they fought for the gristle and marrow of the decayed bones which they were set to grind in their work-hours. In short the Poor Law Amendment Act made old age, infirmity and unemployment all alike a crime in the poor classes, and punished them as such.

Municipal Reform. The Whigs now turned their attention to the reform of municipal government. After abolishing the corrupt system of electing members of Parliament in rotten boroughs under the control of a few landowners, the next step was obviously to abolish similar anomalies in local government. There was immense variety in the systems of government in towns but it can fairly be said that in every case the power was in the hands of a narrow oligarchy. In Birmingham, Sheffield, Halifax, Bradford and Huddersfield the legal authority was simply the lord of the manor. In Leeds the lord of the manor exacted £13,000 from the city in 1839 for leave for the city's corn to be ground in mills other than the lord's. In Liverpool the mayor and aldermen were elected by a select body of 41 voters, in Newcastle by an even more select body of 36. Municipal authorities were not obliged to have their accounts audited and in many cases made large private profits out of the public: in Manchester they established a gasworks which brought them in an average profit of £25,000 a year.

The Municipal Reform Act of 1835 put an end to all this. In 178 chartered towns a uniform system of government was set up, consisting of mayor, aldermen and councillors.[1] The council was obliged to have its accounts audited and published. And the councillors were to be elected by the majority vote of all the ratepayers in the town. The new Act did not go far: it did not give councils wide powers or put them under an obligation to see to the general welfare of the town (for instance only in 29 towns did the council have the exclusive power of draining, cleansing, and paving the streets), but it was a vast improvement on the old system. And it put power into the hands of the middle classes, for the new town councils consisted chiefly of manufacturers, merchants and professional men.

The *tempo* of reform now slowed down somewhat. In 1834 Grey had been succeeded as Prime Minister by Lord Melbourne and that elderly man of fashion, who held office, except for one short Tory interlude, until 1841, was far too easy-going to let himself be hurried. It was his colleague, Lord John Russell, who was responsible for the Municipal Reform Bill and it was left to an outsider, Rowland Hill, to suggest the other great reform of the period: the Penny Post. Under the old system postage was paid on the delivery of a letter, and the rates were inordinately high—the cost between London and Brighton, for example, was eightpence. Under Rowland Hill's system, which came into effect in 1840, adhesive stamps were put on letters before posting and a universal rate of a penny a half-ounce was introduced. At first this seemed like a bounty paid by the Government to the business men: the latter were enabled to correspond cheaply and the Government lost a million pounds in postal revenue and was unable to balance its budget. But soon the amount of correspondence increased to such an extent that the revenues exceeded those under the old rate and the benefit of the Penny Post to the Government was recognized to be as great as the advantage to commerce.

[1] Towns without charters could petition Parliament to come under the Act: Manchester was incorporated in 1838, Birmingham in 1839, Sheffield in 1843 and Bradford in 1847.

The Consolidated Trades Union. The eighteen-thirties go down in the history of the middle class as an age of great reforms. To the working class they wore a very different complexion. The workers gained nothing from the reforms. The Bill of 1832, which their agitation had frightened Parliament into passing, gave the vote not to them but to their employers; the Factory Act did not reduce the men's working hours; the Poor Law Amendment Act made the pauper and the unemployed a criminal and built prisons to house them; the Municipal Reform Act put the workers under middle-class town councils and the Penny Post did not mean anything to them because they could not write a letter.

Robert Owen and a few other long-sighted men soon realized that the Whigs had betrayed the working class. They hit upon a new plan of action which was nothing less than to combine all the workers' unions in the kingdom into one big *Trades Union* which might be able to force concessions from employers by calling a general strike—or National Holiday, as the euphemism of those days had it. In the autumn of 1833 Robert Owen urged " all Trade Unions, Co-operative Societies, Commercial Orders, Benefit Societies and all other associations intended for the improvement of the working classes . . . to form themselves into lodges to make their own laws and regulations—for the purpose of emancipating the industrious and useful classes from the difficulties which overwhelm them." There followed an outbreak of lodges which spread like an epidemic all over the country. Working men met behind locked doors and solemnly enrolled new members by conspirational ceremonies of initiation involving crossed swords, skulls and cross-bones and effigies of death. In January 1834 Owen founded what he pleased to call a *Grand National Consolidated Trades Union* to combine the lodges. The Consolidated Union had an immediate success: within a few weeks it had half a million members—and there were said to be over a million trade unionists altogether at that time.

Melbourne's Government was frightened, and showed it. In March six labourers were holding a ceremony of initiation to their lodge in the village of Tolpuddle in Dorset when they were suddenly arrested. They were accused of "administering an unlawful oath" and were sentenced to the exorbitant punishment of transportation to Botany Bay for seven years. Owen immediately took up the case of the "Tolpuddle Martyrs": he led a deputation to Whitehall and 20,000 workers followed him through the streets. Melbourne called out troops to prevent disorder and refused to receive the deputation.

Now, if ever, was the moment for Owen's general strike. But the Consolidated Union had neither the support nor the discipline that was needed. Owen's fellow-leaders disowned him on the ground that he opposed organized religion—they refused to work any longer with an "atheist." And the rank and file were soon disheartened by the united front of employers and Government which was opposed to them. Here and there they went on strike, but soon their funds were exhausted and they had to return to work. The employers retaliated by "presenting the document" in which it was laid down that no man would be employed unless he openly renounced the Union. In a few months the Consolidated Union withered away. It had been a hot-house growth from the first—all stalk and no roots. The trade unions of which it was composed were in themselves not properly organized and did not command the support of sufficient members of the respective trades. Owen's Consolidated Union was simply not consolidated. In 1926 the close organization of the workers in a few great trades was sufficient for their Unions to combine in an almost General Strike (though that was a failure), but in 1834 such general action was manifestly impossible.

The People's Charter.

The working-class movement—if such ill-directed stirrings of discontent can be called a movement—now took another direction. Direct pressure on the employers through a Consolidated Union had been

THE WHIG REFORMS

tried and had failed. There remained the possibility of direct pressure upon Parliament. The manufacturing class had got the vote and had used it to pass reforms for their own interest; now was the time for the working class to do the same. This at any rate was the opinion of Francis Place and the Cornishman, William Lovett. In 1836 they founded the London Working Men's Association, a sort of Labour Party for men of " good moral character " who were prepared to strive for education and for a democratic reform of Parliament. This Association drew up the People's Charter which they published in May 1836. The Charter consisted of six points:

(1) *Manhood suffrage*, so that all the six million men in the Kingdom should have the vote, instead of only 840,000 as under the 1832 Act.
(2) *Secret Ballot*, so that no one could know how a man voted.
(3) *Annual Parliaments*, so that the people's will could be ascertained every year by a general election.
(4) *Equal Electorate Districts*, so that every M.P. would be elected from a constituency of roughly the same population.
(5) *No Property Qualification* for Members, so that a poor man could stand for Parliament.
(6) *Payment of M.P.s*, so that a poor man could live in comfort if he were elected.

The Charter became the watchword of everyone who felt he had a grievance. The working class believed it to be a sesame which would open the door to the Aladdin's cave of national treasure. All sorts and conditions of agitators called themselves Chartists: the skilled workers of London who wanted cheap newspapers and national education, the trade unionists of the North who wanted " a fair day's wage for a fair day's work," the vast audiences who listened to Oastler's denunciations of the Poor Law and the hardly less vast audiences in Birmingham who listened to Attwood's demands for a reform of the currency. All combined to sign a National Petition which embodied five points of the Charter (omitting the point about Equal Electoral Districts). Each thought that once he was given the vote his own pet reform would follow.

The crisis came in 1839. Over a million working men signed the Chartist National Petition which was presented to Parliament in June. But before the Commons could discuss it an ugly breach occurred in the ranks of the Chartists. Lovett and the Londoners meant Chartism to be a peaceful movement, but the men of the North and Midlands, where distress was more acute, were determined to gain their ends by violence if necessary. Urged on by irresponsible Irish journalists—Feargus O'Connor in his paper *The Northern Star* and Bronterre O'Brien in *The Operative*—they threatened " physical force " and talked of calling a general strike—or " national holiday." The Whig Government, knowing that the northern towns had no police force worth the name and Birmingham none at all, called out the troops and put Sir Charles Napier in command. It was a wise choice; Napier had enough human sympathy to understand the Chartists and enough military ability to keep them in check. " The people should have universal suffrage, the ballot, annual parliaments, farms for the people, and systematic education. I am opposed to landlordism and capitalism," he wrote in his diary, " but," he added, " bad laws must be reformed by the concentrated reason of the nation acting on the legislature, not by the pikes of individuals acting on the bodies of the executive." And when Chartists talked of physical force, " Fools," he wrote. " *We* have the physical force not they. They talk of their hundreds of thousands of men. Who is to move them when I am dancing round them with cavalry and pelting them with cannon shot ? What would their 100,000 men do with my rockets wriggling their fiery tails among them, roaring, scorching, tearing, smashing all they come near ? And when in desperation and despair they broke to fly, how would they bear five regiments of cavalry careering among

them. Poor men ! How little they know of physical force ! "
Thanks to Napier there was martial law but no insurrection
in Birmingham.

Meanwhile the Commons were debating the National
Petition. Not surprisingly they regarded it as the work of
terrorists and rejected it—by 235 votes to 46. Only one
member showed any understanding of the Chartists:
" They are in hostility against the middle class," said young
Mr. Disraeli. " They made no attempt on the aristocracy,
nor on the Corn Laws; they attacked the new class, not the
old. . . . While I disapprove of the Charter I sympathize
with the Chartists."

The year was not to pass without insurrection. A certain
Henry Vincent had preached Chartism in Newport and had
been imprisoned, in spite of the support of a Chartist
draper, John Frost, who was then a J.P. Frost collected a
thousand Chartists in South Wales and on the night of
November 3 marched into Newport to set Vincent free
by force of arms. Napier had heard of the plot and had
secretly posted 35 infantrymen in the town. The Chartists
were taken by surprise and 20 of them were killed and some
50 wounded. Thus ended the " physical force " movement
of 1839.

Meanwhile the Prime Minister, Melbourne, had been
occupied with problems of a very different nature. In 1837
that blustering, indiscreet old man, William IV, had died
and was succeeded by his eighteen-year-old niece, Victoria.
Melbourne made it his duty to be the guardian and tutor
of the ignorant girl; he saw her every day until in 1840 she
married her cousin, Prince Albert of Saxe-Coburg. The
Queen would have liked to keep Melbourne for ever; she
prevented Sir Robert Peel from succeeding him in 1839 by
her refusal to have Tory " Ladies of the Bedchamber " at
her Court. But the Commons were sick of Melbourne's in-
dolent methods and of his continually unbalanced budgets,
and at last the Queen had to give way: Peel became Prime
Minister in 1841 and the nation was swung forward on a
new wave of middle-class reform.

Chapter V: THE EARLY VICTORIAN AGE, 1837-50

The Tractarians – The Political Economists – The Two Nations – Irish Immigration – Peel's Financial Reforms – The Repeal of the Corn Laws – The End of Chartism – The Railway Age.

ONE SOMETIMES HEARS it said that the Early Victorian Age was an age of tranquillity. The very opposite is the truth. It was an age like our own of turmoil, an age of booms and slumps, of profiteering and bankruptcy, of plenty and of poverty. It was an age like our own of triumph in engineering, an age when the face of England was being transformed by a network of railroads as suddenly and disconcertingly as in our times it has been transformed by a network of motor roads. And like our own it was an age of uncertainty, an age of disagreement on the greatest questions of all.

The Tractarians. What is man's duty towards God? In the early nineteenth century Englishmen had been quite sure of the answer. Following the Evangelicals they held that it was a matter for each man's private conscience to decide. But in 1833 there was a group of young men at Oxford who insisted that religion was not so much an individual as a Church matter. Keble and Pusey and Newman and Manning held that the True Faith had been revealed by Christ to the Church and that the Church of England was a true branch of that Catholic Church. They claimed that the English Church had been purified at the Reformation and that, though it had rejected the authority of the Pope, it still remained the same Catholic Church which had been planted in England by Saint Augustine. They wanted to revive the old High Church doctrines of Laud, to restore the seven sacraments and the spiritual authority of bishops and priests whom they believed to be the successors of the Apostles. These views they put forward in a series of *Tracts for the Times*, which earned them the name of Tractarians. The Tracts, carried by young Oxford men on horseback from parish to parish, raised a storm of indignation. The Tractarians were accused of trying to betray the English Church to Rome, a claim which seemed to be justified when Newman in 1844 and Manning in 1851 left the English Church to become Roman Catholics.

The Political Economists. More acute controversy was raised by the question of man's duty towards his neighbour. In the old pre-machine days the answer, at least in theory, had been simple: it was the duty of the father to provide for his family, of the squire to provide for his tenants, of the employer to provide for his employees, of the parish to provide for the poor and of the Government to see that each did his duty to the full. But now all that was changed. Fathers could no longer earn enough to support a family: they had to turn wife and children as well into wage-earners. Landowners had to turn off their cottagers to make way for the new-fangled large-scale farm. Employers paid wages and took no further interest in their workers. The old responsibility of each parish for its paupers was swept away by the Poor Law of 1834. And the whole delicate social structure had been upset by the inordinate growth of the population: for centuries the population of England had been stable in the region of eight million, now it was leaping up and between 1801 and 1841 had actually doubled itself. (*See* p. 17.) What was one's duty towards one's neighbour now?

The answer was given by a group of men known as the Political Economists (or Utilitarians, or Philosophical Radicals). They looked at the new machine-industry and saw that it was good—an immense force adding to the wealth of nations. They looked at the system of competition, under which vigorous men had risen " from nothing " to be masters of great industrial concerns, and found that it too was good—a means of giving scope to the latent energies of mankind. They concluded that if only restrictions were removed from industry and commerce and if employers were allowed really free competition it would, in the phrase of Jeremy Bentham, be " for the greatest happiness of the greatest number." The stock-broker David Ricardo (1772–1823), developing the economics of Adam Smith, insisted that only by removing the restrictions on trade could the wealth of nations be fully developed. The duty of employers to their employees, according to the Political Economists, was to pay them just enough to live on and no more. Robert Malthus, the professor, in his *Essay on Population* (1803) said that if workers were paid more than a " subsistence-wage " they would have more and more children until the population reached the limit that the country could support and then everyone in every class would be reduced to the bare subsistence-level of living. The duty of the Government to the governed, according to the Political Economists, was to leave them alone (*laisser-faire*)—to allow free competition and then merely stand by and see fair play.

This doctrine, which was to become the guiding principle of nineteenth-century England, is known by the French name of *laisser-faire* because it was first advanced by pre-Revolutionary French economists, but it should be noted that neither France nor any other country but England was ever to adopt it. Reduced to its simplest terms, it meant that the Government should leave individual citizens free to employ whom they like how they like, to buy and to sell where and what they like and to invest their money where they like and when they like. The Political Economists believed that enlightened selfishness was more likely to lead to happiness than paternal benevolence. " By making the passion of self-love beyond comparison stronger than the passion of benevolence, the more ignorant are led to pursue the general happiness, an end which they would have totally failed to attain if the moving principle of their conduct had been benevolence," said the Reverend Robert Malthus.

The Two Nations. The gospel of *laisser-faire* was held by all the most progressive thinkers in England in the early nineteenth century. Reformers then were agreed on *laisser-faire* as reformers of every political hue in the 1930's were to be agreed on the very opposite principle, that of Planning. But by the 1840's a few far-seeing thinkers were beginning to oppose *laisser-faire*. Its great drawback was that though it made the rich richer, it made the poor poorer; for under free competition it was in the employers' interest to cut down the wages and to increase the working hours of the employees. This was the contention of Thomas Carlyle who published a short pamphlet, *Chartism* (1840), to draw the attention of the reading public to what he called " the Condition-of-the-People Question," and a longer book, *Past and Present* (1843), in which he soundly condemned *laisser-faire* as the " Gospel of Mammonism ":

" Our life is not a mutual helpfulness; but rather, cloaked under the laws of war, named ' free competition ' and so forth, it is a mutual hostility. We have profoundly forgotten everywhere that *Cash-payment* is not the sole relation of human beings; we think, nothing doubting, that *it* absolves and liquidates all engagements of man. ' My starving workers ? ' answers the rich Millowner: ' Did not I hire them fairly in the Market ? Did I not pay them, to the last sixpence, the sum covenanted for ? What have I to do with them more ? '—Verily Mammon-worship is a melancholy creed. When Cain, for his own behalf, had killed Abel, and was questioned, ' Where is thy brother ? ' he too made answer, ' Am I my brother's keeper . . .'

" The Laws of *Laisser-faire*, O Westminster, the laws of industrial Captain and of industrial Soldier, how much more of idle Captain and industrial Soldier will need to be remodelled and modified and rectified in a hundred and a hundred ways. . . . With two million industrial soldiers already sitting in Bastilles, and five million pining on potatoes, methinks Westminster cannot begin too soon ! "

The same cry that the Scot Carlyle was raising outside

Westminster was being raised within by the Jew Disraeli. He was an extraordinary man. The son of a lifelong scholar, Isaac Disraeli, he had failed in many professions: had gone into a solicitor's office and given it up, had tried to found a daily newspaper (with John Murray as publisher and Sir Walter Scott as patron), had gambled on the Stock Exchange and lost £7,000 more than he possessed. His first novels had a certain success but his attempts to get into Parliament had none: he was defeated four times in elections before the liberality of a rich lady, whom he subsequently married, bought him the votes of the electors of Maidstone. In 1837 he made his first speech, dressed in green coat and white embroidered waistcoat and hung about with jewellery. He was shouted down; his eccentricity blinded the House to his fundamental seriousness, his wit made them overlook his wisdom. Only in 1841 did Disraeli begin to find his true mission in politics, when he gathered together a little group of aristocrats which he called the Young England party to oppose the prevailing attitude of *laisser-faire*. The Young Englanders hated Capitalism and Chartism alike. They wanted to restore a feeling of responsibility between rulers and ruled. They looked back with longing to feudal times when, according to Disraeli's friend, Lord John Manners:

> *Each knew his place—king, peasant, peer, or priest,*
> *The greatest owned connection with the least;*
> *From rank to rank the generous feeling ran,*
> *And linked society as man to man . . .*
> *Now, in their place, behold the modern slave,*
> *Doomed from the very cradle to the grave,*
> *To tread his lonely path of care and toil;*
> *Bound, in sad truth and bowed down to the soil,*
> *He dies, and leaves his sons their heritage—*
> *Work for their prime, and workhouse for their age.*

To call attention to Young England Disraeli wrote a novel, *Coningsby*, in 1844. Next year to call attention to the evils

THE EARLY VICTORIAN AGE

that Young England existed to cure he wrote *Sybil or the Two Nations*. The Two Nations were the rich and poor, and between them there was a great gulf fixed. From the pages of that most readable book the novel-reading public learnt—many of them for the first time—of the degradation into which machine industry and the philosophy of *laisser-faire* had led the vast majority of English people.

Describing conditions in a typical country town, Disraeli wrote: " Marney mainly consisted of a variety of narrow and crowded lanes formed by cottages built of rubble, or unhewn stones without cement, and from age or badness of the material, looking as if they could scarcely hold together. The gaping chinks admitted every blast; the leaning chimneys had lost half their original height; the rotten rafters were evidently misplaced; while in many instances the thatch, yawning in some parts to admit the wind and wet, and in all utterly unfit for its original purpose of giving protection from the weather, looked more like the top of a dunghill than a cottage. Before the doors of these dwellings, and often surrounding them, ran open drains full of animal and vegetable refuse, decomposing into disease, or sometimes in their imperfect course filling foul pits or spreading into stagnant pools, while a concentrated solution of every species of dissolving filth was allowed to soak through, and thoroughly impregnate, the walls and ground adjoining.

" These wretched tenements seldom consist of more than two rooms, in one of which the whole family, however numerous, were obliged to sleep, without distinction of age, or sex, or suffering. With the water streaming down the walls, the light distinguished through the roof, with no hearth in winter, the virtuous mother in the sacred pangs of childbirth gives forth another victim to our thoughtless civilization; surrounded by three generations whose inevitable presence is more painful than her sufferings in that hour of travail; while the father of the coming child, in another corner of the sordid chamber, lies stricken by that typhus[1] which his contaminated dwelling has breathed into his veins, and for whose next prey is perhaps destined his new-born child. These swarming walls had neither windows nor doors sufficient to keep out the weather, to admit the sun, or supply the means of ventilation—the humid and putrid roof of thatch exhaling malaria like all other decaying vegetable matter."

Disraeli's *Sybil* set a fashion for novels dealing with the condition of the people. Mrs. Gaskell's *Mary Barton* appeared in 1848, Charlotte Brontë's *Shirley* in 1849, Charles Kingsley's *Alton Locke* in 1851, and Dickens' *Hard Times* in 1854. Intelligent people could no longer ignore the fact that England had indeed come to consist of two nations. In the lovely smoke-free London of those days where Wren's churches stood out above the City buildings and Nash's parades and crescents ennobled the West End and the press of sailing ships made the Thames the most gracious thoroughfare in the world, there was already a vast slum stretching unbroken from the Tower to beyond Bethnal Green. In the cities of the industrial North five people died of lung trouble every year for every two who died in the country. In a suburb of Manchester the death-rate was 68 per cent higher in the poor streets than in the rich. While wealthy Englishmen were living on the fat of the land the poor lived on bread and cheese, tea and potatoes, with meat—it was usually bacon —twice a week, and doped their children with patent medicines.

Irish Immigration. These evils exist to-day, intensified or mitigated but in no real sense removed. But there were two factors in the condition-of-the-people question in the forties which are gone to-day and which we must therefore

---

[1] In the year that *Sybil* was written 1,462 typhus patients were admitted to the London Fever Hospital, while in Glasgow no less than 32,000 persons were attacked and of these 32 per cent died.

describe at greater length. The first of these was the problem raised by Irish immigration. In the 1840's fifty thousand Irish every year were driven by famine in their own island to seek employment in the industrial towns of England. They were peasants who had never seen a town before and had no idea of how to live in one. Consequently when they found themselves in a town they made, literally, a mess of it. A German observer, Friedrich Engels, describing the *Condition of the Working Class in 1844*, wrote: " The Irishman builds a pig-sty against his wall as he did at home and if he is prevented from doing so, he lets the pig sleep in the room with himself. . . . He eats and sleeps with it, his children play with it, ride upon it, roll in the dirt with it, as one may see a thousand times repeated in all the great towns of England. The filth and comfortlessness that prevail in the houses themselves it is impossible to describe." They were poor people whose ancestors had been poor for centuries and they were used to a standard of living as much lower than that of the Englishman as the Japanese workers' standard is to-day. Consequently employers could take them on for a pittance and dismiss his more expensive English labour. This led Carlyle to write of the Irishman: " He is the sorest evil this country has to strive with. In his rags and savagery he is ready to undertake all work that can be done by mere strength of hand and back—and for wages that will purchase him potatoes. He needs only salt for condiment, he lodges to his mind in any pig-hutch or dog-hutch, roosts in outhouses, and wears a suit of tatters, the getting on and off of which is said to be a difficult operation, transacted only in festivals and the high tides of the Calendar. . . . There abides he, in his squalor and unreason, in his falsity and drunken violence, as the ready-made nucleus of degradation and disorder."

It might have been wise to check Irish immigration as Americans and Australians check immigration from China and Japan to-day. But English industrialists needed labour and they preferred labour that was cheap, so the problem of the Irish-in-England went unchecked.[1]

Another crying evil of the forties which has since disappeared was Truck or " Tommy "—the habit of paying wages in kind instead of in money. Sometimes an employer would pay his workers in the commodities they made for him—six shillings' worth of waistcoats or of stockings instead of six of the Queen's shillings. Sometimes he had the wages paid over the bar of a friend's public house. More often he kept a shop where the prices were fixed by himself and whither the workers were sent with tickets entitling them to their wages' worth of goods which were usually rotten and invariably dear. In *Sybil* Disraeli described a tommy-shop in terms so vivid that one would dismiss it as fiction if one did not know that he had written it almost word for word from the report of a Royal Commission. An Act of 1831 had prohibited truck, but in terms so vague and with so little provision for enforcing them, that it had no effect whatsoever. It was 1896 before truck was really made illegal. It is worth remembering when we read of the increase of wages in the forties (wages were 40 per cent higher and prices 20 per cent lower in 1850 than in 1790. *See* p. 143) that their value to the workers was often diminished by Truck.

Peel's Financial Reforms. The man on whom it fell to choose between *laisser-faire* and its opponents and to steer English policy according to the choice was Sir Robert Peel. He was an exemplary product of the newly rich manufacturing class. His father, the first Sir Robert, had amassed a fortune of a million and a quarter pounds as a pioneer of the Lancashire cotton industry. The son had the stiff, self-conscious dignity of the parvenu. Wellington deplored his breeding: " Peel," he said, " has no manners." The Queen was made uneasy by his stiffness, though later

[1] Here we are concerned only with the effects of the Irish upon England; the effects of the English upon Ireland will be discussed in Chapter X.

she came to trust him. Many people found him alarmingly cold: " His smile," said Daniel O'Connell, " is like the silver plate on a coffin." But nobody could doubt his extraordinary ability. Even the young Disraeli, whom he snubbed by refusing a Cabinet appointment in 1841 and who opposed him bitterly, as we shall see, in the years that followed, admitted that " he is the greatest Member of Parliament that England has ever had."

Peel's greatness lay in the fact that he brought a new standard of values to party politics. The old parties had been founded in the seventeenth century when the great issues lay between the respective rights of Crown and Cabinet, of Established Church and Dissenters (Nonconformists): the Tories had been the supporters of Crown and Church, the Whigs of Cabinet-rule and Dissent. Behind that there lay an economic division: the Tories were the party of the landed gentry, the Whigs of the moneyed men—the rich merchants and financiers. But now the Industrial Revolution had brought new interests to the fore and a new class—that of the manufacturers— into the political limelight. The old issues had lost their importance: the burning question now was how to turn England's new industrial wealth to the best account and Peel was the man to answer it, though it would mean transforming and splitting the Tory party to which he belonged.

Already he had been responsible for a number of remarkable reforms. Back in 1819, when he was a young man of thirty-one, Peel had initiated a measure which gave English banking a degree of stability which no other banking system in the world enjoyed. By " Peel's Act " of 1819 the Bank of England was obliged to give in exchange for gold notes at the rate of £3 17s. 10½d. per ounce. This Act, which came into operation in May 1821, put England on the Gold Standard. Half a century later the other great Powers were to follow our example. This was to be of incalculable benefit to international trade for when traders knew exactly how much their foreign customers' money would be worth in terms of gold they felt infinitely safer in sending goods overseas.

Finance was not the only department in which Peel had distinguished himself. As Home Secretary in 1822 he had reformed the Criminal Code, reducing the offences punishable by death from over a hundred to four—and this in the teeth of the opposition of Tory landowners who wanted poachers hanged and rickburners executed as in " the good old days." Then in 1828 he had provided London with its first police force, setting uniformed constables, known as Peelers, or Bobbies,[1] to patrol the streets in the place of the ineffectual night-watchmen. In 1829 he had put himself at the head of the movement for Catholic Emancipation, and helped Wellington to carry the Bill through Parliament though it meant driving the diehards out of the Tory party. His most remarkable achievement had been accomplished in 1834 when as candidate for Tamworth he had sent a manifesto to his electors announcing that he stood, not for reaction, but for *conserving* what could be proved to be good and for " reforming every institution that really required reform; but gradually, dispassionately and deliberately that the reform might be lasting." The Tamworth Manifesto marked the evolution of the Tory into the Conservative party.

Peel had been Prime Minister in 1834, but he was in power for no more than fifteen months and had no chance to put his principles into practice. Now, in 1841, his opportunity had come. He set to work at once to apply in part the ideas of the Political Economists. His budgets from 1842–45 carried on the work which Huskisson had started, that of sweeping away the heavy duties and indirect taxes which hampered trade. The loss to the revenue he repaired by restoring the *Income Tax* which had first been collected by Pitt as a special war measure and which was henceforth, in spite of the storm of indignation

---

[1] They were dressed in blue coats, white trousers and top-hats, and armed with wooden rattles, and their wages were one guinea a week.

which greeted Peel's sevenpence-in-the-pound levy, to remain as a permanent tax.

At the same time Peel put the financial system of the country on a new basis by the Bank Charter Act of 1844. Hitherto all sorts of banks had the right of issuing paper money. They had abused the right and had issued too many notes, with the result that in times of financial panic when many people rushed to the banks to demand gold for their paper money there had not been enough gold to meet the demand. In 1825, as we have seen, there had been a widespread failure of banks. In 1836 another crisis occurred and the Bank of England had to borrow gold from the Bank of France to strengthen its exhausted reserves. When the time came to renew the Bank of England's Charter in 1844 Peel put a limit on the banks' power to create paper money. The Bank of England was given the sole right of adding to the amount of paper money in circulation and this right was restricted by a clause ordering the Bank to keep £5 in gold in its cellars for every £5 note it printed over and above the sum of £14,000,000.

It should be noted that the Charter, which with trivial amendments has remained the constitution of the Bank to the present day, did not put the Bank under Government control. Nor did the Act of 1844 succeed in its intention of controlling the amount of paper money in circulation. The Bank of England increased its revenues by attracting gold to England[1] and issued more and more paper currency. The joint-stock banks, deprived of the right of issuing new notes, put money into circulation in the new form of cheques.

Yet the new system worked fairly well. It gave business men confidence, and confidence is the first essential of expanding trade. The Bank of England had the Government behind it and when panics occurred, as they did later in the year 1844 and again in 1857 and 1866, and people rushed to withdraw their money from the banks so that the

[1] As luck would have it, the world-supply of gold was increased during the century by the discovery of new goldfields in California (1840), Australia (1851), South Africa (1886), and in Yukon (1898).

reserves of gold in the cellars of Threadneedle Street sank dangerously low, the Government had only to promise to suspend the Bank Charter Act—that is, to allow the Bank to print paper money without having a reserve of gold—and the rush on the Bank ceased. The assurance that the Government was supporting the Bank was enough to allay panic.

Why these panics should have occurred at all, and particularly why they should have occurred as they did with such regularity every ten years or so throughout the nineteenth century, is one of the unsolved problems of economic history. Some economists say that there is a Trade Cycle, meaning that trade must swing from prosperity to depression and back, by the very nature of the capitalist system. Under Capitalism manufacturers do not produce goods to meet a definite demand: they guess what the demand is going to be and regulate production according to their guess. When prospects are good banks lend money to industrialists who extend their works and increase their output. But as the majority of the people are getting no more wages than before they are unable to buy all the new output of goods, so the industrialists are left with a surplus on their hands. They shut down their works and dismiss their workers, and a period of depression sets in and does not end till the stocks in the warehouses are exhausted and industrialists are emboldened to borrow and bankers to lend cheaply once again. After 1866 the bankers learned to guard against the worst ups and downs of this cycle by controlling their loans more carefully.

The Repeal of the Corn Laws. Meanwhile a new agitation had been gathering way in the North, parallel in force and intensity to the agitation for Parliamentary reform in 1830–32. It was a middle-class movement led by middle-class men—by Richard Cobden, a Manchester cotton manufacturer, and by John Bright, the owner of a Rochdale carpet factory. The idea behind the movement was simple: the Corn Laws must be repealed in order to let foreign corn into England so that bread would be plentiful and cheap. From this the whole Free Trade philosophy of *laisser-faire* followed: instead of each nation's striving to be self-supporting, each nation would produce and would exchange its surplus products for the surplus of other countries; thus the world would be linked together in peace by the bonds of commerce.[1] And since England alone at that time produced a surplus of factory-made goods, England would become the workshop of the world, the richest nation the world had ever seen.

These doctrines were not new; Adam Smith, as we know, had announced them in his *Wealth of Nations* as long ago as 1776 and the Political Economists had been expounding them in their tedious books for the last generation. What was new was the methods adopted to popularize them by the Manchester School. They founded the Anti-Corn Law League (1838) and set about building a Free Trade Hall as a monument on the fields of Peterloo. They used the new Penny Post to put their ideas before the electorate—Cobden was the first to see the possibilities of postal propaganda. Then Cobden and Bright began a most remarkable series of lecture-tours. It was a new thing for Members of Parliament to address the electorate when no election was being held. It was a new thing for a man of business to explain the mysteries of economics, as Cobden did, in terms that ordinary people could understand. It was a new thing for a man of religion to make great audiences feel ready, as Bright the Quaker did, to rise on Crusade for Repeal, to cheer and to pray for Repeal, to march in procession with banners bearing the strange device " Down with Monopoly, No Corn Law ! "

---

[1] " Commerce," said Cobden, " is the grand panacea, which, like a beneficent medical discovery, will serve to inoculate with the healthy and saving taste for civilization all the nations of the world. Not a bale of merchandize leaves our shores, but it bears the seeds of intelligence and fruitful thought to the members of some less enlightened community; not a merchant visits our seats of manufacturing industry, but he returns to his own country the missionary of freedom, peace, and good government—whilst our steamboats, that now visit every port of Europe, and our miraculous rail-roads, that are the talk of all nations, are the advertisements and vouchers for the value of our enlightened institutions."

During the early forties Cobden and Bright swept the country with their strange mixture of *laisser-faire* economics and religious revivalism. In the north industrialists flocked to the League, dazzled by the prospects of trade expansion. In the south labourers were easily converted by the prospect of cheap bread: " I be protected and I be starving," said a peasant at a meeting in 1843. Only the Tory landlords and farmers resisted: they saw nothing attractive in having to compete with foreign wheat and maize.

In 1845 Peel was wavering. His Bank Charter Act had been designed to put an end to *laisser-faire* in banking. He was becoming convinced that Free Trade was right, but his own party were Protectionists whereas the Opposition headed by Lord John Russell were disciples of Cobden and Bright. To repeal the Corn Laws would be to ruin the Tory party. Back-bench Tories were goading him for contemplating treachery. Disraeli raised cheers and laughter in the House by his taunts: " The right honourable gentleman has caught the Whigs bathing, and walked away with their clothes. He has left them in the full enjoyment of their *liberal* position, and he is himself a strict *conservative* of their garments. . . . I remember him making his Protection speeches. They were the best I ever heard. It was a great thing to hear the honourable gentleman say, ' I would rather be the leader of the gentlemen of England than possess the confidence of sovereigns.' That was a great thing. We don't hear much of ' the gentlemen of England ' now."

Then a calamity happened which threw Peel finally on to the side of the League. In Ireland a blight ruined the potato crop. The Irish had no alternative food. The English had no surplus grain to send them, for the harvest of 1845 was spoilt by rain. The Corn Laws prevented foreign food from coming into the United Kingdom. Therefore the Corn Laws must go.

So on the night of June 26, 1846, while Peel's government was being defeated on another issue in the House of Commons, Repeal of the Corn Laws was carried in the Lords, and England became a Free Trade country. This

THE EARLY VICTORIAN AGE 93

was an epoch-making reform, if ever there was one. In a sense the rest of our history has been a history of the consequences of the Repeal of 1846. But in tracing these consequences we must be careful to note that they meant different things at different times.

The End of Chartism. The immediate result of the Repeal was not to usher in the millennium promised by Bright. The rest of the 1840's were still " the Hungry Forties." The price of bread did not fall: it was merely prevented from rising by the Repeal. The Chartist leaders soon realized that they had been side-tracked by the Anti-Corn Law League as they had been side-tracked by the Reform Bill Whigs in 1832. They clamoured now for the Ten-Hour Day Bill which Lord Shaftesbury had been attempting to pass for years. Bright and the manufacturing interests in the Commons opposed the Bill. Though it was intended to limit merely the hours of " young persons " between 13 and 18, it was seen that it would in fact be extended to adults, for machinery cannot be run for fifteen hours for one set of workers and for ten hours for another. At last, in 1847, the Ten-Hour Day Bill was passed. Employers in future tended to stabilize the working day at from 6 a.m. to 6 p.m. in summer, from 7 a.m. to 7 p.m. in winter, with intervals for meals.

This was a long step forward and the workers' champions would have been well advised to confine their attention to reforms of that sort. But the Chartist movement had fallen under the leadership of Feargus O'Connor and dreams of " physical force " still chased each other across that crazy Irishman's brain. In 1842 a second National Petition had been presented to Parliament, only to be rejected by 287 votes to 49. Its rejection had been followed by widespread strikes in the north. They had failed, and their failure should have taught O'Connor a lesson; but now in 1847 he planned a third National Petition. It was to have five million signatures; it was to be carried to the House by a procession of half a million Chartists; it was to be followed, if rejected, by insurrection. So much for O'Connor's intentions. In fact some 30,000 Chartists met on Kennington Common on April 10, 1848, and found their way to Westminster barred. The Government had called on the aged Duke of Wellington to bar the way to London with a military force and had enrolled a body of 170,000 special constables. The Chartists had to bundle their leaders and the innumerable pages of the Petition into three hackney cabs. So the march on Westminster was a fiasco. And the Petition was a fiasco too, for when a Parliamentary committee came to examine it they found the " signatures " numbered less than two million and included—by a stroke of Irish humour singularly unsuited to English taste— those of Queen Victoria, the Prince Consort and the Duke of Wellington.

Chartism dissolved in ridicule. The six points of the Charter were all very well in abstract justice (all except one have since been granted), but as a practical cure for the diseases of the workers in the thirties and forties they were worse than useless. Chartism had told the worker to demand the vote when what he really wanted was bread. Chartist leaders had told him to use physical force when his real weapon, as he was later to discover, was passive resistance by means of the trade union and the industrial strike.

The Railway Age. If the immediate consequences of 1846 were disappointing, its later consequences exceeded the fondest dreams of the Political Economists. By 1850 English industries were ready to take advantage of Free Trade. Already the main lines of our present railway system had been laid. The first railway of all, from Stockton to Darlington, was opened in 1825 and designed to take coal from the South-West Durham Coalfield to the Tees, and thence to the sea. The second, from Liverpool to Manchester, was opened in 1830 and designed to carry cotton and other raw materials from the port to the great new manufacturing centre round Manchester. The engineer and supervisor of both was George Stephenson. To him and to the Cornishman, Robert Trevithick (1771–1833), the credit must go for turning the stationary steam engine into a locomotive railway engine. Stephenson designed his railways to carry freight between industrial centres in the north, and on these lines development continued throughout the thirties. In the forties a new development was begun, that of connecting London with the provinces. In those years most of the great lines we know to-day were laid down: by 1850 there were through trains from London to Lancaster, to Taunton, to Southampton, to Brighton, to Dover (*see* map on page 96). The small companies which had built the first lines for coal purposes soon combined into a few great companies: in 1846 there were 200 railway companies, in 1848 there were only 22.

The man behind these amalgamations was George Hudson, the " Railway King." A farmer's son who had gone into business as a linen-draper in York, Hudson financed half the railways in England, became a banker, a Tory M.P., a millionaire, a multi-millionaire. He raised his money largely by swindling the public with cooked accounts and false balance-sheets, and he spent it on enriching his friends and his beloved city of York. Half crook, half public benefactor, George Hudson was a typical " self-made man " of the Early Victorian Age.

There was widespread resistance to the railways at first: landowners detested the "locomotive monster with a tail of smoke"; farmers complained that it frightened their cattle to death; travellers refused to risk their lives to it and stuck to their coaches. But gradually they all bowed to the inevitable: landowners sold land to the companies at fantastic prices; farmers found the railways a wonderful means of conveyance for their produce; passengers forsook their nine-miles-an-hour coaches for the trains—which by 1850 were running at 50 m.p.h. By the mid-forties it was obvious that the railways had come to stay. Investors let their optimism run away with them and plunged their money into railway shares to such an extent that the public

became alarmed and rushed to the banks to withdraw their money. Panic was narrowly averted in 1847 by the suspension of the Bank Charter Act, in other words by giving the Bank of England permission to issue new paper money if the rush continued. The rush did not continue. A few local banks collapsed, but thereafter investment in railway development continued at a steadier and more healthy pace, making England the first nation in the world to have a railway system for the transport of her industrial goods, as the Industrial Revolution had made her the first nation to turn to manufacture on a large scale by machinery.

In 1850 Peel died—the result of a fall from his horse in Hyde Park. The Early Victorian Age, the age of uncertainty and civil conflict, died with him. Peel had found England at the cross-roads, hesitating between the sign which pointed to Self-Sufficient England and that pointing to Industrial Expansion. He had put England firmly upon the latter road, by repealing the Corn Laws. The problem that lay before the future rulers of England was to find buyers for our coal and iron, for our woollen and cotton goods, and sellers from whom to obtain increasing quantities of raw wool and cotton and of the food which we were no longer growing in sufficient extent to feed our rising population. We shall see how they opened up new colonies to supply us with food and raw materials; how they interfered in Europe to keep ports open to our goods; how they wrung trading concessions from the peoples of the Far East. We shall see that the years between 1850 and 1873 were the years of England's unchallenged supremacy, for then we alone held the secret of machine-industry. And later we shall see how, after about 1873, cheap foreign food ruined our farmers, and other nations learned our secrets and entered into competition with us for colonies and foreign markets, a competition which ended in a great war between the industrial powers in 1914–18, and in the subsequent abandoning by England of the principles of Free Trade which had been adopted amid such enthusiasm during the Hungry Forties.

Chapter VI: AN EMPIRE IN THE MAKING, 1815-70

The Empire in 1815 – Wakefield and the Colonial Reformers – The Durham Report – India: annexations and reforms – Mutiny – Trade with the Far East – Trade with the White Colonies.

THE MOST SURPRISING THING about the British Empire is its newness. A hundred years ago it consisted of nothing more than a few islands and coastal settlements which were inhabited chiefly by Frenchmen and Dutchmen, white convicts and black slaves. The British Government had lost one Empire in the American War of Independence (1783) and was not inclined to acquire another. It regarded the remaining colonists as potential rebels and sent out army officers to govern them, and to wring what revenue they could for the mother-country out of colonial trade.

The Empire in 1815.   The West Indies were the most important of the British colonies in the first part of the nineteenth century. Until as late as 1842 the West Indian trade was worth much more than the trade of all the rest of the Empire together. The islands provided the United Kingdom with its sugar supply—and with its rum. They were owned by rich planters and worked by negro slaves.

Next in importance were the North American Provinces, thanks to their trade in ships and naval equipment. But three-quarters of the Canada we know to-day were then unexplored: the prairies were unknown and no Canadian corn found its way to the British Isles. Of the colonists the oldest established were the French, who since their defeat in 1759 had quietly accepted English rule on the understanding that they should be left in the enjoyment of their French language and law and their Roman Catholic religion. They had naturally little affection for their English rulers but

AN EMPIRE IN THE MAKING 99

they looked to England to protect them from the Americans who were threatening to absorb them into the United States and from the newcomers who had fled from the States after the American Revolution. The latter, the United Empire Loyalists, had settled in Upper Canada (Ontario) and in the east and were a perpetual menace to the French colonists of Lower Canada (Quebec). As for the rest of Canada, the Maritime Provinces of the east, Nova Scotia, New Brunswick and Prince Edward Island, were inhabited by sturdy British fisher-folk and had a flourishing industry in building ships of the soft woods of the Canadian forests. Nearly a third of the ships in the British Mercantile marine in 1826 were built in the North American Provinces.[1]

Of the African continent, Cape Colony was the only part which was inhabited by white men in 1815, and the white men there were Dutch. England had seized the Cape from the Dutch in 1806, when Holland happened to be the unwilling ally of Napoleon, and after the war had paid Holland £6,000,000 for the right to retain it. The Dutch Settlers (Boers) hated British rule from the beginning. They hated it more in 1820 when the first batch of English colonists arrived and settled, with the aid of a Government grant, at Port Elizabeth. They hated it still more in 1828 when English was proclaimed the official language in courts and schools in place of Dutch, and when the natives (Hottentots) were declared to be the equals of Europeans before the law. The last straw was the Act of 1834 which abolished slavery and thus deprived the Boer farmers of their unpaid labour. Some of the Dutch decided to leave the colony: in 1836 they piled their wives and children, their furniture and Bibles into ox-wagons and made the Great Trek into

[1] *Yes, we did a heap o' riggin'*
In those rampin', boomin' days
When the wooden ships were buildin'
On their quaint old greasy ways:
Craft of every sort and fashion,
Big and little, lithe and tall,
Had their birthplace by the harbour
And we rigged them one and all.

the unknown North until they found new pastures beyond the Orange and the Vaal Rivers. Even here the English claimed to be their overlords; it was not until 1854 that Westminster recognized the independence of the Transvaal Republic and of the Orange Free State. The motive of this harrying of the Boers was humanitarian, not economic. The mineral resources of South Africa were still undreamed of and the only value of the colony to England lay in the convenience of Cape Town as a port of call on the way to India and in the possibility of sheep-farming on a modest scale in the hinterland. The Boers were harried because they enslaved the natives. The head of the Colonial Office between 1836 and 1847 was Sir James Stephen, the friend and nephew of Wilberforce.

Finally Australia. It too was almost an unknown continent in 1815. Captain Cook had planted the British flag on some points of the eastern coast in 1770, but there was no settlement by white men until 1788 when a Captain Phillip reached Botany Bay with a cargo of 717 convicts and 250 guards. The custom of transporting convicts as slaves to the colonies instead of shutting them in prisons at home was an old one. Their usual destination had been Virginia and the Carolinas until the American Revolution made it necessary for a new dumping ground to be found. In 1787 George III announced to Parliament that he intended to transport convicts to Australia " to remove the inconvenience which arose from the crowded state of the gaols in different parts of the kingdom."

Captain Phillip was only just in time. A few days after he landed a French ship arrived to plant the French flag on the coast and to claim Australia for France. Perhaps it is well that the French were forestalled, for like the English they would have peopled the new country with convicts, and with convicts of the worst character. Most of the first men and women to be transported from England were guilty of nothing more shocking than resisting and criticizing the Government, and later batches of convicts consisted of men sentenced for crimes still less heinous: for example, a batch sent out in the year of Queen Victoria's coronation included men guilty of slaughtering butcher's meat without a licence, damaging trees and saplings, stealing oysters from an oyster bed, defacing marks on Government property, and poaching.

Altogether 130,000 convicts were transported to Australia. The contractors who shipped them got £20 or £30 per head from the Government and invariably overcrowded the ships so as to increase their profit; it was not unusual for one convict out of every four to die on the voyage out as a result of overcrowding and bad feeding. The survivors were sold as " assigned servants " to settlers who came out to try their luck at farming with this unpaid labour the coastlands of Australia which they could buy for a paltry 2s. an acre. Beyond scattered settlements on the coast the continent was still unknown: it was 1829 before even the Murray River was explored.

Wakefield and the Colonial Reformers.

In this miserable state the British Empire might have remained had not the prevalence of unemployment induced the British Government to consider the possibility of relieving the pressure of population at home by assisting emigration to the colonies. A few settlements were established in the twenties, but they were not notably successful (and one in Western Australia was a notable failure) because the Government was interested only in getting emigrants out of England and not in their welfare when they reached their destination.

In 1829 articles began to appear in the *Morning Chronicle* and the *Spectator* exposing in a lively style the cause of the failure. The articles were anonymous because the author, Edward Gibbon Wakefield, was serving a term in Newgate Gaol. Wakefield had had a stormy career. Born in 1796, the son of a Radical who was a friend of Francis Place, he had entered the diplomatic service and secured promotion at the age of twenty by marrying an heiress after a daring elopement. His wife died in 1820 and six years later he tried to repair his fortunes by marrying another heiress. This time the elopement was even more daring. The heiress, whom he had never met, was a school-girl. Wakefield called at the school in a closed carriage, got the girl into it on a pretext and drove to Gretna Green where the marriage service was read by the blacksmith. This escapade was followed by his arrest; he was tried and sentenced to three years' imprisonment. Seeing no future for himself in England, he became interested in the colonies and from this interest was born a series of ideas on which the British Dominions as we know them to-day were founded.

Wakefield showed that the new settlements had failed because the Government was interested in emigration rather than in colonization. Decent people would not settle in countries where the only amenities were provided by the company of convicts and where neither the comforts nor the liberties of the home countries could be enjoyed. He therefore laid down four new principles of colonization. First the transportation of convicts should cease. Secondly settlers should be obliged to pay for land they acquired in the colonies; he suggested a minimum price of £2 an acre, intending thus to attract a rich type of settler and also to provide a fund out of which the passage-money of emigrant labourers—preferably respectable married couples—could be paid. Thirdly the cultural and devotional needs of settlers should be provided for by the establishment of schools and churches. Finally their liberties should be secured by the grant of self-government through colonial parliaments.

These excellent ideas were rejected in Government circles for reasons almost equally excellent. In the first place their execution would cost a great deal of public money, and the Colonial Office from that day to this has been disinclined to support colonial settlement until individuals have proved by private enterprise that it can be made to pay. In the second place the establishment of white men's colonies in black men's countries would lead to the corruption of the natives. The Evangelicals, who as we have seen had great influence with the Government in the early thirties, urged this point strongly and were supported by the evidence of missionaries who reported that the association of civilized with primitive people was invariably disastrous to the morals and religion of the latter. Only on the question of transportation was the Government as a whole prepared to change its policy, and that was not so much because of the arguments of Wakefield as of those of the Evangelicals. In 1840 the last batch of convicts was sent to New South Wales.

Meanwhile Wakefield, released from prison, had gone to work on his own account. He managed to persuade a new Colonial Secretary, Stanley, who had been at school with him at Westminster, to countenance the foundation of a colony on the new principles at Adelaide in South Australia. This was in 1837. In the same year he founded the New Zealand Company and sent his brother to establish the first British settlement in New Zealand at a place which he called Wellington (1839). This time the Colonial Office was against him, but he urged that if Britain did not annex the islands France indubitably would. Indeed a certain Baron de Thierrey had already bought some land from the natives (Maoris) and was calling himself King of New Zealand. This argument prevailed, and the Government declared New Zealand to be annexed to the British Crown, salving its conscience by signing with the Maori chiefs the Treaty of Waitangi (1840) by which the Crown guaranteed to them " the full, exclusive and undisputed possession of their lands and estates," on condition that they yielded to the British " the exclusive right of pre-emption over such lands as the proprietors thereof may be disposed to alienate." Wakefield then cast round for new supporters at home and found them in the leaders of the Presbyterian Church and of the Church of England. These connections led to the establishment of the Scottish colony of Dunedin and of the Anglican colony of Canterbury. A decade of wars against the Maoris followed; the heads of the Churches at home had none of the missionaries' qualms about the effects of white penetration upon the natives.

The Durham Report. The next stage in the work of Wakefield and his friends was to win the right of self-government for the colonies. The opportunity came in 1837—a memorable year in the history of the Empire. A rebellion, or rather two rebellions, broke out in Canada. The French Canadians under Papineau rose in revolt against their English Governor and his irresponsible Council. The United Empire Loyalists, under Mackenzie, rose in revolt against their equally irresponsible Governor and Council. Lord Melbourne sent out Lord Durham, the most virile—and incidentally the most awkward-tempered —of his colleagues, with special powers to deal with the situation. Durham took Gibbon Wakefield with him as his secret adviser, and Charles Buller, a wise and witty young pupil of Carlyle. He soon crushed the rebellions but his autocratic methods aroused a storm of indignation both in Canada and in England, and in five months Lord Durham was recalled in disgrace. Yet the report on colonial government which he drew up with the help of Wakefield and published on his return laid down the principles on which the Empire is now governed.

The Durham Report proposed that colonial Governors should always act on the advice of ministers acceptable to a parliament elected by the colonists, and should become constitutional rulers like the King of England. In Durham's words, " I know not how it is possible to secure . . . harmony in any other way than by administering the government on those principles which have been found perfectly efficacious in Great Britain. I would not impair a single prerogative of the Crown. . . . But the Crown must . . . submit to the necessary consequences of representative institutions; and if it has to carry on the government in unison with a representative body, it must consent to carry it on by means of those in whom that representative body has confidence."

The Durham Report also proposed that French and

AN EMPIRE IN THE MAKING

English Canada should be united in a single province with a single parliament. This reform was not quite so disinterested, for it was designed to give the English a majority in parliament with the power of out-voting French interests on every point. The report was adopted in 1840. There remained the gigantic task of putting its principles into practice.

Luckily for the future of Canada, a great man was sent out as Governor-General in 1847. He was Lord Elgin, the son-in-law of Durham. Canada is indebted to him for four great achievements. First and foremost, he made responsible government possible by choosing as his ministers popular reformers, even though they had been connected with the recent rebellions. Secondly he taught the French and English members to work together in parliament for the common good of Canada. Thirdly he induced the Westminster Government to abandon the vast reserves of Canadian land that had been set aside to furnish revenues for the Anglican Church (which was destined never to win a preponderant influence over Canadian souls). Fourthly he made in 1854 a treaty for comparatively Free Trade with the United States, and so began that close commercial relationship which, in spite of setbacks, has done so much to add to the prosperity of both countries.

By the middle of the century the principle of self-government had been accepted for all British colonies where white settlers predominated. In North America there were three self-governing colonies—Canada, Nova Scotia and New Brunswick; in South Africa there were three—Cape Colony, Transvaal and the Orange Free State; in Australia there were five—New South Wales, Victoria, Queensland, South Australia and Van Diemen's Land (Tasmania); and in New Zealand there was one. Wakefield had a marvellously clear vision of the future of the colonies which comprised this new Empire: " At some future time our Colonies, powerful as the Parent State or more so, must either, thanks to mismanagement, have become independent states more likely to be its enemies than its hearty friends, or else, through a wise foresight, have been kept closely bound to it,—confederacy, in some shape, by degrees, taking the place of the old bond of union,—the British nation continuing still united, so far as perpetual peace, mutual good understanding, freedom of commerce, and identity of foreign policy can unite it,— these Islands still its Metropolis, though their people be no longer the admitted holders of its whole Imperial power."

But the British Government had conceded the principle of self-government not out of far-sighted policy but out of apathy. Colonies cost more than they were worth: in 1846, for example, they bought only £8 million worth of British goods and the British Government spent £4 million on colonial defence. Until about 1870 the Government was on the whole profoundly unconcerned about the Empire. Huskisson had had visions of an Empire united by commercial Preference, but Huskisson had died in 1835—run over by the Liverpool–Manchester train on its opening day. Wakefield and Durham had had visions of a more personal bond of union, but Wakefield died forgotten in 1862 and Durham was distrusted by his colleagues. The prevailing attitude of the Government was that the colonies should go their way as the States of America had gone theirs. Their independence was regarded as "an inevitable step" by *The Times* of February 11, 1850. "These wretched colonies," said Disraeli in 1852, "will all be independent in a few years and are a millstone around our necks."

India: Annexations and Reforms.

The only country that England cared about keeping in those days was India, and that was not, properly speaking, a colony at all. Three-quarters of that vast sub-continent (India is as big as Europe excluding Russia) was ruled by independent and mutually antagonistic native princes. The remaining quarter was ruled by the British directors of the Honourable East India Company which had been chartered for trade with the Far East as long ago as 1600. The primary motive of the British in going to India was profit: they went for

AN EMPIRE IN THE MAKING

trade in the spices and ivory, in the precious stones and woods of the East and later for the cotton, tea and hemp which could be grown abundantly on Indian plantations. Huge fortunes were made by the officers and shareholders of the Company and the " nabob " or retired Anglo-Indian was the typical profiteer of Georgian England. But profit was not the only motive which drew Englishmen to India: many went in a missionary spirit to convert the natives to their Western religion of Christianity and to their Western ideals of honesty and humane law. They regarded the native Hindu and Moslem religions as little better than superstitions and they dismissed the age-old moral and social codes of the East as mere barbarity. This attitude may seem more than a trifle narrow-minded, but it must not be forgotten that a spirit comparable to that of the Crusaders animated many of the leaders who spread British rule in the Indian Peninsula.

The most memorable of the early nineteenth-century rulers of India was Lord William Bentinck who was Governor-General from 1828–35. In those years—it was the period of the first Whig reforms in England—he applied many liberal and humane measures to the Company's territory. He established local courts, so that natives could have justice done without travelling long distances; he allowed natives into certain lower ranks of the Civil Service; he set up a Medical College for Indian students in Calcutta; he established a system of education for rich natives. His reforms were not always appreciated: the justice administered in the Courts was British and seemed strangely unjust to the native mind; the medicine taught was European medicine and ignored completely the traditional herb-cures and spells of the East; the education provided was in the English language and took no account of the native tongues and literature of India. But Bentinck was convinced of the absolute rightness of the English outlook. He had no hesitation in abolishing the custom of *suttee* by which widows used to throw themselves to be burned on the funeral pyres of their dead husbands. To

Bentinck and the British *suttee* was criminal suicide and the idea that a wife should follow her husband in death as in life was mere superstition.

The next two Governors, Lord Auckland and Lord Hardinge, deliberately undertook a policy of extending British rule by force of arms. The first act of aggression was in Afghanistan, the mountainous kingdom which lies between India and Russia. In 1839 Lord Auckland sent an army to put a pro-British ruler on the throne of Afghanistan. After two years the Afghans threw that ruler out and the British army (690 British and 3,800 Indians) was annihilated so completely while trying to make its way back over the mountains to India that only one man reached the British base alive. A second army was sent to Kabul in 1842 and avenged the disaster, but the plan of establishing British control over Afghanistan had to be abandoned and Indians never forgot the lesson that the British Army was not invincible.

The next act of aggression was round the Indus, the great river which drains the Punjab with its tributaries and flows into the sea through the province of Scinde. Sir Charles Napier conquered Scinde in 1843; it was, he said, " a very advantageous, useful, humane piece of rascality." To the Sikhs who inhabited the Punjab the rascality was more obvious than the advantage. They resisted the British with all the force of their arms and their religion (the Sikhs are a dissenting Hindu sect), and it cost the British five years of hard fighting before they could establish control of the Punjab. In January 1849 the Sikhs came within reach of ultimate victory at the battle of Chilianwala, but they were defeated in the following month at Gujerat.

Lord Dalhousie who was Governor from 1848 to 1856 combined the reforming zeal of Bentinck with the aggressive tendencies of Auckland and Hardinge. He introduced railways and six thousand miles of telegraph. He laid down a great road from Calcutta to Peshawar. He started works of irrigation to check the floods and droughts which were the age-long curse of India. At the same time he annexed

AN EMPIRE IN THE MAKING

Lower Burma (1852) which was inhabited by people quite different in race and religion (they were Buddhists) from any of the people of India. He invented a doctrine of " Lapse " according to which an Indian Prince who had no male heir was forbidden to adopt one and was bound to make over his land to the British; this convenient doctrine brought Nagpore and seven other Indian states under British rule in Dalhousie's time. Finally, in 1856, he seized Oudh.

Dalhousie's intention was to confer the blessings of British civilization upon the Indians. Holding Cobden's doctrine (*see* page 91, footnote) that civilization follows trade, he set himself to increase the trade between England and India, and in this he succeeded. But he failed to realize that the people of India often did not want British civilization, which seemed to them wholly materialistic and dangerous to the religion that they valued above all else. They distrusted the telegraph as black magic and the railway because people of different caste were made to travel in the same carriage. For the same reason they distrusted Dalhousie's opening of the lower ranks of the Civil Service to competition, which enabled low-caste Hindus to rise above members of higher castes. The people of India resented any interference with their caste system as we would resent any attempt to abolish marriage or the authority of parents over their children. They suspected that in changing their way of life and in taking over their government the English were trying to change their religion.

The Mutiny. In 1857, a year after Dalhousie had been replaced by Lord Canning, the statesman's son, insurrection broke out. As might have been expected, the insurrectionaries were the soldiers who had been enrolled in the British Army; they were the best-armed section of the population, as well as the section which came into closest contact with the British. They had been contemplating mutiny for some time. They liked fighting rival tribes with the excellent new European weapons, but they were alarmed by Dalhousie's innovations and encouraged in their discontent by the reverses which the British had recently suffered at the hands of Russians, Afghans and Sikhs. The immediate cause of the Mutiny was an order that they should use cartridges greased with a preparation made up of cow-fat and pig-lard, that is, with the fat of the animal which the Hindus hold sacred and with the lard of the animal which the Moslems consider it an abomination to touch.

The Mutiny began at Meerut. Seventy sepoys had been condemned to ten years' penal servitude for refusing to use the new cartridges. On May 10 the garrison murdered its officers and set out for Delhi, the ancient capital of the Moguls, not fifty miles distant, and there proclaimed a new Mogul Emperor. The insurrectionary movement spread down the Ganges like a forest fire. Lucknow rose and besieged the British in the Residency. Cawnpore rose and for three weeks besieged a few hundred British civilians, who eventually surrendered on the promise of safe conduct.

It was September 14 before the British could bring down from the Punjab a relieving army strong enough to recapture Delhi. It was November before troops arrived from England to recapture Lucknow and Cawnpore.

Mutiny was over but trouble was not. The events of the summer had aroused a terrible blood-lust in both Indians and British. In the first days of the Mutiny English commanders on several occasions tied prisoners to the muzzles of guns and blew them into fragments so that their bodies could not be given the burial which, according to their religion, is necessary to salvation. " If I had them in my power," wrote Sir John Nicholson of the mutineers, " I would inflict the most excruciating tortures I could think of, with a perfectly easy conscience." On the Indian side Nana Sahib, the conqueror of Cawnpore, alarmed by rumours of the atrocities inflicted by the British Army on its march to recapture the city, determined to violate the promise of safe conduct and to put his British prisoners to death; when his guards refused to carry out his orders he empolyed five professional murderers to do it. All but four of the prisoners were massacred. Fear of wholesale British reprisals[1] gave Indians the courage of despair. A national rising broke out in Oudh and a gallant princess, the Ranee of Jhansi, conducted a guerilla war against the British until the spring of 1858, when she was defeated and killed at Gwailor.

The Mutiny was really more than a mutiny but less than a wholesale rebellion. The Indian Princes in nearly every case were on the side of authority. The Sikhs and the Gurkhas were glad of an opportunity to fight the Hindus, and for that reason remained faithful to England. The rising was confined to parts of Bengal, the Central Provinces, Oudh and Rohilcund.

The result of it all was that a new order began in India. The Honourable East India Company, after 260 years of existence, was brought to an end. India was annexed to the Crown and in an attempt to please the Indian people was called thereafter the Indian Empire, a name which in fact gave little satisfaction in India or in England.

Trade with the Far East. The shock of the Indian Mutiny roused the Government from its apathy towards Imperial trade, at least in so far as trade with the Far East was concerned. Three events that took place in the year 1858 show that the Government was awakening to the possibilities of Eastern commerce. First India was brought under the British Crown and the new Indian Civil Servants set to work to build roads and dams and railways to increase the value of trade with India. Lord Stanley announced in 1859 that exports to and imports from Great Britain had doubled within the last twenty years. This was nothing to the progress which followed. In 1854 the first consignment of Indian tea was shipped to England; it was to be the forerunner of a huge trade. After the fifties practically the whole of the Indian cotton crop was shipped to Lancashire.

[1] After the Mutiny when Canning insisted that the innocent should not be punished with the guilty he was contemptuously nick-named "Clemency Canning."

The Indians thus lost their basic occupation—that of spinning and weaving cloth—as English domestic workers had done a generation earlier. In return they gained cheap Lancashire clothes. Not for another half century did they begin to learn the secret of factory production and to set up mills to manufacture their own cotton in India.

Secondly, the year 1858 marked the establishment of British ports in China, on the banks of the great Yangtse River. Sixteen years before the British had won their first port in China. The story is not pleasant. British traders had insisted on selling Bengal opium on the Chinese coast. When the Emperor objected to the introduction of the drug into his dominions England went to war with China to force him to accept the opium trade, and the Opium War of 1842 led to the acquisition of Hong Kong, the island at the mouth of the Si Kiang.

Thirdly, in 1858 the first commercial treaty was made with Japan. Ever since the sixteenth century, when the Mikado had expelled the Jesuits, Japan had lived in seclusion, forbidding natives to leave and foreigners to come to her islands. But in 1853 an American fleet forced its way into her ports and soon the Mikado had to abandon his policy and open Japan to the trade of the West. This was to prove a very mixed blessing, as Lord Elgin foresaw. Japan, he said, was " a land with a perfectly paternal Government, a perfectly filial people, a community entirely self-supporting, peace within and without; no want; no ill-will between classes. That is what I find in Japan in the year 1858 after two hundred years of exclusion of foreign trade and foreigners. Twenty years hence what will be the contrast ? "

Trade with the White Colonies.

But if the Government was taking a lead in opening the East to British commerce, it was doing nothing to help the development of the self-governing colonies. In the fifties and sixties that development was being carried out at an astonishing pace by the enterprise of individual Britons. Manufacturers pressed their goods upon the colonists, investors lent them money, engineers went out to build the railways which were to open up the hinterlands to the trade of the outside world.

In the fifteen years between 1855 and 1870 the trade between the colonies and Britain doubled and more than doubled in value[1]—and this in spite of the Free Trade policy which spoiled the market for West Indian sugar and which gave the United States a larger share than the Mother Country in the trade of Canada. The Canadian shipbuilding industry was reaching its height and the trade in timber was being developed (it was not yet the time for corn exports: throughout the nineteenth century the United States, Argentine and India were each outpacing Canada in their export of corn to Great Britain). In South Africa farmers were exporting wool and sheepskins and ostrich feathers (it was not yet the time for diamonds and gold whose existence there was still unsuspected). More valuable to us than the trade of either of these colonies was the trade of Australia, thanks to her exports of wool and of gold. In 1804 one of the early settlers, John MacArthur, had taken out a few merino sheep and three years later the first consignment of wool —245 lbs.—was sent from Australia to Britain. By the fifties Australia had become the first wool-growing country in the world. In 1851 gold was found at Ballarat and crews of adventurers more independent and more lawless than the old convicts rushed out to seek their fortunes in the diggings. " The colony," in Wakefield's words, " was

		Worth of Goods to Britain £		Worth of goods from Britain £
[1] In 1855 Canada	sold	4,600,000	and bought	2,500,000
In 1870 ,,	,,	8,500,000	,,	6,200,000
In 1855 S. Africa	,,	778,000		
In 1870 ,,	,,	7,788,000		
In 1855 Australia	,,	6,500,000	,,	10,600,000
In 1870 ,,	,,	13,000,000	,,	14,000,000
In 1855 New Zealand	,,	31,000		
In 1870 ,,	,,	4,639,000		

precipitated into a nation." The population which in 1851 was 405,000 reached 1,145,000 in 1861; and in that decade £110,000,000 worth of gold was mined in Australia. Even more rapid was the commercial development of New Zealand. In those days her riches, like Australia's, lay in wool and gold (the days when refrigeration was to make possible the export of meat and dairy produce to Britain had not yet come).

This rapid increase of trade with the farthest corners of the earth was made possible by the improvements in communications. The first ocean-going steamships were being launched in the sixties and in those same years the sailing ship reached its finest form in the *clippers*, vessels with frame of iron and planks of oak and teak which could make the 11,000 mile voyage from Australia in eighty days. It was in the sixties too that the first cable was laid across the Atlantic.

By 1870, therefore, the colonies had developed in a manner which no one in 1815 could have imagined. In the last thirty years a million people from Great Britain and Ireland had settled in Australasia and almost as many in British North America. (Incidentally over three-and-a-half million emigrated to the United States during the same period.) From the few islands and coastlines inhabited by foreigners, convicts and slaves had grown a group of self-governing colonies which were rapidly developing into nations in their own right. But the British Government was still not awake to the importance to the Mother Country of fostering officially the development of Imperial trade.

Chapter VII: REVOLUTION IN EUROPE, 1830-71

Palmerston – The Revolutions of 1848 – The Russo-Turkish War, 1853–56 – The Crimea – Italian Unity – The American Civil War – German Unity – The Paris Commune.

The people of Europe looked on England in the mid-nineteenth century much as we look on Russia to-day. That is to say, the rulers thought we were revolutionaries, and some advanced thinkers among the ruled thought we were inspired reformers. The rulers distrusted our parliamentary rule, our strictly limited monarchy, our middle-class franchise and our belief in self-government for colonies; and the Liberals admired them.

Neither attitude is surprising if we remember that the ruling class all over Europe still believed in despotism. Nicholas was ruling over Russians and Poles with the *knout*; Metternich was ruling Austrians, Czechs, Magyars, Slavs and Venetians with the iron fist in the velvet glove; thirty-nine princes tyrannized the thirty-nine states of the German Confederation; and Spain, Portugal and Naples were suffering under despotic monarchies. Everywhere the revolutions of 1830 had been followed by repression; nowhere was there freedom of speech or of press, nowhere had the middle class the right to vote. France alone was an exception: there the revolution of 1830 had succeeded and King Louis Philippe had given one citizen in a hundred the right to vote; but the ineffectiveness of his government was soon to turn all classes against him.

The British Government, for its part, had a quite definite attitude towards Europe. Our traditional policy was to keep the ports of the continent open to our ships. We were on the side of small nations in their struggles against foreign despots because the small nations were most likely to welcome our commerce and also because we did believe in national liberty. But we were not prepared to let our sympathy lead us into war on their behalf nor to interfere in the struggles of foreign liberals against governments of their own nationality.

Palmerston.   For more than a generation England's foreign affairs were conducted by Henry Temple, Viscount Palmerston. Born into the Whig aristocracy in 1774 and educated conventionally at Harrow and Cambridge, he served a long apprenticeship of twenty years among the dusty files of the War Office before being rewarded with the post of Foreign Minister. Though he was twice Prime Minister (1855–58 and 1859–65) his real interest lay in foreign affairs and he was the guiding spirit of the Foreign Office from 1830 until his death in 1865. The great work of this dapper, debonair, dauntless nobleman lay in raising the prestige of England abroad. His jaunty self-confidence and love of bluff antagonized the Queen and the Prince Consort, but in spite of their opposition he steered England firmly, if a trifle hazardously, on the traditional course of her foreign policy.

His first triumph was in out-manœuvring Louis Philippe. Mehemet Ali of Egypt was bidding fair to make himself master of the Near East. France sympathized with Mehemet. Turkey in despair turned to Russia for help, offering in return to allow Russian warships into the Black Sea and through the Dardanelles (Treaty of Unkiar–Skelessi, 1833). This was a menace to British naval power in the Mediterranean, so Palmerston offered England's help to Turkey. It was the English fleet which in 1840 defeated Mehemet by capturing Beyrout and Acre, so it was to England, not to Russia, that Turkey's gratitude went. At the Treaty of London, 1841, Turkey promised to close the Dardanelles to warships. As for France, she had the humiliation of seeing her Egyptian protégé crushed and disgraced.

On two other occasions French policy was frustrated.

Some Swiss Catholics had made a *Sonderbund* to oppose the Protestants (who were also liberals). When France joined Austria in supporting the Catholics, Palmerston protested with such vigour that France withdrew her support, lamely. Then Louis Philippe attempted interference in Spain. The problem there was to find a husband for the Spanish Queen. Louis was suspected of wanting to marry her or her sister to a French prince so as to secure the Spanish succession for France. A promise was extracted from him that the Queen's sister should contract no such marriage until the Queen had married a non-Frenchman, but Louis treacherously got round this in 1846 by arranging for the Queen to marry the weakling and presumably impotent Duke of Cadiz at the same time as he married his own son to the Queen's sister. This time it was not Palmerston who defeated Louis Philippe's aim. The Queen had a son and the French claim to the Spanish Succession was lost.

The Revolutions of 1848. Then suddenly the storm that had been gathering over Europe through the long years of repression burst. In every continental country there was a revolution in 1848. In every continental country men rose for the three great ideals which the French revolutionaries of 1789 had set before them, which the Congress of Vienna had denied them and which the risings of 1830 had failed to win. They rose for Liberty, for Equality and for Fraternity. And now Liberty meant being governed by a parliament elected by manhood suffrage, and Equality meant a living wage and a share in the profits of industry for workers, and Fraternity, as we have said, meant nationalism—the right of people of a common language and traditions to be united under a common rule.

The first outbreak came in Paris in February. Workers from the poor quarters pulled up the paving-stones and barricaded themselves against the military. They forced Louis Philippe to abdicate and Lamartine, the poet, who was head of the Provisional Government, to apply some of the ideas of their prophet Louis Blanc and to find work for the unemployed in national workshops.

In March the revolution spread over Europe. Everywhere except in Paris it was a rising of the educated middle class. In Berlin the King of Prussia bowed before the storm and promised a constitution on the English model. The kings of the smaller German states saw no way of saving their crowns except by following his example. In Vienna the students and their professors rose against the aristocracy: Metternich fled to Brighton. The Czechs of Bohemia, and the Magyars of Hungary were up in arms for national independence. While they were breaking away from German rule, German Liberals were trying to unite the German-speaking peoples. Meeting at Frankfurt as the elected representatives of their people they set to work in an orderly and peaceable way to draw up a constitution which would ensure both Liberty and Unity to the Germany of the future.

At the same time revolution was spreading beyond the Alps. Inspired by the teachings of Mazzini and led by the King of Sardinia and by Cavour his Minister, the Italians rose against their Austrian oppressors. The Piedmontese marched on Milan, the Venetians declared an independent Republic. But the Austrians had a good army in Italy; the revolutionaries were defeated in 1849. The Pope himself had declared against them and their ideals.

By this time the forces of reaction had collected themselves in every other country, and every other revolution was on the point of collapse. The Viennese Army had restored the Emperor; the Czechs were forced into submission; in Hungary, after a long and valiant resistance by Kossuth, a terrible reaction set in under General Haynau. The Prussian King, on the advice of a young landowner, Otto von Bismarck, turned against the Liberals, refused to recognize the Frankfurt Parliament. All over Germany the mighty were restored to their seats.

In France the Revolution had a more chequered career. The peasants disapproved of the Socialist ideas of the Paris revolutionaries. They armed themselves and came to Paris in the new railway trains and defeated the Socialists. It seemed that France was in for a civil war. There was only one name that could have commanded the loyalty of all classes of Frenchmen and that name was Napoleon. Bonaparte was dead, of course, but his nephew Louis Napoleon presented himself as a candidate for the Presidency. Never was nephew less like his uncle. Louis Napoleon was a sad little man with a parrot profile and a gentle manner. He had been brought up in Italy, had been imprisoned in France for leading a pitiful private insurrection with two or three followers (and a tame vulture in place of an imperial eagle), and had long lived in England where he had rowed Victoria on Virginia Water and had acted as special constable during the Chartist scare of 1848. But his name worked wonders. He was elected President of France by a huge majority. Three years later he made a *coup d'état* and declared himself Emperor, as Napoleon III.

The revolutions of 1848 had failed. Most countries were under their old monarchs once more and France had exchanged a King for an Emperor. But it was not a failure like that of 1830. After 1848 nothing would be quite the same again. The most reactionary rulers began to admit that it would be necessary to give the Liberals their pet reforms—constitutionally limited monarchy, manhood suffrage, freedom of speech and the rest. Only in a few countries, such as Russia, Prussia and Spain, were there rulers able enough to make liberal concessions on paper without sacrificing any of their despotic power in fact.

In all this Palmerston had been in his element at the Foreign Office. Working continuously, writing despatch after despatch in his model handwriting, he was prodigal of advice and approval. He believed in using England's diplomatic influence to further the cause of Liberalism abroad. His Chief, Lord John Russell, the Prime Minister, was nervous of this policy. His sovereign and her Consort were horrified by it. Palmerston did not care a button: he openly approved the revolutions of 1848. He rejoiced when

Haynau, the reactionary Hungarian general, on a visit to England in 1850, was nicknamed Hyena and given a beating by the draymen of Barclay & Perkins' brewery; he publicly entertained the Hungarian Liberal, Kossuth. "Pam" was the hero of the nation in those days. He could do nothing wrong. He was applauded even for his disgraceful action in the affair of Don Pacifico, a Gibraltar Jew who had got into trouble in Athens. The Jew claimed British citizenship and Palmerston insisted that the Athenian authorities should give an explanation. Lord John and the Court were shocked but the public were delighted by his impudence. The Prime Minister and the Court were both shocked and delighted in 1851 when Palmerston went too far and sent an official message of congratulation to Louis Napoleon on his *coup d'état*, for which indiscretion he was dismissed from office.

Palmerston was too popular to be kept out of power and a few months later he was back in the Cabinet. The nation knew that the alternative to Palmerston in control of foreign policy was the Prince Consort, and the nation hated Albert. He was handsome and hardworking, he deserved gratitude for the reform he had carried out in the Royal Household, which had been fraudulently and wastefully conducted, and for his encouragement of science and the industrial arts, which had been completely neglected by other eminent men; but he was young, humourless and a German, and the English people resented these characteristics in a man who had increasing influence over their sovereign. If anyone was to browbeat the Queen, Englishmen preferred that it should be Palmerston.

The Russo-Turkish War, 1853–56.

Soon Palmerston was involved in international conflict. Early in 1853 the Eastern Question came up again, this time in a more serious form. The Tsar proposed a partition of the tottering Turkish Empire: England was to have Egypt, France to have Syria and the Turks were to be expelled from Europe—Serbia and Bulgaria becoming self-governing States under

Russian protection and Constantinople a free city. In the light of future events this seems a reasonable proposal, the acceptance of which might have saved untold bloodshed, but to Palmerston and the English Government of the time it seemed an insidious step towards the Russian seizure of Constantinople. The Emperor of France also distrusted the Tsar with whom he was quarrelling over the right to protect the Christian subjects of Turkey. Napoleon III supported the claim of Roman Catholic priests to have the keys to the Holy Sepulchre in Jerusalem, and the claim was allowed by the Turkish Government. The Tsar countered by demanding that his right to be guardian of the Christian population of Turkey should be recognized. On the advice of Lord Stratford de Redcliffe, the British ambassador at Constantinople, the Turkish Government refused the Tsar's claim.

Realizing that English and French opinion was against him the Tsar launched his attack on Turkey. In July 1853 his armies moved into Moldavia, over which the Russians had already established a protectorate, and in November the Russian fleet wiped out what there was of a Turkish fleet at Sinope.

At this point England and France sent warships into the Black Sea. They had no great objection to Russian aggression in the Balkans but they had every objection to Russian expansion by sea. The presence of allied fleets in the Black Sea was enough to put heart into the Turks. In June 1854 they held up the Russian advance at Silistria. The Tsar abandoned his plan of attack and by August there was not a Russian soldier in the principalities of Moldavia and Wallachia.

There the war should have ended. Turkey had Austria's promise to secure the Principalities for the future and the promise of England and France to secure the Black Sea. But by now the Allies had caught the war-fever. Louis Napoleon, remembering his uncle, wanted to attack Russia. As for England, the whole country was clamouring for war. Led by *The Times*, public opinion was raging against the

Russians, as it was to rage against the Germans in 1914. The Prime Minister, the gentle Lord Aberdeen, had wanted peace, but Palmerston, at this time Home Secretary, was too much for him and in March war had been declared. By July England was committed to a joint attack with France on the Russian naval base at Sebastopol in the Crimean Peninsula.

The Crimea. England had muddled her way into the war; she was to muddle her way through it. In charge of the expedition to the Crimea were sent two Admirals and a Chief Engineer who were all over seventy and a Commander-in-Chief, Lord Raglan, who was sixty-six and who, having fought in the Peninsular War and lost an arm at Waterloo, still persisted in speaking of the enemy as " the French." The French commanders were rather less aged but considerably less competent. In September the joint expedition landed at Eupatoria, crossed the Alma river and on the wooded hills beyond fought the Russian Army and routed it. The obvious course now, as Lord Raglan pointed out, was an immediate advance upon Sebastopol. But this the French Commander, St. Arnaud, refused; his men were tired, he said. So the Allies abandoned the open road to Sebastopol and settled down to a long siege.

A new British base was formed to the south of Sebastopol in the little inlet of Balaclava. The object now was to seize the Worontzow Road which ran along the heights above Balaclava and to take the Russian forts which lay on the shoulders of the Mount Inkerman. The attempt failed, but not before it had cost two bloody battles which well illustrated the disgraceful staff work and the admirable courage of the British. The battle of Balaclava (October) will always be remembered for the misinterpreted order which sent the Light Brigade charging up a valley that was guarded on three sides by Russian guns, and the battle of Inkerman (November) as the " soldiers' battle " which was fought in a fog that made generalship impossible and left the rank and file to fight it out in futile hand-to-hand encounter.

Now the cold weather came and the armies settled down to winter quarters. The Crimean winter is not exceptionally severe; indeed the coastal climate of the peninsula is the mildest in Russia—a fact that has made it the most popular of Russian holiday resorts. But the winter of 1854–55 was wet, cold and prolonged and the British Army was not equipped for even the mildest and shortest of winters. The men were left in leaky tents to sleep on the sodden ground. They had no fuel and their food was served to them raw—uncooked salt beef and unroasted coffee. Naturally enough, scurvy broke out, yet the officers did not, for four whole months, issue the lime-juice from the stores, nor had they enough acumen to buy the cargoes of fresh meat and cabbages which traders brought to Balaclava. The sick were left under canvas on the bare ground until they were shipped off to the hospital base at Scutari where even worse conditions of disease and neglect awaited them. In December, January and February 7,400 British soldiers died and 23,000 were on the sick-list.

When in February Palmerston became Prime Minister the whole conduct of the war changed. Florence Nightingale was sent to reorganize the hospital system: she succeeded in actually halving the death-rate in the hospitals. The War Office was galvanized into action. Young officers replaced the old. By the end of the summer the British Army had been well-equipped, well-provisioned and reinforced; roads and a light railway had been built across the Crimea from Balaclava and all was ready for a final assault upon the forts which guarded Sebastopol. On September 8 the assault was made. Though the English failed to take the Redan fort, the French captured fort Malakov and the Russians evacuated Sebastopol.

The capture of Sebastopol ended the fighting in the Crimea. The new Tsar, Alexander II (Nicholas I had died of exposure in the war), continued to fight the Turks in Asia Minor until the end of the year and then gave in.

The Russians had lost over half a million men. At the peace treaty which was signed at Paris in 1856 Russia gave up her claim to protect the Orthodox Christians and to occupy the Danubian Provinces. Also she recognized that there should be no warships in the Black Sea.

The Crimean War settled nothing. The Ottoman Empire had been saved from extinction but continued to be the sick man of Europe. The Danube remained neutral but within fifteen years of the Peace of Paris there were Russian troops in Bessarabia and Russian warships in the Black Sea. Alexander continued to rule as a despot[1] and the imperial ambitions of the Russian Government, so far from being checked, took a course which threatened the British Empire more directly than expansion in the Black Sea. Russia began to extend her frontiers in the direction of British India, capturing Bokhara, Khiva and Samarkand.

Italian Unity. After this Eastern interlude the attention of the world was drawn to three great national movements in the West. The conscious need of the Western world was still for Liberty, Equality and Fraternity, but the failure of the 1848 revolutions had taught reformers that strength lies in unity. They believed now that unity was the *first* necessity.

The first blow for unity was struck in Italy. The Kingdom of Sardinia had taken the lead in the movement to rid Italy of the Austrians. It was the policy of Cavour, the Sardinian Minister, to secure the help of England and France. By sending a small Sardinian force to assist them in their war against Russia he had succeeded. Louis Napoleon promised military support in return for Savoy and Nice, and Palmerston promised moral support for nothing. In 1859 French and Sardinian troops defeated the Austrians at Magenta and Solferino. A soldier of fortune named Garibaldi led a private army of a thousand " red-shirts "

---

[1] One of the advantages of this was that he was able to liberate the serfs in 1861—a measure which no Russian Parliament would have been strong enough or disinterested enough to put through.

to capture Naples and Sicily. In 1860 Victor Emmanuel of Sardinia became King of all Italy with the exception of Rome, which was still under the rule of the Pope, and Venice and Trentino, which were still held by the Austrians. A congratulatory despatch reached him from London: " Her Majesty's Government can see no sufficient grounds for the severe censure with which Austria, France, Prussia and Russia have visited the acts of the King of Sardinia. Her Majesty's Government will turn their eyes rather to the justifying prospect of a people building up the edifice of their liberties and consolidating the work of their independence among the sympathies and good wishes of Europe."

The American Civil War. America was the scene of the next struggle for national unity. The United States at this time were united in little but name. Each state had the right to make its own laws and each used its right to work for its own economic prosperity without thought for its neighbours. The movement for a more real Union began in the northern states which were rapidly becoming industrialized. Roads and railways are the enemy of local divisions: they need complete absence of local barriers if they are to operate to the best advantage. Also industrial centres need raw materials. The Southern States were great producers of raw materials: they were not industrial but feudal in outlook, were controlled by aristocratic planters who raised cotton, rice and tobacco with the labour of negro slaves. These gentlemen sold their crops to the highest bidder and saw no reason why they should give buyers from the Northern States preference over buyers from England.

The leaders of the Northern States made the abolition of slavery their excuse for forcing the South into a closer Union. The Southerners replied by breaking away altogether. The President of the Union, Abraham Lincoln, replied by declaring war on them. For four years (1861–65) the civil war raged, a war made all the more devastating by the participation of the civilian population and by the use, for the first time, of such new instruments as railways, steamships and the telegraph. In the end the North won: the Union was preserved, slavery was abolished, the centre of prosperity moved from the South to the North and the United States entered in earnest upon a career of industrialism.

The war had a serious repercussion upon England. The ports of Virginia, Maryland and the Carolinas had been blockaded, with the result that the usual cotton cargoes could not be sent to England. Lancashire mills stood empty and Lancashire workers were unemployed. Some idea of the distress caused by this " cotton famine " can be gained by the fact that at Christmas 1862 there were no less than 500,000 people in Lancashire out of work and dependent on public relief.

It is not surprising that Palmerston was anxious to interfere on the side of the Southerners. He did all that he could to encourage them without actually declaring war on their side. English merchantmen were allowed to run guns into the Southern ports. An English mail boat, the *Trent*, was allowed to give a passage to two Southern diplomats destined for England. When the *Trent* was held up by a Northern cruiser and the diplomats put in prison Palmerston had Lord John Russell pen a threatening despatch to President Lincoln. The last action of the Prince Consort on his death-bed (1861) was to persuade Palmerston not to send that despatch. But Palmerston was irrepressible: he allowed a privateer, the *Alabama*, to be fitted out in Birkenhead for the Southerners' use. The *Alabama* captured 69 prizes before she was sunk. When the war was over and the Northern States had won, the British Government had to pay £3,250,000 for its complicity in this affair.

German Unity. The last of the great modern nations to achieve its unity was Germany. The German intellectuals who met at Frankfurt in 1848 had wanted to unite Germany under the ideals of liberalism. But Bismarck, now Chancellor of Prussia, realised that liberalism was not enough. Germany had no natural boundaries like Italy. She was not isolated from all rivals like the United States. The problem of launching her as a united nation was much more difficult: the Austrian Empire had designs upon South Germany, France had designs upon the Rhineland. Bismarck realized that only by rigid discipline and an invincible army could the new German Empire be brought into being. That discipline and that army he created in the Prussian State. Then he set about securing the adherence of the other states of Germany.

The work of German unity was accomplished by three blows, each carefully prepared and perfectly timed by Bismarck. The first came in 1864 in Schleswig-Holstein. Palmerston once said that only three people understood the Schleswig-Holstein case: a German professor who was mad, the Prince Consort who was dead, and himself—and he had forgotten it. Actually the question was not so difficult. Schleswig was a duchy inhabited largely by people of Danish race, Holstein a duchy inhabited largely by Germans. They were under a separate Government but their Duke was the King of Denmark (much as Canada and Newfoundland are under different Governments though they have the same king, the King of England). When the King of Denmark suggested bringing the duchies under the Danish Government in 1852, Palmerston, amongst other Foreign Ministers, guaranteed their integrity. Then in 1864 Bismarck persuaded Austria to join him and jointly they attacked the duchies. England was in honour bound to go to war to defend them. But in his old age Palmerston's nerve failed him; he left Denmark to her fate. In the next year Palmerston died.

As for Bismarck, he seized Schleswig-Holstein; and then he turned on Austria, who now, thanks to the part he had led her to play in the affair of the duchies, was without an ally in Europe. In a seven weeks' war in 1866 Prussia defeated Austria. Bismarck could have partitioned Austria, but once he had made sure that not she but Prussia would be master of Germany in future, he left her intact, thus winning the support of the Austrians for his lenience. In 1870 their support was useful. In July of that year, having picked a quarrel with Louis Napoleon, he went to war with France and defeated her at Sedan on September 1. Siege was laid to Paris, which surrendered in January. In that month in the Hall of Mirrors in the Palace of Versailles he signed the document which united the Kingdoms of Germany in the German Empire. Public opinion in England supported Prussia in this: Bismarck had played his cards so cleverly that Louis Napoleon was made to appear the aggressor. "There can be no doubt," said *The Times* on July 16, 1870, "as to the side on which the world's sympathies will be enlisted, and, whatever may on former occasions have been the offences of Prussia, she will in this instance have on her side all that moral support which is seldom denied to those who take up arms in self-defence."

The first result of Bismarck's policy was that Germany became the second richest nation in Europe. In addition to a heavy indemnity Bismarck took Alsace from France, and the rich iron districts of Lorraine. These, joined to the coal mines of the Saar and connected with the mines and factories and cheap water transport of the valleys where the Ruhr flows into the Rhine, made an industrial unit second only in value to that of Northern England.

A second result was that Bismarck's wars helped to complete the unity of Italy. His defeat of the Austrians enabled the Italians to occupy Venice; his defeat of Napoleon III, the champion of the Pope, enabled them to occupy Rome. The Popes who for many centuries had ruled central Italy and had taken their place among the monarchs of Europe were henceforward deprived of all temporal power except in the precincts of the Vatican; it was a loss which did not diminish their moral and spiritual power. All Italy was now—for the first time since the days of Imperial Rome—united under a single Government. But with the new Italy as with the new Germany unity was still an artificial thing; it would need many years of trials borne and perils braved before in either country the ideals of 1848 could be achieved.

The Paris Commune. A third result of Bismarck's victories was that France became a Republic again. The Empire collapsed when Napoleon III was taken prisoner. Some middle-class leaders set up a republican government while the Prussians were besieging Paris. After six months' siege Paris surrendered. But her troubles were only beginning, for civil war followed. A working-class party, the Communists, seized control of the city and drove the Republican leaders outside the walls. While the Russian invaders watched, French Republicans fought French Communists from March 1871 to the end of May. At last the middle-class leaders won, executed 25,000 Communists and set up the Third Republic to receive the terms of Bismarck. The Third Republic differed from the Empire of Napoleon III in that it was middle class in outlook and not allied to the Church of Rome and not interested in any European conquests—except such as might lead to the recapture of Alsace-Lorraine.

Europe had not heard the last of this Communist movement. Its founder was Karl Marx, a German Jew who with his friend Friedrich Engels wrote the *Manifesto of the Communist Party* in 1847. This was a call to the workers of all countries who were suffering from the deprivations consequent upon the Industrial Revolution to combine against their employers: " Workers of the world, unite ! You have nothing to lose but your chains." After the publication of the *Manifesto* Marx came to London and there, working in the Reading Room of the British Museum while his children were dying of starvation in a tiny flat in Dean Street, Soho, he wrote his great work *Das Kapital*. In this he drew a terrible—and true—description of the sufferings of the poor since the Industrial Revolution, and came to the conclusion that those sufferings would continue and grow worse as long as the capitalist system was allowed to go on. For under that system employers were bound to pay their employees less than their work was worth; if they paid high wages they would be driven out of business by employers who paid low wages and could consequently sell their goods more cheaply. Thus one class could get rich only at the expense of the other and there was a constant antagonism—which Marx called a Class War—between the two. Marx insisted that employers would never surrender their profits and be content with a humble wage like the workers; the only cure for the latter was therefore to rise in revolution against the capitalists and to *force* them to share the wealth of the country evenly by establishing a society in which class-distinctions would be abolished and in which land, factories and all other means of production would be owned by the public (the State) in the interests of the people as a whole. The publication of *Das Kapital* (1867) was preceded by the meeting of the *First International Working-Men's Association* in London in 1864, when Marx, in his address, called on the representatives to unite for the conquest of political power. The movement had little following in England, but the *First International* met in continental cities every year—with a break caused by the Franco-Prussian War—until 1872, when it was split by a quarrel between Marx, who wanted to work through parliaments for social reform, and other Communists who wanted immediate revolution.

The years 1848 to 1871 had seen a long succession of wars and revolutions involving every country but England. With the exception of the misadventure in the Crimea, England had kept clear of these tangles and had concentrated on growing rich.

Chapter VIII: THE MID-VICTORIAN AGE, 1850-74

The Bases of Prosperity – Gladstone and Finance – Disraeli and the Second Reform Bill – Gladstone's First Ministry – Mid-Victorian Comfort – Mid-Victorian Culture – The first " Great Depression."

THE MID-VICTORIAN ERA was a Golden Age of English history. In that third quarter of the nineteenth century England's wealth increased out of all reckoning; during that brief generation she became the richest nation the world had ever seen.

The Golden Age may be said to have begun in 1851, the year after Peel's death, with the Great Trade Exhibition. The idea of this gigantic display of the fruits of the Industrial Revolution was the Prince Consort's; he worked on the plans for two hard years, persuaded the Government to lend a site in Hyde Park, chose the design of Joseph Paxton for a building to house it—this was the Crystal Palace, that first and most fantastic example of " modern " architecture—and eventually devoted the profits to the foundation of the Science Museum in South Kensington. Hundreds of British manufacturers displayed their products at the Exhibition alongside those of foreigners—the silks and velvets of the French and the hand-wrought steel of the German firm of Krupp's. Six million people visited the Exhibition in six months and no doubt all went away convinced of England's industrial supremacy.

It is less easy to give a date for the end of the Golden Age. Perhaps 1874 may be taken as the year in which the gold—for reasons to be given later—ceased to glitter quite so brightly. Wages continued to rise fairly steadily until 1897, but it was in 1874—the year when Gladstone's first and greatest Ministry came to an end—that the economic calamity known as the Great Depression overtook England.

The Bases of Prosperity. England's prosperity during that age was based on three foundations. The first was the vast increase in industrial output. The most important of our products were coal and iron, cotton and woollen goods. During the period we have called the Golden Age the output of coal doubled: and the output of iron trebled: and the output of cotton goods doubled: and the output of woollens trebled. And this was not all. In 1856 a French immigrant's son called Bessemer[1] discovered a new way of converting iron into steel. In two years the price of steel dropped to half. The Bessemer process made the mass-production of steel possible; soon steel rails, steel machinery and steel ships were being produced, and the whole world bought its steel from England until it stole the Bessemer secret or developed new processes for itself. All this increased production meant of course increased prosperity for England. The value of our exports was almost quadrupled during the period; England had become the world's clothier and the world's workshop.

The second basis of England's prosperity was the growth of shipping. The mid-Victorian age saw the transition from sailing ships to steamships and from ships of wood to ships of iron. The old windjammer and the new clipper began to be replaced by the paddle steamer in about 1840 when the Cunard Line, consisting of four paddle ships, was founded. The paddle began to give way to the screw propeller after 1858, the year of the launch of the ironclad *Great Eastern*.[2] The transition from sail to steam was slow: the troops sent to quell the Indian Mutiny in 1857 went

---

[1] Amongst other things Bessemer invented an unforgeable perforated stamp, a sugar press, a process of embossing velvet, plate-glass, and an unrockable steamship. The last-named alone was not a practical success.

[2] This 18,000 ton ship was 672 feet long and remained for 50 years the biggest afloat. She was designed by Brunel, another French immigrant's son, who was also the pioneer of the Great Western Railway.

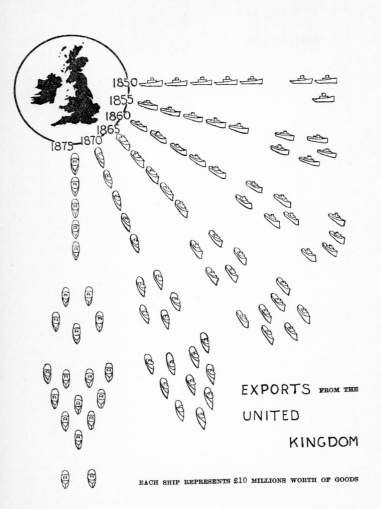

out under sail, and the *Great Eastern* herself was equipped with sail as well as with paddle and screw; it was not until the seventies that ships began to give up the use of sails altogether. The transition from wood to iron was faster. The first steamships had wooden hulls but it was found that the vibration of the screw was too much for the beams. In the sixties iron began to come into general use—the Navy launched its first ironclad in 1861 and the first iron Cunarder followed in 1864. The number of British steamships increased from 1,187 in 1850 to 5,247 in 1880, and the new type of vessel not only sailed with greater speed and regularity but carried four times as much cargo as the old. Altogether the British shipping business earned £50,000,000 in the year 1872. Shipowners had become the latest class of *nouveaux riches*, and England had become the world's carrier.

The third foundation of our national prosperity was increased investment. Without capital—which simply means money saved—no business can be started or extended: no coal can be mined, no invention utilized, no ship built or put to sea. Every business enterprise incurs expenses before it can be got going sufficiently to make a profit, and to meet those expenses someone must be found to invest his spare money in the business. In the old days people had kept their spare money in a stocking or under their mattress. Most forms of lending money for profit were frowned upon until the sixteenth century as constituting the sin of usury. After that a few " business men " put their money into " ventures," helping to fit out ships in the hope of a share in the profits of the voyage. The business men of the early days of the Industrial Revolution put their own savings into their businesses but could not count much on the savings of other people. If they wanted to extend their factories they put their own profits back into the business. That is why thrift was considered such an important virtue in Early Victorian days: only by thrift on the part of industrialists could capital be found for new industries. The general public dared not invest their

BRITISH INDUSTRIAL OUTPUT AND SHIPPING

1850   1873

PRODUCTION
EACH SQUARE REPRESENTS ONE MILLION TONS

COAL   COAL

PIG-IRON   PIG-IRON

EXPORTS
EACH SQUARE REPRESENTS £1 MILLIONS

COTTON (GOODS)   COTTON (GOODS)

WOOLLENS   WOOLLENS

SHIPPING
EACH SQUARE REPRESENTS ONE MILLION TONS CLEARED THROUGH U.K. PORTS

1850   1873

savings in a company because if that company failed they might be liable to lose not only what they had invested but their house and their land and everything that was theirs. Their " liability," in business language, was " unlimited." While investment was discouraged in this way business development was bound to be slow. But in the mid-Victorian age a new way was found to tempt savings out of the stocking and the mattress into industry. In 1856 a Joint Stock Companies Act was passed which provided that investors' liability was to be limited: in other words, investors in a company that failed were to be liable to lose nothing more than the sum they had invested. Investment was now a fair risk; at the worst one might lose one's share, at the best one might receive a huge dividend.

The Joint Stock Companies Act had most important results. Companies could be floated for any purpose that had a fair prospect of success and the capital could always be raised by inviting the public to buy shares in its profits through financial houses which existed for that purpose. Shares could be sold or re-bought on the Stock Exchange, a central agency which had been set up by some private dealers in 1804.

As time went on, increasing amounts of the Englishman's spare money found their way into foreign countries. Foreigners caught the infection of the Machine late, and caught it severely because England was ready to supply them with the means and the materials and with the machines ready-made. All over Europe railways were being built— in France, Germany, Austria, Italy, Spain, Belgium and Roumania—and everywhere the builders needed capital. Englishmen, knowing by experience how profitable railways could be, lent the money. Often they supplied the skilled workmen and the materials[1] and sometimes they provided

[1] Railways in five continents, stretching over 8,000 miles in all, were built by one English firm, that of Brassey. Thomas Brassey was a quiet dignified man who lived simply as a country estate-agent until George Stephenson brought him into prominence by buying stone from one of his quarries. Soon he was the best-known contractor in England, and when foreign countries took up the idea of railways it was to Thomas

directors for the continental companies: there was an English representative on the directing Board of the French *Compagnie de l'Ouest* as late as 1914. And Europe was not the only field for our overseas investment. We have seen how Englishmen lent—and lost—money to the South American republics in the twenties. In the mid-Victorian age there was a new and more judicious bout of lending to South America. Altogether the amount of British money invested abroad in the years 1870–74 reached an average of £61,000,000 a year—a huge sum for a country of 23,000,000 inhabitants. (*See* Appendix III.) Britain, or rather the City of London, where Britain's money business was transacted, became the banker of the world.

On these three bases then—production for export, shipping and financing—England's prosperity was founded. We have now to see what England's rulers did to shape and develop that prosperity and what effect it had on the lives of Englishmen in the mid-Victorian age.

Gladstone and Finance.

Three great statesmen, Palmerston, Gladstone and Disraeli, dominated the political life of the time. Three more different men can hardly be imagined. Palmerston, whose work has been described, was born into the Irish peerage. William Ewart Gladstone was a chip of a very different block. He was born in 1809 (thirty-five years after Palmerston), the son of a rich Liverpool merchant and slave-owner who sent him to Eton and Oxford, where he gained the highest academic honours. He was a man of a formidable earnestness of outlook and of an unusual capacity for work. He first attracted attention by a book on *The State in Relation to the Church*; his ambition was to take Holy Orders, and it was with the greatest difficulty that his friends persuaded him that he could do most for the Church by becoming a politician. In 1832 he sat in Parliament as a member of the Tory

---

Brassey that they entrusted the work of construction. At one time he had 80,000 men in his employ. Examples of his work can be seen to-day in every country of Europe.

party, which was the traditional champion of the Church.

Though Gladstone was by inclination a Churchman he was by nature a financial genius. He was in the tradition of Huskisson and Peel, those other north-country men whose work had been to build a financial and economic system that would give England's trade its fullest scope. So when the Tory party refused to follow Peel after the Repeal of the Corn Laws, we find Gladstone coming over to the party of Free Trade and rising to fame as a Whig Chancellor of the Exchequer. This fame rests on a series of Free Trade Budgets of which the most noteworthy were those of 1855 and 1860. His object was to make life less expensive for Englishmen. He achieved it by bold policy and incessant work (twelve hours a day at his desk was nothing to Gladstone) directed towards reducing the duties on goods coming into the country. He abolished duties on three or four hundred articles: in 1860 only forty-eight duties remained and these were left not in order to " protect " English industries but to yield a revenue to the Exchequer by taxing luxuries.

Four of the abolished duties are worth particular notice. By abolishing the tax on soap Gladstone made the English the best-washed people in the world. By reducing the tax on tea to 6*d*. a pound he made tea the drink of the poor.[1] By abolishing the tax on paper and the newspaper stamp duty he made it possible for books and newspapers to be sold more cheaply, and therefore to be more widely read. By abolishing the tax on advertisements (which had been 1*s*. 6*d*. per advertisement) he unwittingly paved the way for a movement the consequences of which still defy calculation.

These reforms Gladstone accompanied by stringent economies in Government expenditure. He hoped to be able to abolish the Income Tax, but in spite of all his efforts

---

[1] Between 1870 and 1900 the amount of tea drunk in England doubled. The amount drunk before that had not been inconsiderable. Mr. Weller in Dickens's *Pickwick Papers* (1836) remarked: " There's a young woman in the next form but two, as has drunk nine cups and a half; and she's swelling wisibly before my wery eyes."

the tax on incomes remained as a permanent tax. All he could do was to reduce it from 1s. 4d. in the pound sterling —the figure it had reached in Peel's day—to 3d. in the pound, which was the figure for 1874.

Disraeli and the Second Reform Bill.
As time went on Gladstone turned more and more to the radical Reformers. He became a friend of Cobden and Bright and the " Manchester School." Cobden, with Gladstone's support, went to Paris and negotiated a commercial treaty with France (1860) which made trade between the two nations almost completely free. Bright had Gladstone behind him in working for a more important reform: the enfranchisement of the working man. " Every man who is not presumably incapacitated by some consideration of personal unfitness or political danger, is morally entitled to come within the pale of the constitution," said Gladstone in 1864. When his old chief, Palmerston, died in the following year he sponsored a Bill in the House to give the working man a vote. The Bill was thrown out and the Liberals went with it. They were succeeded by a Conservative Ministry with Lord Derby as its figure-head and Disraeli as its guiding hand.

Disraeli was Gladstone's opponent throughout his public life. The two had absolutely nothing in common. We have seen how the young Jew made his name as a novelist and as the founder of a Young Tory Party to oppose Peel's Free Trade policy. He found Gladstone's moral earnestness tedious and distrusted his windy, benevolent manner. " The Honourable Member," he once said of him in the Commons, " is intoxicated by the exuberance of his own verbosity." But Disraeli knew that Gladstone was right about the working-man's vote and in 1867 he calmly " dished the Whigs " by passing through Parliament the Bill which the Whigs had failed to get through. The Second Reform Bill gave the vote in borough constituencies to every payer of rates, that is to every urban householder. This was rather less than " the working-man's vote," for it excluded agricultural labourers and miners who lived in county constituencies. But it did give the working class a voice in government. Politicians henceforward had to remember to win the goodwill of the workers.

Dishing the Whigs brought little good to Disraeli; at the election which followed the new electors voted against him and Gladstone became Prime Minister. The ambition of " Dizzy's " life—the Premiership—was dashed from him at the moment of achievement; now, at the age of sixty-four, he found himself once more in opposition, apparently for ever.

Gladstone's First Ministry, 1868–74.

Gladstone was the first Whig Prime Minister to have a desire for radical reform. Under him the Whigs gained—and on the whole earned—the name of Liberals. When he was told that he was to be Prime Minister he was wielding an axe on his estate in Cheshire. Throughout his ministry he continued to wield a metaphorical axe, hewing his way through forests of corruption. His first " mission," he said, was to pacify Ireland. In this we shall not follow him until a later chapter; there are more urgent matters nearer home to be described. The first of these is the need for educational reform.

The Scots were a literate people for there had been a school in every Scots parish for the last two centuries. The English and the Welsh were not. Half of them could neither read nor write, and most of the other half had acquired but the barest smattering of education at Church Schools or at schools run for private profit after the fashion of Dickens's "Dotheboys Hall." To remedy this an *Elementary Education Act* was passed in 1870. In parishes where there was no adequate school in existence the ratepayers were to elect a School Board which was to provide education for children between five and twelve years of age. The cost of these " Board Schools " was to be borne by the Government, the parents and the ratepayers of the parish in equal proportion.

The Act of 1870 went far, but not far enough to make

England a nation of literate people. It was 1880 before elementary education was made compulsory and, oddly enough, it was 1891 before it was made free.

Until 1870 education was the monopoly of the children of a few rich men. These rich men also monopolized the best posts in the Army and the Civil Service. Commissions in the Army were bought and sold like shares on the Stock Exchange. Posts in the Civil Service were distributed by politicians to relatives and supporters with little regard to their abilities. In 1870 Gladstone changed all that. He applied one great principle of the French Revolution—that of " the career open to talents "—by insisting that the entry into the Civil Service should be by public examination, and by persuading the Queen to abolish the purchase of commissions in the Army. The new system was not perfect: the Services remained the domain of rich men's sons, for only those who had had an expensive education had a chance of success in the examinations, and besides, it has so far passed the ingenuity of man to devise a form of examination which will bring all the best men to the top. But it was better than " old corruption."

One glaring example of " old corruption " remained, in the system of voting at parliamentary elections. By custom voters mounted a hustings (or platform) and recorded their votes publicly. It was not unusual for landlords and employers to turn out men who voted against them, or for candidates to pay " roughs " to keep voters of the opposite side away from the hustings. For generations reformers had protested against this custom. The Chartists had made secret ballot one of their six demands. In 1872 the Secret Ballot Act was passed. Instead of appearing in public on a hustings each voter goes alone into a polling booth and there puts a cross against the name of a candidate on a piece of paper, folds it, and slips it into a sealed box. No one can know which way anyone else has voted. Thus the evils of bribery and intimidation, which had accompanied parliamentary elections since the beginning, were swept away—at least in their more blatant forms.

Meanwhile Gladstone was not unmindful of the working men whose votes had brought him into power. He annoyed them by his *Licensing Act* (1872) which gave magistrates the right to grant or refuse licences to public houses and which insisted on those houses being closed at eleven o'clock in the provinces and twelve in London. But he had delighted them by his *Trade Union Act* of the previous year. This Act extended to the workers' Trade Unions and their funds the protection of the law. It did not, however, legalize peaceful picketing. In the very year that it was passed seven women were sent to prison for saying " Bah " to a worker who refused to go on strike.

Mid-Victorian Comfort. The prosperity of mid-Victorian England was enjoyed by all classes. The workers were better off now and the voice of working-class distress which had been raised so persistently and inarticulately in in the first two quarters of the century was raised not at all in the third. Factories and foundries were working in full blast; there was little unemployment. Hours had been cut down to ten a day and conditions improved by a hundred Factory and Mines Acts. Wages were rising fast: between 1850 and 1875 real wages rose by one-third. (If a man's wage in money goes up by a third and the prices he has to pay go up to the same extent, then he is no better off, for he can buy no more than before. But if his money wages increase faster than prices then his *real* wage has increased.)

While the prosperity of the working class had increased by a third, that of the middle class had increased thirty-fold. The mid-Victorian bourgeois lived in a state of luxury which would have startled their ancestors by its opulence as much as it shocks us by its bad taste. Their fortune had come so fast that they had no traditions to guide them in the spending of it. They built themselves vast houses of brick and twisted the windows and porches into shapes copied from mediæval Gothic churches. They filled their rooms with furniture from every corner of the world: occasional tables and *étagères* of bamboo from the farthest

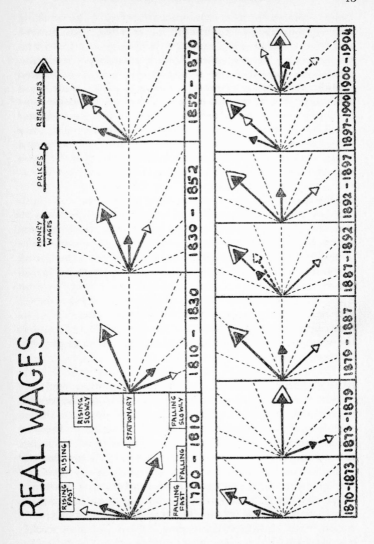

East; tables and chairs of mahogany from Jamaica or of walnut from Spain, upholstered in horsehair from Arabia and covered with plush embossed by a process discovered by Bessemer; carpets from Turkey, aspidistras from the Himalayas and curtains of machine-made lace from France (thanks to Cobden's treaty). By 1875 their walls were decorated with heads and antlers of the first big game shot in Africa, and with Landseer's pictures of lions and Bengal tigers. The lines of their furniture, chandeliers and vases were ornate and intricate, twisted in imitation of the shapes characteristic of India, Burma and China. And the food they sat down to was as rich and exotic as the furniture. For dinner, served in the evening, the soup was turtle or mulligatawny, the fish Russian sturgeon or salmon brought fresh by the Flying Scotsman; the joint was always English (the first chilled meat was not to come until 1880), but the sauces were flavoured with Eastern spices, and of the condiments, which were many, the salt alone came from England. The dessert, too, was exotic: nuts from Brazil, ginger from China, oranges from Seville, Tangerines from Tangier.[1] Everything in those mid-Victorian *ménages* reflected sudden prosperity and far-flung commerce. The first diamonds from Kimberley sparkled on the fingers of the women, and the luxuriant hair of the men shone with oil from Macassar.

Mid-Victorian Culture. The mid-Victorian age produced a remarkable civilization. Gone were the doubts and troubles of Early Victorian days. The men of the Golden Age had an unshakable faith in the goodness of God, in the greatness of England and in their own ability to change the world. This mood of optimism liberated their energies to achieve great works of art. They painted bad pictures and they wrought bad plays (the Puritan attitude towards the

[1] Bananas did not make their appearance until Alfred Jones of Liverpool began to introduce them, about 1885, with his famous after-dinner invitation: " Have a banana ? " As a partner in the Elder Dempster shipping company he was interested in popularizing the products of the Canary Islands.

theatre was revived and no well-bred girl or man could go on the stage without loss of good repute), but they wrote fine novels: Thackeray was hard at work until his death in 1865 and Dickens until 1870. And they wrote memorable poems: Tennyson became Poet Laureate in succession to Wordsworth in 1850 and Browning was doing his best work between 1840 and 1870. One of the greatest of English literary critics, Matthew Arnold, was a mid-Victorian. So was John Stuart Mill, the individualist philosopher, who published *On Liberty* in 1859, *Representative Government* in 1861 and *The Subjection of Women* in 1869 (the titles of his books give the best clue to his ideas).

Much of the energy of the age went into scientific discovery. The first submarine cable was laid from Dover to Calais in 1850; Singer invented his sewing machine in the following year; Bessemer's steel-converter appeared in 1856. The sixties were years of immense activity in perfecting iron ships, and the seventies saw invention after invention in the application of electricity to the telephone and to lighting.

Perhaps the figure most typical of the age is Charles Darwin. That handsome, bearded man, pious and abstemious, industrious and kind, spent his life (1809–82) in biological research. He made a voyage round the world and wrote a valuable travel-diary. Then in 1859 he published his *Origin of Species* which was to become the most influential book of the century. In this he worked out an idea, long familiar to philosophers, that life has evolved from simple forms—from primeval mud, through plants, jelly-fish, reptiles, animals to Man himself. He suggested that some species died out and others flourished because the " struggle for existence " always ended in the " survival of the fittest."

Darwin's theory of the origin of species profoundly shocked his contemporaries because it seemed to contradict the Bible and leave no room for the finger of God. Out of the ensuing controversy, in which Darwin himself took no part, there developed a common notion that Science and

Religion must be opposed to each other. Churchmen accordingly opposed the teaching of science in the schools and universities of Victorian England, and the dispute spread to America where in the twentieth century the State of Tennessee forbade any teacher " to teach any theory that denies the story of the Divine creation of man as taught in the Bible, and to teach instead that man has descended from a lower order of animals."

If Darwin may be taken as the typical figure of the mid-Victorian age, its greatest advocate was Macaulay. He was the master rhetorician of a rhetorical age. His *History*, which appeared between 1848 and 1861, described the revolutions of the seventeenth century as a mere prelude to the glories of Victorian England. "Nowhere," he wrote of the England of 1685, " could be found that sensitive and restless compassion which has, in our time, extended a powerful protection to the factory child, to the Hindoo widow, to the negro slave, which pries into the stores and watercasks of every emigrant ship, which winces at every lash laid on the back of a drunken soldier, which will not suffer the thief in the hulks to be ill-fed or over-worked and which has repeatedly endeavoured to save the life even of the murderer." And he added: " It is now the fashion to place the golden age of England in times when noblemen were destitute of comforts the want of which would be intolerable to a modern footman, when farmers and shopkeepers breakfasted on loaves the very sight of which would raise a riot in a modern workhouse, when men died faster in the purest country air than they now die in the most pestilential lanes of our towns, and when men died faster in the lanes of our towns than they now die on the coast of Guinea. We too shall, in our turn, be outstripped, and in our turn be envied. It may well be, in the twentieth century, that the peasant of Dorset may think himself miserably paid with fifteen shillings a week; that the carpenter at Greenwich may receive ten shillings a day; that labouring men may be as little used to dine without meat as they now are to eat rye bread; that sanitary police and medical discoveries may have added several more years to the average length of human life; that numerous comforts and luxuries which are now unknown, or confined to a few, may be within the reach of every diligent and thrifty working man. And it may then be the mode to assert that the increase of wealth and the progress of science have benefited the few at the expense of the many, and to talk of the reign of Queen Victoria as the time when England was truly merry England, when all classes were bound together by brotherly sympathy, when the rich did not grind the faces of the poor, and when the poor did not envy the splendour of the rich."

The First "Great Depression." The tide of mid-Victorian prosperity rolled steadily on until 1872. In 1873 it was still rising, though more slowly. In 1874 there were signs of an ebb. Then came a slump which hit three groups of Englishmen in particular. The first was the farmer. He had always specialized in wheat: the Repeal of the Corn Laws had not affected him much, for in all but very bad years he could grow wheat more cheaply than foreigners could grow it and ship it to England. In the fifties three-quarters of the wheat consumed in England was home-grown. But by the early seventies continental producers had railways and swift steamships to transport their produce. Canada too had begun growing foodstuffs on a huge scale now that she had a means of transporting it from the prairies. The English farmer could not compete. In all counties except Norfolk he ceased specializing in wheat and took to mixed farming and stock-raising. In the twenty years after 1874 the number of acres under wheat in England sank from 3,500,000 to 1,500,000 and since then England has never been able to grow her own food.

The second group to be hit consisted of the ship-builders and owners. They had built too many ships in the previous years and now that the fashion for steel ships was beginning they found many of their vessels out of date and redundant. More serious was the distress felt by the third group, the iron industry. England was used to supplying the world with iron rails, which soon cracked and had to be replaced —meaning new orders for English firms—every seven to ten years. Now railways were using steel rails which lasted much longer. And foreigners were making steel from their own iron. The new processes favoured Germany in particular, for since 1870 she held the rich iron deposits of Lorraine. Germany had spent most of the £200,000,000 paid her by France in buying industrial equipment from England. In 1874 those orders ceased to come in; Germany was ready to rival England at her own game of being the workshop of the world.

It must not be supposed that the men of 1874 realized what was happening. They simply blamed the Government—which Disraeli called " a range of extinct volcanoes " —for the ebb in prosperity. They blamed the Income Tax which Gladstone had so often promised to abolish and which was still in force. So at the 1874 elections Gladstone and the Liberals were thrown out and Disraeli achieved the ambition of a lifetime and became Prime Minister with a strong parliamentary majority behind him.

Chapter IX: EMPIRES OR NATIONS? 1874-86

Disraeli's Social Reforms – The Route to India – Eastern Question Again – Discovery of Africa – The Zulu War – Gladstone's Second Ministry – Egypt and the Sudan – Failure of Gladstone's Policy.

More clearly than anyone else at that time, Disraeli realized that England had raised up rivals to her own industrial supremacy by selling to other nations rails, engines, machines and all the means of industrial production; he concluded that if England was to maintain her lead it must be by concentrating less on trade with Europe and more on trade overseas, especially with the Empire. The years of his great Ministry (1874–80) are therefore famous in history as a period of imperial expansion.

Disraeli's Social Reforms. Before Disraeli could turn to the task of making his dreams of Empire come true he had a promise to fulfil. Thirty years ago he had formed the Young England group to bridge the gulf between what he had described in *Sybil* as " the two nations," the rich and the poor. In thirty years he had lost some of his romanticism but none of his human sympathy. There was little enough that he could do for the working class without losing the support of his Conservative followers, but that little he did. He made the first serious attack on the slums by an *Artisans' Dwellings Act* which authorized and encouraged town councils to pull down insanitary buildings and to replace them by decent houses for working men and their families. He checked the enclosure of common land, which had done such harm to the poorer country people in the previous hundred years, by an Act which came into force just in time to prevent the enclosure of Epping Forest (to-day Epping is the property of the City of London). He prevented the overloading of ships which had cost so many lives at sea by supporting the Bill of a private member, Samuel Plimsoll, providing that all ships must bear along their hulls a mark, the *Plimsoll line*, showing the depth to which they may safely be loaded. He safeguarded the working people who had put by their scanty savings in Friendly Societies by passing a *Friendly Societies Act* insisting on the adoption of sound rules and public audit of accounts. There were hundreds of these societies, ranging from the Oddfellows and the Druids to the Ancient Order of Foresters, the Buffaloes and the Hearts of Oak. After Disraeli's Act they attracted more and more of the poor man's savings until in 1934 they had 5,000,000 members and funds amounting to £70,000,000.

Then, most important of all, he capped Gladstone's *Trade Unions Act* by an Act laying down the principle that nothing is a crime if done by two or more persons which was not a crime if done by one. This meant that peaceful picketing was henceforth legal. In 1876 Disraeli wrote proudly to the Queen that " representative working men . . . and the great employers of labour . . . equally hailed these measures as a complete and satisfactory solution of *the greatest question of the day, the relations between Capital and Labour*."

The Route to India. From this time until his fall Disraeli was engrossed in the problems of Empire. They were two : India and Africa.

The key to the first problem lay in keeping the route to India in British hands. When Napoleon III had proposed cutting a canal through the isthmus of Suez, Disraeli had opposed it on the ground that a canal shared with other Powers was worse than no canal at all. But France went on with the canal on her own account and completed it in 1869 with French engineers (notably de Lesseps) and Egyptian labour. The money for building the canal was subscribed partly by Frenchmen and partly by Ismail, the successor of Mehemet Ali as Khedive of Egypt.

It so happened that both France and Egypt were too weak to take advantage of their new investment. Napoleon III was defeated by Russia in 1870 and for some time after was in no mood to follow up his plans for expansion in the East. As for Ismail, he was up to his eyes in debt; and on November 14, 1875, the news reached the British Foreign Office that he was anxious to raise money by selling his shares in the Suez Canal.

Disraeli saw at once that this was the opportunity of a lifetime. Parliament was not sitting and therefore could not vote the money—four million pounds. Yet it was necessary to act at once because there were other buyers in the field. Gambling on the chance that Parliament would vote the money when it met, Disraeli borrowed the four millions from Rothschild, the banker, and bought the shares. Everyone congratulated Disraeli and his Queen. It may be amusing to note that Victoria's sixteen-year-old grandson wrote to his mother: " Dear Mama, I must write you a line because I know you will be delighted that England has bought the Suez Canal. How jolly ! " The boy was later to become Kaiser Wilhelm II.

The British Government was now the chief partner in the Suez Canal.[1] But holding shares in a business enterprise in a foreign country usually has political consequences. One needs to be sure that the Government of that country is safe and sound, so that dividends may continue to be paid. If the foreign Government is neither, one is tempted to interfere politically in order to secure the dividends. That is what happened in Egypt. The Khedive's Government went bankrupt. The Turkish Government, which was the overlord of Egypt, was too weak to save it. England and France consequently came in and took control of Egyptian finances.

---

[1] The canal is owned by the Egyptian Government but is leased to a Company until 1968. On the Board of this Company are ten British directors, twenty-one French, and one Dutch. The British Government holds seven-sixteenths of the shares and receives a large annual dividend from the canal.

The Eastern Question Again. The weakness of the Turk was a help to England and France in Egypt but it was a menace to them elsewhere. If the Turkish Empire broke up Russia would extend her frontier to the Mediterranean—a prospect which British statesmen had been dreading since the beginning of the century. Fear of this expansion had brought England and France into the Crimean War; the Russian bear had been checked by the Treaty of Paris (1856), but now, twenty years later, it was on the move again. The way had been opened for it by the failure of the Turk to keep his promise to defend his Christian subjects. The latter were in rebellion all over the Balkans by 1876, and Russia was preparing to help the rebels.

Gladstone, had he been in power, would have given England's help too: he was shocked by the Turkish atrocities in Bulgaria where, to give one instance, twelve hundred rebels had surrendered on condition that their lives would be spared and had been burned to death in the village church by Turks. But Gladstone was not in power. And Disraeli cared less for avenging Bulgars than for checking Russia. Parliament granted him £6,000,000 for armaments and he sent the British fleet to the Sea of Marmora. Public opinion was behind him and the popular song of the winter of 1877-78 went:

> *We don't want to fight,*
>   *But by Jingo if we do!*
> *We've got the ships, we've got the men,*
>   *We've got the money too.*
> *We've fought the Bear before,*
>   *And while we're Britons true,*
> *The Russians shall not have Constantinople!*

The Russians had declared war on the Turks in April 1877 and after a short campaign during which the Turkish soldiers had shown unexpected but unavailing powers of resistance at Plevna, had reached the gates of Constantinople. England's threat of intervention caused them

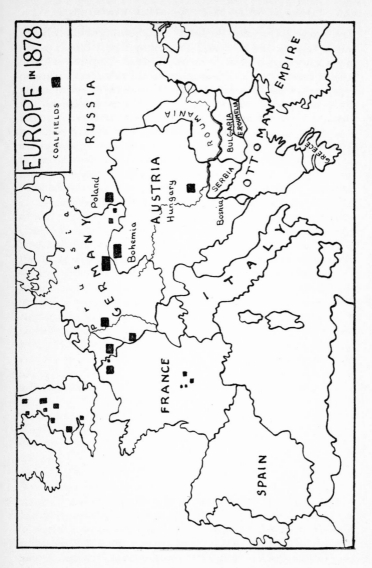

hurriedly to conclude the Treaty of San Stefano with the Turks in March 1878. By the Treaty Turkey was to renounce all her European provinces except eastern Thrace and Albania. Serbia, Montenegro and Roumania were to be independent; Bosnia and Herzegovina were to be under Austrian control; and a big Bulgaria, stretching from the Danube to the Aegean, was to be under Russian control. Russia was also to have Batoum, Kars and Bessarabia.

It was not a bad proposal for a settlement, especially in view of the fact that the Tsarist Government was too inefficient to control Bulgaria, big or little, for long. But Austria would not hear of it; she was frightened of Russian influence with the Balkans and threatened Russia with war. Nor would Disraeli hear of it: he bluffed Russia into thinking that England was ready to fight by bringing 7,000 troops from India to Malta by the new Suez Canal route. At this point Bismarck offered to play the "honest broker" and advised Russia to refer the peace terms to an international congress. Before the Congress of Berlin met Russia gave way to Disraeli's demands and modified the treaty so that Bulgaria became a small country and Turkey kept Macedonia and the control of a new state of Eastern Roumelia.

Disraeli returned to England in triumph, claiming that he had secured " Peace with Honour." Actually the peace was short-lived, for Eastern Roumelia was absorbed by Bulgaria in 1885 and the Turks were massacring Christians again by 1896; and honour was smudged by the annexation of Cyprus, which Great Britain received as a reward for Disraeli's services at Berlin. It would be more accurate to say that he had secured independence for eleven million people in the Balkans, amputation instead of extinction for the Turkish Empire in Europe, and diversion of the ambitions of Russia from the Near to the Far East.

The route to India was still not safe. Disraeli had secured the Suez route for England and had prevented the possibility of Russia's eastward expansion through Turkey by buttressing the toppling Ottoman Empire. But there was still, in Disraeli's mind, a fear that Russia might win over the Emir of Afghanistan, a policy which would bring Russia up to the very gates of India. To guard against this he sent as Viceroy of India Lord Lytton, the bellicose son of Bulwer Lytton the novelist, with instructions to bind Afghanistan to an alliance with England. Lytton knew no method but force. He seized Baluchistan. Then he seized the Kandahar province of Afghanistan. At the point of the sword he forced the Kabul Government to accept a British "adviser." When this official was murdered at Kabul in 1878 England sent two armies to avenge him. It seemed that neither Afghans nor English had learned much since 1842.

The Discovery of Africa. At this point the attention of Englishmen was diverted to even more dramatic events in Africa. Here the problem was very different. The Indian sub-continent had been explored and subjugated; the problem there was merely one of finding a suitable form of rule and of securing and developing the trade-routes. The African continent was unexplored. Something was known of the coastline: Englishmen had settled in the extreme South, Frenchmen had conquered Algiers in the North, there were several European colonies on the West coast and in the East the Portuguese had a colony on the mouth of the Zambesi, but of the interior Europeans were profoundly ignorant. Rumours of fantastic wealth hidden in the Dark Continent brought out explorer after explorer to seek the sources of the Nile, round which it was believed would be found a country of fabulous riches—the lost kingdom of Prester John—and the sources of the Niger, where there was said to be a town called Timbuktu, a veritable El Dorado of Africa.

The most successful of the early explorers were Scotsmen. James Bruce discovered the source of the Blue Nile in the Abyssinian Lake Tsana in 1769. Mungo Park died in 1805 exploring the Upper Niger, Alexander Gordon Laing reached Timbuktu in 1826, and within the next twenty-five years the mystery of the course of the Niger was solved. There remained the mystery of the White Nile. In 1861 the source of that river was found by Captain Speke and Captain Grant in Lake Victoria Nyanza. The greatest of all the Scots explorers was the missionary David Livingstone, who between 1840 and 1867 worked in Bechuanaland, in Lake Ngami, in Nyasaland and the territory round Lake Tanganyika—countries which no European had penetrated before. In 1867 Livingstone was reported missing and his loss was taken as a national tragedy in Britain. There was public rejoicing when the news came that he had been found on Lake Tanganyika by H. M. Stanley,[1] who had been sent out by an American newspaper and who had crossed the whole continent in search of him.

The first military expedition of the British into the African interior was made in 1867 when an army was sent from India against the Negus Theodore of Abyssinia. Theodore had ruled with the help of British consuls until suddenly he became angry at the failure of the British Government to answer his letters (in one of which, it is said, he proposed marriage to the widowed Queen Victoria) and clapped consuls and missionaries into prison. An army of 12,000 British Indian troops under Sir Robert Napier was sent to procure their release and after a fierce battle at Magdala (1868), in which breech-loading rifles were used by the British for the first time, the troops of the Negus were defeated. Theodore shot himself[2] and Napier, seeing the country relapsing into anarchy, lost no time in evacuating his troops. The expedition cost a good deal more than it was worth.

Much more favourable to British imperial expansion were the fertile and temperate plains in the south of the

[1] Stanley was not his real name; it was that of a rich American who had adopted him as a lad from a workhouse in Wales.

[2] He left a letter for Napier: " Believing myself to be a great lord, I gave you battle; but by reason of the worthlessness of my artillery, all my pains were as naught. Out of what I have done of evil towards my people may God bring good. His will be done. I had intended, if God had so decreed, to conquer the whole world; and it was my desire to die if my purpose could not be fulfilled.

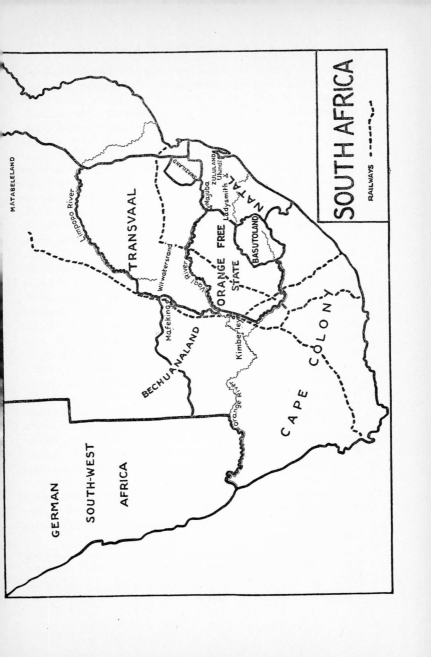

continent. There were four white settlements in South Africa: Cape Colony and Natal which were British colonies, and Transvaal and the Orange Free State which were Boer Republics. The white population of all four was less than that of Birmingham, but their disputes soon became a matter of European importance.

The Zulu War. The Boers hated the British for depriving them of their slaves and for virtually driving them out of Cape Colony on the Great Trek. They hated the British for driving them out of Natal: a British Governor, Sir Benjamin D'Urban, had asserted that the Boers needed protection from the Zulus and had made this an excuse for annexing the coastal strip of Natal and Zululand which lay beyond it. They hated the British for claiming a little hill which lay on the borders of the Orange Free State and Cape Colony. This hill had been discovered in 1870 to be rich in diamonds: a rush of foreign adventurers followed and the hill, first called New Rush and later Kimberley, made fortunes for all concerned except the Boers.

It was Disraeli's policy to bring the Boer Republics of South Africa under British rule. In 1877 he sent to the Transvaal a certain Sir Theophilus Shepstone, who had no difficulty in persuading the rascally President Burgers to agree to the annexation of his country by Britain. Burgers did this to save himself from the Zulus, whom his Boers had ill-treated—from their first arrival in Africa until to-day the Dutch settlers have attempted to enslave and oppress the native races. The Zulus belonged to the fighting race of Bantus, black men who had been spreading southward over the lands of the degenerate native races of South Africa. A chieftain called Chaka had organised them into a nation-at-arms at the beginning of the century and now King Cetewayo, a successor of Chaka, was threatening further conquests with his army of 40,000 picked warriors. Disraeli appointed as High Commissioner of South Africa Sir Bartle Frere, a man who had made his name for firm handling of native races in India. Frere sent an ultimatum to

Cetewayo ordering him to disband his troops. Then, as Cetewayo preserved a dignified silence, he declared war.

Three divisions of British and native troops marched into Zululand in January 1879 under the command of Lord Chelmsford. They were armed with breech-loading rifles and had a few guns. The Zulus, in full war panoply of leopard-skins, feathers and ox-tails, had only spears and hide-shields. But they knew their ground and out-numbered their enemy. The British were defeated at the battle of Isandhlwana and it was all they could do to hold their camp at Rorke's Drift. Hastily reinforcements were sent out from England and India—over 10,000 men, and horses and Gatling guns—and at last, over five months after Isandhlwana, the Zulus were defeated and their capital, Ulundi, captured.

By the Zulu War England had lost men, money and prestige. She had also lost her hold over the Transvaal. While Cetewayo was a menace the Boers had been willing to accept British protection; now that his power was destroyed they had no intention of abandoning their independence. Perhaps it was well for Disraeli that his Ministry fell in April 1880, leaving Gladstone to take the consequences.

Gladstone's Second Ministry, 1880–85. No one can envy Gladstone his position in 1880. As a good Liberal one of the first tenets of his creed was the right of every nation, however small and primitive, to its own laws and religion. In the great electoral campaign which he had fought in his Midlothian constituency in the autumn of 1879 he had constantly stressed the virtues of Nationalism in attacking Disraeli's policy of Imperialism: " Remember," he had said, " that the sanctity of life in the hill villages of Afghanistan, among the winter snows, is as inviolable in the eye of Almighty God as can be your own. Remember that He who has united you as human beings in the same flesh and blood, has bound you by the law of mutual love; that that mutual love is not limited by the shores of this island, is not limited by the boundaries of Christian civilisation; that it passes over the whole surface of the earth, and embraces the meanest along with the greatest in its unmeasured scope." Disraeli had violated the rights of Nationalism in Afghanistan and in Africa. Gladstone's task was to make good these errors. It involved him in terrible contradictions and in ultimate failure.

The Afghan problem proved the easiest of solution. Early in 1880 a very able savage, Abdur Rahman, a nephew of the deposed Emir, seized the throne of Kabul. Gladstone, reversing the policy of Disraeli, recognized Abdur Rahman and paid his price, which was the restoration of Kandahar to Afghanistan.[1] This settlement was not popular with Englishmen, who were ashamed at what seemed a surrender, or with Afghans, who hated being kept in order by the strong hand of their new monarch. But it proved an admirable conclusion of the two difficulties which Gladstone had most at heart: the national independence of Afghanistan was assured, and Russia's advance towards India was checked. After one more fruitless attempt to advance into Afghan territory (when they seized and tried to hold the village of Pendjeh in 1885) the Russians turned their attention to expansion further East and set about the construction of the Trans-Siberian railway.

The South African problem proved more difficult. At Midlothian Gladstone had said: "If Cyprus and Transvaal were as valuable as they are valueless, I would repudiate them because they are obtained by means dishonourable to the character of the country." The Boers of the Transvaal took this as permission to assert their independence. Under the excellent leadership of Paul Krüger they raised their national flag (December 1880) and proceeded to drive the British troops out of the country. For this first Boer War the British commander, Sir George Colley, had no more than 2,000 men at his disposal and they were no match for the Boers who, well mounted and well armed and

[1] Disraeli made his last appearance in Parliament to protest against the cession of Kandahar. Two months later, in 1881, he died.

most of them crack shots, defeated the British three times in a couple of months. In the last encounter, at Majuba Hill, Colley was killed and nearly three hundred British were killed, wounded or captured while the Boers lost scarcely a man. Gladstone accepted the defeat. He refused to send the British Army from the Cape to punish the Boers; instead he signed a treaty recognizing their independence. The first draft of this treaty (March 1881) contained a vague reference to British suzerainty, but in 1884, thanks to Krüger's insistence, even this claim over the Transvaal was abandoned.

Egypt and the Sudan. In Egypt a similar situation faced Gladstone. Disraeli had asserted large imperial claims and had resigned, leaving his successor to do the fighting. Under Disraeli England had joined France in taking control of Egypt. In 1883 a nationalist revolt against the dual control flared out under Arabi Pasha, an Egyptian soldier. Arabi stood for "Egypt for the Egyptians" and began his campaign by murdering fifty Europeans at Alexandria. Gladstone was in a quandary. He believed in Egypt's right to national independence but he could not stand by and watch his countrymen being slaughtered. He invited the European Powers to join him in suppressing Arabi, but the Powers were otherwise engaged. Even the French refused to take any further responsibility. So Gladstone had no alternative but to send a British expedition to deal with Arabi's soldiers. The expedition was led by Sir Garnet Wolseley whose successes had become proverbial—"All Sir Garnet," meaning "everything all right," was already a phrase in common use. He destroyed the fortifications of Alexandria and defeated Arabi at Tel-el-Kebir in 1882.

The British Government now found itself in an absurdly false position with regard to Egypt. Dual control by France and Britain was ended, thanks to French passivity. Britain had already vast financial interests in Egypt. Now she had soldiers there. Yet Egypt was nominally part of the Turkish

Empire though the Turks were too weak to exercise any real supervision and left the country to the rule of an aged and corrupt set of Pashas. Gladstone could not bring himself to leave Egypt to the Pashas; nor could he establish British rule over the land by annexing it to the British Empire. He compromised: British officers stayed in Egypt, nominally as officials of the Egyptian Khedive and of his overlord the Turkish Sultan-Caliph, and Sir Evelyn Baring (later Lord Cromer) was sent out as Consul-General to " advise " the Khedive Government. On paper Egypt was Turkish; in fact it came increasingly under British control. Cromer set to work to establish an honest financial system and to organize works of agriculture and irrigation so that the lives of Egyptian peasants should be lightened and the dividends of British shareholders increased. The paradox of British rule in a Turkish dominion lasted until 1914.

Gladstone had lied to himself over Egypt. He had crushed Egyptian nationalism in the interests of British prestige and commerce. One lie leads to another: Gladstone was at once involved in crushing another national rising, this time in the Sudan.

The Sudan is a vast territory covering the upper valleys of the White and the Blue Nile. It is inhabited by black races which are quite distinct from the Egyptians— " Sudan " is an Arabic word meaning " the blacks." Under Mehemet Ali the Egyptians had conquered the Sudan and had built Khartoum to keep the natives in awe. But now, when the news spread up the Nile that the Egyptians under Arabi had failed to throw off the yoke of the Europeans, some Sudanese tribes made an attempt to throw off that of the Egyptians. Their leader was a prophet who called himself the Mahdi, or Messiah. He proclaimed a Holy War and set up a new Moslem Kingdom in the Sudan.

Again Gladstone was in a quandary. He could not help sympathizing with the Mahdi and his Dervishes; they represented a genuine religious and national rising against

Egyptian conquerors who had done nothing for the Sudan but enslave its people and remove its wealth. " Those people are struggling to be free," said Gladstone in the House, " and they are rightly struggling to be free." Yet the Sudan controls the water supply of Egypt, and whoever controls the Sudan controls Egypt. Besides, the Egyptian Pashas had sent out a miserable army of convicts under Colonel Hicks, a British officer, to suppress the rising, and Hicks and his men had been annihilated by the Mahdi at El Obeid in 1883. And now the Mahdi's men were rounding up British traders and missionaries in the Sudan and were putting them to the sword.

Something had to be done to rescue the survivors. Gladstone agreed that an expedition should be sent out " to report on the best means of evacuating the Sudan." Someone suggested that General Gordon should lead the expedition, and Gladstone gave his consent. It was the greatest mistake of his career. Gordon's life had been spent in *suppressing* national risings. He had won thirty-three battles in China suppressing the Taiping rebellion against the Manchu emperors. He had been employed by the Egyptian Government for three years as Governor-General of the Sudan. Now his orders were to evacuate the very territory over which he had once ruled. Not for a moment did he intend to obey them. He marched to Khartoum and entrenched himself there, declaring that he would stay until the British Government came to its senses and sent an army to take control of the Sudan. To his mind it was a Holy War of Christian against Moslem.

Gladstone hastened to recall his insubordinate officer. But Gordon refused to leave Khartoum, and in England public opinion, fanned by the newspapers, supported him and clamoured for an army to be sent out. Gladstone would not abandon his principles; he would not send an army to the Sudan. Then came news that Gordon was besieged in Khartoum and that his life and those of his men depended on relief being sent at once. Gladstone hesitated, and Gordon was lost. When at last Wolseley was sent with a relief expedition to Khartoum it was too late: Gordon was dead and the Dervishes were masters of Khartoum.

From 1885 to 1897 the Dervishes ruled the Sudan. The Mahdi died and the religious inspiration went out of the movement, but the kingdom which he had created survived under his chief supporter, Abdullah, the Khalifa. Year after year there was fighting with the British outposts on the Egyptian frontier until at last, when Gladstone was dead, the imperialist policy which he had opposed and which Gordon had sponsored was adopted in deadly earnest by the British Government.

Failure of Gladstone's Policy. Gladstone had grappled with four national movements. In Afghanistan, in the Transvaal and in the Sudan he had fulfilled his Midlothian promises; in Egypt he had broken them. Both his successes and his failures made him unpopular, for the public were more interested in Empire than in the rights of small nations, more interested in Gordon's life than in Gladstone's promises. At the elections of 1885 Gladstone was defeated.

His second Ministry had not been without its triumphs. It is memorable for the passing of the third Reform Bill (1884) which gave the vote to agricultural labourers and to miners in country districts. A million and a quarter new votes were created by this—a greater number than had been enfranchized by the first two Reform Bills put together. It was becoming possible to speak of England as a democratic country.

Meanwhile it was a fifth nationalist movement that finally defeated Gladstone. The Irish were in revolt. Twice again Gladstone became Prime Minister—for a few months in 1886 and between 1892 and 1894—and on each occasion he brought forward a new Bill for Irish Home Rule and on each occasion he was defeated. The Liberal party split. A number of Liberals calling themselves Unionists, because they favoured the preservation of the Union with Ireland, broke away and subsequently joined

EMPIRES OR NATIONS?

the Conservatives. A number of others broke away under Lord Rosebery, calling themselves Liberal Imperialists, because they believed in the extension and consolidation of the British Empire. In the following chapter we shall digress from the history of Victorian England to consider the problem of Ireland as a whole.

It was an irresistible force that had defeated Gladstone. He stood for Liberalism—for the freedom of individuals and of nations from their oppressors. At the time of his first Ministry (1868–74) it had been possible to take this attitude successfully, for then England was without serious rivals in the commercial world: she could afford to let the small nations have their liberty. But the Great Depression which began in 1874 changed all that. Henceforth England had to struggle to compete with other industrial countries and this competition involved securing fields for investment, sources for raw materials and safe markets in distant territories; and the securing of these involved the conquest of small nations as colonies and the binding of them into a strong colonial Empire. Disraeli stood for Imperialism and Gladstone for Nationalism; and because England could not maintain her commercial supremacy without an Empire, the policy of Disraeli was bound to prevail.

Chapter X: THE LIBERATION OF IRELAND, 1815-1935

The Grievances of the Irish – O'Connell and Catholic Emancipation – Young Ireland and the Famine – The Fenians and the Land League – Gladstone and Home Rule – Ulster and the Irish Nationalists – The Irish Free State.

THE STORY OF IRELAND in the last century and a half is the story of a revolution; it is blackened by famine and murder, smudged by bribery and corruption, yet lighted by the pure flame of undying ideals and by the steady approach of victory.

The causes of this revolution lie deep in Ireland's past. In the twelfth century the island was invaded by the knights of Henry II. "A hostile and separate power," as Lecky says, "was planted in the centre of Ireland, sufficiently powerful to prevent the formation of another civilization, yet not sufficiently powerful to impose a civilization of its own. Feudalism was introduced, but the keystone of the system, a strong resident sovereign, was wanting, and Ireland was soon torn by the wars of great Anglo-Norman nobles, who were, in fact, independent sovereigns, much like the old Irish kings." It took the English four hundred years to complete the conquest of Ireland; not until Mary and Elizabeth had settled hordes of Englishmen on the lands of Southern Ireland, not until James I had settled hordes of Scotsmen on the lands of Ulster in the north, was the conquest accomplished. And then, in 1641, the Irish rose in rebellion, a rebellion which lost them half their population and all their liberty.

There were now two races in Ireland: the native Gaelic-speaking Irish who were Catholics, and the English-speaking Anglo-Irish who were Protestants. The settlement which was imposed by the English Government at the end of the seventeenth century made the former the subjects, almost the serfs, of the latter. The Anglo-Irish *Ascendancy*, though a small minority of the island's population,[1] alone voted and sat in the Dublin Parliament and ruled the island in its own landowning interest until the end of the eighteenth century, when there was a rebellion of the poorer classes under Wolfe Tone. At this point the English Government stepped in and took control over Ireland by an Act of Union (1800) which gave the Westminster Parliament the right to make laws for Ireland, allowing a hundred members of the Ascendancy to sit as M.P.s.

The Grievances of the Irish. At the beginning of the nineteenth century the Irish had three just grievances. The first was a *religious* grievance. The Irish were (and are) a Roman Catholic people. When England broke away from the Papacy in Tudor times the Irish became more loyal to Rome. In 1800 three-quarters of the population were Papists. The remaining quarter were not Irish by race: they were either Dissenters, most of whom were descended from the Scots whom James I had planted in Ulster, or members of the Church of Ireland which was a branch of the Church of England and was supported almost exclusively by the Anglo-Irish landowning gentry of the Ascendancy. The Catholic majority had to pay tithes to support the parsons and buildings of the latter. What was worse, Catholics could not sit as Members of Parliament; they were debarred from taking any part in the government of their country. No wonder the Irish were ready to fight for Emancipation—that is, for political toleration. At the time of the passing of the Act of Union, Pitt had promised that Catholic Emancipation would be the first Act to be passed by the new Parliament. In 1815 that promise was still unfulfilled and the Irish were still

[1] It is altogether extraordinary how many great men that small minority produced. Among soldiers, Marlborough, Wellington and Roberts were Anglo-Irish. Among statesmen Castlereagh, Canning and Palmerston. Among writers Berkeley, Swift, Steele, Burke, Goldsmith, Sheridan, Congreve, Wilde, Shaw, Synge and Yeats.

suffering from a degrading form of religious persecution.

Secondly, there was an *economic* grievance. The soil of Ireland was owned by the Protestant Ascendancy. And most of these Anglo-Irish landowners did not even live in Ireland. They made no attempt to understand or to look after their tenants but lived comfortably in England on the money the Irish paid them in rent. To collect the rent and supervise the running of the estates they sent agents to Ireland. The first duty of the agent was to send money to his master in England; the more money he sent the better he was thanked. He therefore did everything he could to put up the Irishman's rent. If a tenant fenced his fields, his rent would go up; if he repaired his cabin or built new farm buildings, his rent would go up; and if he refused to pay, then he would be turned out and a new tenant found who would be glad enough to get the land with its new fences and buildings, even at the high rent that was asked. There were, of course, some landowners who cared for their Irish estates as well as any squire cared for his English village, but they were exceptional. The Irish had an economic grievance such as we cannot think about to-day without indignation.

Circumstances made the economic grievance more acute after 1815. During the long French wars food was scarce and Irish wheat and meat and dairy produce fetched high prices. When the war ended prices fell and the Irish, who had no other resource but agriculture, felt the pinch worst. The landowners adjusted themselves to peace conditions and Ireland continued to be the granary of England until 1846; then her chief exporting industry was fatally damaged by the Repeal of the Corn Laws.

Thirdly the Irish had a *political* grievance. They were governed by Englishmen. There was an English garrison at Dublin Castle, an English administrator at Government House and an English Lord-Lieutenant in the Residency. And though there were a hundred Anglo-Irish representatives at Westminster they could get nothing done without the support of English Whigs or Tories. It is true that in a sense the Dublin Parliament had brought this upon Ireland by voting for the Act of Union, but the alternative to Union was to go on with a Dublin Parliament (which since 1782 could make laws for Ireland, though it could not appoint the men who enforced them) and to go on with Englishmen at the Castle and the Residency—they remained whether there was a Union or not.

The history of Ireland resolves itself into one long struggle for the removal of these three grievances. The political grievance was just as real as the other two, but it was the last to be fought against: religion and land lie nearer to a people's heart than politics.

O'Connell and Catholic Emancipation.

The movement for Catholic Emancipation began peaceably enough. Grattan, an Anglo-Irish Protestant M.P., raised the question repeatedly at Westminster between 1812 and 1819, but always his motion was defeated. This failure drove the Irish to more original methods. A great leader arose in the person of Daniel O'Connell, a Papist of Papists and an orator such as only the Irish race can produce. He was a master of political agitation. Up and down the country he held mass meetings, forming a " Catholic Association " which half Ireland joined, even though it meant paying a penny a week into the Association's funds. By 1835 when the Association was suppressed by Parliament, O'Connell, " The Liberator," was the uncrowned king of Ireland. In 1829 he stood as a candidate for County Clare and was elected by a huge majority over Vesey Fitzgerald, the Protestant candidate. Yet by law O'Connell, as a Catholic, could not take his seat. Clearly the law would have to go, or the green fields of Ireland would be stained with blood.

The law went. Peel and Wellington (the latter an Anglo-Irish landowner himself), showing great courage in beating down the prejudices of the Tory supporters, forced the Roman Catholic Emancipation Bill through Parliament in 1829. George IV signed it reluctantly, grumbling that: " Now Wellington is King in England, and O'Connell is

King in Ireland and I am only Dean of Windsor." The Act made all offices in England and Ireland, except two or three, open to Roman Catholics and allowed them to sit in Parliament.

O'Connell had won a great victory but he was anything but satisfied. For one thing, Emancipation was accompanied by an Act depriving the Irish Catholic peasants of their vote: formerly the 40s. freeholder had a vote, now the qualification was raised to £10. For another, the Irish members of the Westminster Parliament, though now they might be Catholics, were still a minority in an assembly of non-Catholic Englishmen. O'Connell turned his talents to agitation for the Repeal of the Union Act—for what later generations were to call Home Rule for Ireland.

"Young Ireland" and the Famine. But though O'Connell was an unequalled agitator he shrank from openly breaking the law. When in 1843 the Lord-Lieutenant forbade him to hold a projected mass-meeting at Clontarf he abandoned the project. There were young men in Ireland who despised this respect for English law. Led by Smith O'Brien and Gavan Duffy they formed a Young Ireland party to rouse the country for Repeal. In their papers, the *Nation* and the *United Irishman*, they threatened violence. This startled the English Government into doing something for Ireland. A Commission under the Earl of Devon was sent to investigate the land question; it reported that tenants should be compensated for improvements they made on their land. Lord Stanley urged the Commons to pass a *Land Act*; but the Commons refused. In the same year, 1845, Peel succeeded in passing a Bill to raise the Government grant for education in Ireland: the education of Catholics was improved by raising the grant to Maynooth College—the training college for priests—from £9,000 to £26,000 a year, and of Protestants by the foundation of three new University Colleges, known as Queen's University, at Cork, Galway and Belfast.

At this point calamity overtook Ireland. In the autumn of

1845 the potato crop all over Europe was ruined by a blight. It was the greatest natural calamity that Europe had known since the Black Death. It hit Ireland hardest because potatoes were the only one of her food crops which was not ear-marked for export. During the famine landowners went on selling wheat and meat to England while the Irish peasants died for want of food. In four years the population of Ireland was reduced from 8,175,000 to 6,500,000. Nearly a million Irish people died of starvation and nearly a million emigrated to the United States. For the rest of the century the drain of emigration went on; Irish farmers could not afford to keep their sons at home and could not pay their rents except with the aid of the remittances which those emigrants sent home from America.

The Fenians and the Land League. It is not surprising that the next movement for the relief of Ireland's grievances came from America. When the American Civil War was over many Irishmen who had fought in it came home determined to organize an armed insurrection in Ireland. After all, they argued, the English never listened to Irish grievances until there was a disturbance. O'Connell's agitation had won Emancipation, O'Brien's agitation had won at least the Maynooth Grant; they would see if more forceful agitation would not win Home Rule itself. So they formed the Fenian Society, or Irish Revolutionary Brotherhood, and under O'Donovan Rossa and James Stephens they planned jail-breaking and similar outrages. Their methods were not unsuccessful. Again the British Government apparently yielded to violence when it had refused to yield to argument. In 1869 Gladstone carried a Bill for the Disestablishment of the Irish Church. The Protestant Church of Ireland ceased to be supported by the State; henceforth it must rely on its own resources. Since the members of this Church were then not more than a tenth of the population of Ireland, disestablishment seemed only just.

The religious grievance of the Irish was now in some

measure removed. The land grievance was more pressing than ever. The Irish always regarded the man who worked the land as the owner of it; they could never get used to the English idea that the farmer was only a tenant—only a borrower, so to speak—of the land from a landlord. In Ulster there was still a custom that a tenant could not be turned off his land as long as he paid his rent. The Irish, with the Fenians at their head, were agitating that " Ulster tenant right " should be extended to the rest of Ireland. Mr. Gladstone met them half-way. In 1870 he passed his first Land Act making it obligatory for the landlord to compensate a tenant whom he turned out of his holding and to pay for any improvements the outgoing tenant had made in his land.

This was a half-measure. The Irish wanted what they called the Three F's: that is *Free Sale*, or the right of tenants to sub-let at will; *Fair Rents*, or the assessment of rent by impartial tribunals, and *Fixity of Tenure*, or the right of tenants not to be evicted without long notice. They hit upon new methods of agitation. Charles Stuart Parnell, an Irish M.P., who though a Protestant landowner made himself the champion of the cause of the Catholic tenants, began the practice of talking endlessly in the Commons, so that no business could be finished unless the House was prepared to vote the redress of Irish grievances. This method was strangely effective: it gave the Irish party the greatest possible advertisement in England. Even more effective was the scheme for a Land League put into practice by a young Irish labourer, Michael Davitt, who was the son of evicted peasants and had lost an arm while tending machinery in a Lancashire mill and had spent ten years in Portland gaol on a conspiracy-to-murder charge. Now he returned to Ireland and organized a Land League of Irish farmers on the lines of an English Trade Union. The Leaguers' methods were the strike, the " boycott " and " moonlighting." If they felt their rent to be unfair they went on strike against paying, and if they were evicted by force they picketed the farm so that no other tenant dared

THE LIBERATION OF IRELAND 173

to take it. If they disliked the conduct of a particular landlord they refused to speak to him or to have any dealings with him whatsoever: this practice got its name from Captain Boycott, one of the first landlords against whom it was applied. If they felt themselves wronged in any way they went out by night (hence " moonlighting ") and burned ricks and destroyed crops; there were no less than five hundred of these outrages in the year 1880.

Again terrorist tactics were successful; again Gladstone yielded. In 1881 he passed his Second Land Act which gave Ireland the Three F's. Courts were set up to decide on fair rents—and this led to a general reduction of rents by 25 per cent. Land Commissioners were empowered to lend money to tenants who wished to buy their holdings.[1]

The Land League had won its cause, but Parnell, like O'Connell after Emancipation, was not satisfied. The Land Act, like the Emancipation Act, was accompanied by repressive measures. A Coercion Bill gave the Government power to imprison suspects without trial. In 1881 Parnell himself was put in gaol. He warned the Government that if they locked him up they would leave " Captain Moonlight " in charge of Ireland; and he was right. There were crimes all over Ireland in 1881 and in the following year a little group of terrorists (of whom Parnell disapproved as much as any Englishmen) murdered Lord Frederick Cavendish, the new Secretary for Ireland, in Phœnix Park in Dublin.

Gladstone and Home Rule.

Parnell was released and devoted the rest of his life to an attempt to remove the remaining grievance of the Irish, the political grievance against English rule. The elections of 1885 gave him his chance for they returned Liberals and Conservatives in such even proportions that Gladstone could not count on a majority unless the Irish members supported him. Gladstone now declared himself converted to Home Rule and

[1] These powers were gradually extended, notably by the Wyndham Act of 1903, until the peasant proprietor became the typical figure of Ireland.

in 1886 he brought in his first Home Rule Bill. Like the first Land Act, it was only a half-measure: it was proposed that the Irish should have their own Parliament in Dublin, but that they should contribute to the Imperial exchequer and should leave the Army, Navy, Foreign Policy, Customs and Excise in English hands. The Bill split the Liberal party, as the Emancipation Bill had split the Tory party half a century earlier. Home Rule was thrown out; eighty-three Liberal " Unionists " voted against it and later joined the Conservatives.

The Conservative Government was determined to put an end to lawlessness in Ireland. In Dublin Mr. Arthur (later Lord) Balfour ruled with the firmest hand Ireland had known since the Union. In London every attempt was made to ruin Parnell. *The Times* published in facsimile a letter, purporting to be written by Parnell, in which he gave his approval to the murder of Cavendish. This was proved to be a forgery. Then detectives were set to watch Parnell on his visits to a certain Mrs. O'Shea with whom he was in love. In 1890 Mrs. O'Shea was divorced by her husband, and Parnell was the co-respondent. In Catholic Ireland this was enough to end a man's public career. Parnell died in disgrace in 1891.

The Home Rule Movement did not die with him. In 1893 Gladstone, now in power for the last time, tried to pass a second Home Rule Bill. It was rejected by the House of Lords. Gladstone retired from politics and the Conservatives resumed unopposed their traditional policy, which was to give Ireland good government rather than self-government. To show that they were not unmindful of Ireland's grievances they passed a Land Purchase Act voting the sum of £5,000,000 a year to Irish peasants with which they could buy their farms from the landlords, on undertaking to pay the English Government back on easy terms.

The rest of the story of Irish liberation belongs to a later period and should properly find its place later in this book, but for the sake of continuity we shall tell it here.

THE LIBERATION OF IRELAND 175

Ulster and the Irish Nationalists. The Liberals returned to power in 1906 and in 1911 introduced a third Home Rule Bill. This time the opposition did not come from the Lords (their power had been curtailed by a Parliament Act, as will be seen by a glance at page 214) but from a section of Ireland itself. Unlike the rest of Ireland, the majority of the inhabitants of Belfast and East Ulster were Protestants. They were opposed to Home Rule because it would leave them at the mercy of the Catholic majority of Southern Ireland. Led by Sir Edward Carson the Ulstermen began to form a private army. They declared their intention to fight against the rest of Ireland if a Home Rule Parliament should be set up in Dublin. The rebellious example set by Carson's Volunteers was followed by the Irish Nationalists, who armed against the Ulstermen.

The Prime Minister, Mr. Asquith, was powerless against Carson's threat of civil war because he knew that the people of England did not care enough for Irish Home Rule to let him send soldiers to suppress the Ulster Volunteers. General Gough and fifty-seven cavalry officers resigned because they refused to face the possibility of being sent to fight their friends in Ulster—the incident was known as the " Curragh Mutiny." The Secretary of State for War, Colonel Seely, and the Chief of the General Staff, Sir John French, resigned because they sympathized with General Gough. At the same time arms were being landed in Belfast from Germany: a quarter of a million rifles and three million rounds of ammunition were unloaded in the last week of April 1914. All through that spring and summer attention was turned to the Ulster crisis rather than to the gathering storm over Europe. King George V called a conference of leaders of all parties—Conservative as well as Liberal, Ulstermen as well as Nationalists—at Buckingham Palace, but on July 24 the conference broke down. Arms were being landed at Dublin now. It seemed that nothing short of an earthquake could save Ireland from civil war.

In the following week the earthquake came. The Great

War broke out and the Irish question was shelved. Even the Home Rule Bill which had now become law was not put into force because of the Government's pre-occupation with the war.

It was a tragedy for the Irish Nationalists that the Government withheld the cup of triumph from them at the very moment when it had been put to their lips. They could not appreciate what the war meant to Englishmen; it was not Ireland's war. They had been told they must wait, but as the war dragged on month after month they got less and less able to wait. At last a group of idealists planned an insurrection. At their head was Patrick Pearse, a poet who had founded a school near Dublin where he brought up the sons of Nationalists in the language and lore of Gaelic Ireland.[1] He had his brother with him, and Thomas McDonough the poet, and Sir Roger Casement and others. The plan of rising in arms against the might of England seemed desperate, but there was the ghost of a chance that it would succeed. It was timed for Easter, 1916, and that spring England had her hands more than full on the Continent. Casement's job was to run arms in from Germany. At the last minute he was caught and his cargo captured. The official leader of the movement, Eoin MacNeill, called the rising off, but Pearse was determined to go on with it. He and six friends called themselves the " Provisional government of the Irish Republic " and issued the following proclamation: " We declare the right of the people of Ireland to the ownership of Ireland, and to the unfettered control of Irish destinies, to be sovereign and indefeasible. The long usurpation of that right by a foreign people and government has not extinguished the right, nor can it ever be extinguished save by the destruction of the Irish people. In every generation the Irish people have asserted their right to national freedom and sovereignty: six times during the past three hundred years they have

[1] It is worth noting that Pearse, like most of the Irish Nationalist leaders from Tone to Parnell, was of Anglo-Irish, not of Gaelic-Irish, descent.

asserted it in arms. Standing on that fundamental right and again asserting in arms in the face of the world, we hereby proclaim the Irish Republic as a Sovereign Independent State, and we pledge our lives and the lives of our comrades-in-arms to the cause of its freedom, of its welfare, and of its exaltation among the nations. . . ."

At the appointed time the contingents outside Dublin, reluctantly obeying MacNeill's orders, did not rise, but in the capital Pearse's men seized the strategic points—the Customs House, the Post Office, the Four Courts, the Gresham Hotel and Boland's Mill. They had rifles and a few machine guns. The British garrison were superior in numbers and arms, and they had light artillery. Yet for the whole of Easter Week the insurrectionists held out. Only when the British threatened to burn the Post Office and its occupants did Pearse surrender.

Dublin still bears the marks of that rising, physically in the bullet-scarred walls of her public buildings and morally in her mourning for the men who suffered in it. Fifty-eight Irishmen were killed in the fighting. The British held a court martial and sentenced ninety-seven others to death as rebels. The sentence was actually carried out in the case of sixteen men: Pearse and fifteen of the leaders were shot. Only one leader was reprieved—the Commandant who had held Boland's Mill—and that was because he had been born in America and the English were anxious not to offend the United States just when there was a chance that they would come in to the World War on the English side. The name of the reprieved man was Eamonn de Valera.

In April 1918 the British Government made the biggest of all mistakes that have been made in relations with Ireland. They proposed to apply the Conscription Law to Irishmen. If there was one thing that could rouse the more peaceable Irish folk to hatred of England, it was this. The English Government made itself hateful by trying to force Irishmen to join the colours, and it made itself ridiculous by failing. When the Great War ended the British

Government found a new insurrection brewing in Ireland which had ten times more popular support than that of Easter Week.

The Irish Nationalists proclaimed Ireland to be a Republic. They set up a revolutionary Parliament—the Dáil—in Dublin and organized an Irish Republican Army (I.R.A.) to carry out its decrees by force. There were still the official British Government and police in Dublin, but the Nationalists proclaimed that their attitude towards them was " that of the Belgian people to the German army of occupation." In May guerilla war began. The I.R.A. raided police stations and army posts for arms. They broke into prisons, shot warders and set prisoners free. They shot policemen, and no coroner's jury dared bring in a verdict for murder.

In face of this reign of terror Lloyd George's Government had two alternatives: to crush the Nationalists by overwhelming force or to grant their demands. Neither course was taken. Instead, the police force in Ireland was reinforced by 60,000 regular soldiers and by specially enlisted gendarmes known as Black-and-Tans. They answered terror by terror. They ambushed leaders of the I.R.A., they raided Republicans in their houses. The I.R.A. retaliated by new outrages. They broke into the quarters of British officers and shot them dead in their beds. Until the summer of 1921 this wretched war of reprisals and counter-reprisals went on. Then in July there was a truce. Lloyd George agreed to negotiate with Sinn Fein and the Dáil sent plenipotentiaries to Dublin. Lloyd George offered to give Ireland the status of a British Dominion—that is, Home Rule from Dublin subject to their recognition of the British Crown. And the Irish representatives accepted, some like Arthur Griffith and the young I.R.A. leader Michael Collins, because they believed that it gave Ireland the substance of political independence, others like Gavan Duffy, the son of the Young Ireland leader, because they felt it was forced upon them by the threat of war *à outrance*.

But when the plenipotentiaries returned to Dublin with the Treaty, they found that a large party in the Dáil would have none of it. Eamonn de Valera, the President, and the out-and-out Republicans refused to accept the status of a British Dominion or to take any oath to the British Crown: they would have complete independence or nothing. The very men who had done most for Irish nationalism were now at loggerheads and Ireland drifted into one more reign of terror, a guerilla war between Republicans and " Free Staters." It was the worst type of civil war—a war in which the men of each side knew the habits and hiding places of the other. It did not end until 1923 and by that time Arthur Griffith had died and Michael Collins had been killed in an ambush.

The Irish Free State.

The Free State party prevailed. William Cosgrave set up the first native Government which Ireland had known for centuries. While accepting Dominion Status, Cosgrave worked for cultural independence, carrying on the movement which Thomas Davis, a Young Ireland leader, had started for the revival of the Gaelic language and culture. For ten years, from 1922 to 1932, relations with England were, on the surface, friendly: English people were encouraged to invest money in the Free State and trade arrangements favourable to both countries were concluded.

But this solution was in reality a poor compromise, for two reasons. First, the Free State did not include the whole of Ireland. In 1920 a separate Government had been set up at Belfast with jurisdiction over six counties of Ulster. These six counties became known as " Northern Ireland," a largely Protestant, wholly pro-British area which, though it had a provincial Parliament of its own, was an integral part of the United Kingdom and continued to make payments towards Imperial defence and in return received large sums of money from Great Britain to pay for its large police force and for the relief of its unemployed. Thus Ireland was absurdly and dangerously divided into two mutually hostile and suspicious States. Secondly, the old political grievance still rankled in Southern Ireland: the desire for complete independence of Great Britain was not satisfied by the Free State Constitution or by Cosgrave's conciliatory methods. At the elections of 1932 the Fianna Fail (Republican) party was returned to power and Eamonn de Valera became President. He set himself to break the remaining bonds which tied Southern Ireland to Great Britain. He refused to take the oath to the King. He refused to pay the land annuities which Irish farmers had contracted to pay by way of wiping off the debt they had incurred to buy their farms from the landlords. The British Government retaliated by putting heavy taxes on the cattle, meat and dairy produce which are the staple exports of Ireland.

Meanwhile Mr. de Valera put into practice more positive measures to restore Ireland's independence. He tried to make her *economically* independent of England by subsidizing farmers to produce for the home market instead of for export, by encouraging the establishment of factories in Ireland to make the boots and shoes, clothes and crockery which the Irish had been used to buy from England. He carried out Cosgrave's policy of making her *culturally* independent by having the ancient Irish language taught in the schools, broadcast on the wireless, written in textbooks; by moving Gaelic-speaking fisher-families of the West to other parts of Ireland where the English-speaking peasants might be tempted to acquire their old tongue again; by encouraging the peasant-crafts and the study of the history and traditions of the Ireland of the pre-Conquest days.

One question remains: How far did the grievances which Ireland has struggled so long to redress still exist in 1935? The old religious grievance was gone. Although Dublin's buildings were still dominated by two huge and empty Protestant cathedrals while there was no cathedral for the Catholics, and although the Protestant University known as Trinity College occupied the finest site in the city while the Catholic, or National, University was of very inferior standing as a cultural centre, the Free State in 1935 was ruled by Catholics. The old economic grievance was gone. Ireland was a country of peasant proprietors and the relatively few large Anglo-Irish landowners who remained were rapidly becoming more Irish and less English in sympathy. And though there was still an economic grievance in the shape of a tariff war with England, this was bound to be of short duration. The old political grievance remained in a new form: before long the problem of the relations between Northern Ireland (Ulster) and the Free State would have to be settled and the problem of the relations between England and the Free State, which was a Republic in fact but not in law, would have to be settled too.

So this chapter on the liberation of Ireland must remain unfinished. In 1935 Ireland was liberated from everything except the quarrels in her own camp and the bitterness in her own heart which centuries of foreign rule had engendered.

Chapter XI: THE LATE VICTORIAN AGE, 1886-1906

Rhodes in Africa – The South African War – The Grab for Africa – Joseph Chamberlain – Free Trade *versus* Tariff Reform – The Passing of Victorianism – The Emancipation of Women.

A NEW AGE opened for Great Britain with the return of the Conservatives to power in 1886. The mid-Victorian age with its serene faith in *laisser-faire* had come to an end in 1874. Then the Depression had forced England to experiment with new policies: Disraeli had undertaken wars of aggression to extend the Empire; Gladstone had tried to secure the Empire while renouncing aggression. Now, in 1886, the wavering was over: the late Victorian age was to be an age of conscious and aggressive Imperialism. An Oxford undergraduate had written in his diary nine years before: " I contend that we are the first race in the world, and that the more of the world we inhabit, the better it is for the human race." This was now becoming the creed of the whole nation. Englishmen really believed in what a young poet called Rudyard Kipling was writing of *Pride of Race* and *The White Man's Burden*; they really believed that it was good for all non-European peoples to be ruled by Great Britain.

Behind that comforting creed was stark economic necessity. The United States, France, Belgium and Germany—especially Germany—were all highly industrialized nations now; their merchants were supplying continental demands and were competing for our trade with Africa and Asia. A Commission on the Depression of Trade reported in 1886: " In every quarter of the world the perseverance and enterprise of the Germans are making themselves felt. In actual production of commodities we have few, if any, advantages over them, and in a knowledge of the markets of the world, a desire to accommodate themselves to local tastes and idiosyncrasies, a determination to obtain a footing wherever they can and a tenacity in maintaining it, they appear to be gaining ground over us." England had therefore to extend her own Empire if she was to retain her economic supremacy and keep her men at work in mine and factory. "There is no way of securing plenty of employment except by creating new markets and developing old ones," said young Joseph Chamberlain, who was to be Colonial Secretary from 1895 to 1903. Disraeli had despised Chamberlain, the Birmingham hardware manufacturer who, he said, "looked like a cheesemonger and spoke like one"; but it was on Chamberlain that the mantle of Disraeli fell, rather than on Lord Salisbury, the dignified aristocrat who was Prime Minister from 1880 to 1892 and whose policy has been described as one of "splendid isolation" for England. There was no one who did more for the British Empire than Chamberlain, unless it was Cecil Rhodes, the Essex parson's son whose undergraduate diary we have quoted above.

Rhodes in Africa.   As a boy of eighteen, Rhodes went out to South Africa in the diamond rush of 1870. In intervals between making his fortune in the mines he worked for Matriculation and kept his terms at Oxford where he was Master of the Drag and eventually took his degree. From the beginning he realized the possibility of a great British Dominion stretching from Cape Colony along the highlands of east-central Africa to the lakes of Tanganyika and northward to the Nile. By incredible pertinacity, effrontery and lack of scruple he almost realized his ambition.

His first concern, as he confessed to his friend General Gordon, was to make a fortune so as to have the power of the purse behind him. With the help of a Hamburg Jew, Alfred Beit, he bought up claim after claim near Kimberley, finally forming the De Beers Diamond Company which bought up the rival combine made by a Whitechapel

Jew, Barney Isaacs ("Barney Barnato"), and so won a monopoly of the diamond output.

By this time the whole situation in South Africa had been changed by the discovery of gold—rich unending seams of gold—in the Witwatersrand, in the Dutch Republic of Transvaal. A swarm of adventurers, mostly Jews and Englishmen, rushed to the Rand; the town of Johannesburg sprang up and soon the "Uitlanders," as the newcomers were called, outnumbered the Dutch in whose Republic they were prospecting. Rhodes came to the Rand and founded in 1887 the company known as Gold Fields of South Africa.

Rhodes was now one of the richest men in the world; it was time to turn to his imperial projects. His first concern was to develop the unknown lands north of the Limpopo River. For this purpose he went to London and secured a Royal Charter for a British South Africa Company (1889). A year later he became Prime Minister of Cape Colony. He had now all the power he wanted. His way to the north was barred by the lands of the Matabele tribes. Their king, Lo Bengula, a majestic and amiable savage, was no match for Rhodes, who sent his friend, the plausible Dr. Jameson, to wring from him permission to march an army through Matabeleland. Rhodes wanted more than a right of way; he wanted the land itself. In 1893 he picked a quarrel with Lo Bengula and sent Jameson to fight the Matabele and capture their capital, Bulawayo.

An orgy of land-grabbing followed. In 1895 the Queen was pleased to give the name of Rhodesia to the country north of Matabeleland. Rhodes was now monarch of all he surveyed. From Lake Tanganyika to the Cape, British territory stretched unbroken save for the two Boer Republics of Transvaal and the Orange Free State. Rhodes was now forty-two; like Napoleon at the same age, he let ambition become a disease. He determined to make South Africa a British dominion. To placate the Dutch he promised equal rights for Boer and Briton. Krüger saw in this nothing but a trap laid by English capitalists to get the wealth of the Transvaal into their hands. He and the Boer farmers, living their simple life like Old Testament patriarchs, with their cattle and horses and Kaffir servants, already hated the English for the way their prospectors, the Uitlanders, had swarmed over the Rand. All through the nineties the Uitlanders grew richer and their complaints against Krüger grew louder. Krüger replied by taxing them more heavily and refusing them the right to vote for the Transvaal Parliament. If they disliked his system, they might go back to their own country.

The South African War. Rhodes decided to help the Uitlanders to make a revolution against Krüger. He sent them arms and he encouraged Jameson to collect an army on their northern frontier to help them as soon as they should rise. Jameson could not wait; at Christmas 1895 he marched into the Transvaal. The Jameson Raid was a failure, and an inexcusable failure since it was made before the Uitlanders had risen against Krüger or been attacked by him.[1]

Krüger was convinced now that the British Government was out to exterminate his Boers. Lord Milner, sent out as High Commissioner to negotiate with him, was anything but conciliatory. Krüger demanded the withdrawal of British troops from South Africa, and when Milner refused he declared war in October 1899, pitting his 30,000 men against the whole British Empire.

The second Boer War began like the first, with Boer victories. There were not more than 12,000 British troops in South Africa; they were well armed and equipped but

---

[1] The spirit of England at the time may be judged by this verse written by the Poet Laureate, Alfred Austin, to commemorate the Jameson Raid:

> *I suppose we were wrong, were madmen,*
> *Still, I think on the Judgement Day,*
> *When God sifts the good from the bad men,*
> *There'll be something more to say.*
> *We were wrong, but we aren't half sorry*
> *And, as one of the baffled band,*
> *I would rather have had that foray*
> *Than the crushings of all the Rand.*

were stiff with parade-ground notions of warfare. The Boer farmers, riding hard and shooting straight, trapped one British detachment at Kimberley on the Orange Free State frontier and another at Mafeking on the frontier of the Transvaal. Advancing into Natal the farmers surrounded the main body of the British at Ladysmith and held the half of Natal which lies north of the Tugela River. Four battles were fought and lost (at Colenso, Spion Kop, Vaalkranz and Pieter's Mill) before the British were able to force the line of the Tugela and relieve Ladysmith.

The second stage of the war began in February 1900, when Lord Roberts, England's most famous soldier, was sent to South Africa with a strong army and Kitchener as Chief-of-Staff. England was taking no chances. The British force in South Africa was brought up to 150,000 by the enlistment of volunteers from all over the Empire; for the first time Canadians, Australians and New Zealanders were fighting England's battles.

The people of England were delighted by the news of victory after victory. The British won their first battle under Kitchener in February at Paardeburg; Kimberley was relieved, and Ladysmith; Lord Roberts marched in triumph into the capitals of the Orange Free State and the Transvaal, and in May the little force under Colonel Baden-Powell was set free by the relief of Mafeking. In London on the night when the news of the relief of Mafeking arrived the crowds in the streets went crazy with joy. In South Africa it seemed that the war was over; Lord Roberts sailed for home.

But the war was not over. The Boers were still at large, mounted still and equipped with rifles and ammunition captured from the enemy. A third stage of the war began and lasted for eighteen months. It was guerilla warfare, the Boers swooping down upon British outposts and supply convoys, the British under Kitchener carefully building lines of barbed wire and block-houses and cutting the Boers off from their supplies and interning their women and children in concentration camps where 20,000 of them died. At last, in May 1902, the Boer leaders surrendered on condition of being given self-government within the British Empire. The settlement was completed in 1909 when an Act of Parliament combined the four states of South Africa into a Union with Dominion Status. Rhodes's dream was realized: Africa was British (directly or indirectly) from the Cape to Alexandria. The realization of the dream had cost Britain nearly 6,000 dead and 23,000 wounded in the second Boer War.

The Union of South Africa created as many difficulties as it settled. First there was the Anglo-Boer problem: was the new Union to be Boer or British in character? The first two Union Prime Ministers, Botha and Smuts, themselves Boers who had fought under Krüger, decided that it should be British, but there was a Boer rebellion in 1914, headed by de Wet and encouraged by Germany, and after the war there was an increasingly strong Boer nationalist party in the Union. Secondly, there was the native problem: what were to be the rights of the five million Bantus on whose labour the one and three-quarter million whites of the Union were dependent? The Boers hankered after the old slave-owning days and were anxious to force the natives into the crudest, worst-paid labour. But the British Government, which had laid down in the Act of Union that the natives must have "the utmost consideration and the most impartial justice," felt responsible for the future of the Bantus. No way has yet been found of solving the native problem.

The Grab for Africa. The exploits of Rhodes and the British colonists in South Africa were but one episode in a general "grab for Africa" which was indulged in at the end of the nineteenth century by the four industrialized nations of Europe—France, Belgium, Germany and Great Britain. Each fought with the same weapon: the machine gun, of which H. M. Stanley had said, when first shown it in 1880, that "it would be a fine weapon for subduing the heathen." Each fought for the same purpose: to secure materials for its factories and markets for its industrial goods. The object was not so much colonies as commerce. Private traders opened up new districts and then their home Governments stepped in to protect them. The process was always the same: the flag followed trade.

The French had penetrated Algiers between 1830 and 1847 and their traders had crossed the Atlas Mountains; now in the eighties and nineties they sent native troops and the notorious Foreign Legion to conquer the Sahara. German traders had settled in Togoland, in Cameroon, in South-West Africa, and in East Africa; in 1884 and 1885 Bismarck adopted these five areas as German colonies. A Belgian trading company took over the vast and rich basin of the Congo and, though it was not adopted as a colony until 1907, the chief shareholder was the King of the Belgians, Leopold I, who was responsible for the enslaving and frightful oppression of the natives which the Company perpetrated. British chartered companies, the Royal Niger Company and the British East Africa Company, paved the way for the foundation of the Crown Colonies of Nigeria and Kenya. The work of Rhodes's South Africa Company we have already described.

By the nineties the Governments of the industrial countries were alive to the need for colonies and no longer left the initiative to private traders. The British Consul-General in Egypt, Lord Cromer, made Egypt a British Protectorate in everything but name. He dammed the Nile and irrigated the fields so that the cotton crops flourished and the export of raw cotton to Lancashire increased. He also trained an army of Egyptians, and in 1896 Kitchener persuaded the Government to let him use this force for the conquest of the Sudan. Since Gordon's death the Dervishes had maintained a typical Eastern despotism in the Sudan. The British had nothing against them except that they practised slavery. This was a sufficient *casus belli* for Kitchener. After very careful preparations, which included building a railway, he advanced step by step across the Nubian desert until he totally defeated the Khalifa at Omdurman near Khartoum in 1898, the year of Gladstone's death.

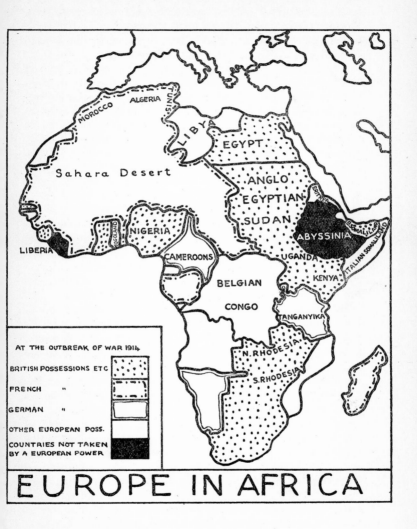

Joseph Chamberlain.

Behind all these conquests there was a man of vision in the British Cabinet. Joseph Chamberlain's life-work was to increase the value to the mother-country of trade with the colonies. We may examine his achievement from three points of view: his development of the tropical colonies, his encouragement of commerce with the white Dominions, and his campaign for Tariff Reform.

Chamberlain realized that the first thing to be done in the tropical colonies was to make them inhabitable by Englishmen. Fever was the greatest enemy that Englishmen had to face in the tropics: West Africa was still " the white man's grave," and parts of East Africa were not much better. Of all types of fever malaria was the most prevalent. Nothing was known about its causes until in 1897 Sir Ronald Ross discovered that the germ was carried by mosquitoes. To make the most of this and other discoveries Chamberlain made a Government grant to the London School of Tropical Medicine which was opened in 1899. Sir Alfred Jones (the shipowner who introduced bananas to England) founded a similar school in Liverpool. An offensive was launched against tropical diseases which had better results in five years than a generation of military warfare. King Edward VIII has said that Ross " made a quarter of the globe habitable." Without Chamberlain's ready support his discovery might never have been utilized.

The next need of the tropical colonies was capital with which to build roads and railways to open up their hinterlands, and ports and steamships with which to connect them with England. Chamberlain made it possible for them to raise the capital by a Crown Colonies Act (1899) empowering the Treasury to lend money to the colonies, and by an Act of 1900 which allowed trustees to invest in colonial stocks. Railways were built from Capetown to Rhodesia, and from the coast to the interior of Kenya and Nigeria. England was realizing now that money spent on colonial development was a profitable investment.

The white settlements presented a different problem. The many small self-governing colonies of the middle of the century had now linked themselves up by federation into a few vast Dominions. By the British North American Act of 1867 the two Canadas, New Brunswick and Nova Scotia, while each retaining its own parliament, had united in the Dominion of Canada, with a federal Government at Ottawa. Australia became a federal Dominion in 1900. England had given the colonies self-government thinking that they would use it to introduce Free Trade on the English model, but they had used it to impose tariffs on overseas goods. Foreign countries too had disappointed English expectations by not adopting Free Trade, so now every country in the world was able to get its goods into the United Kingdom duty free while English goods were everywhere met by tariffs. In 1897 the Canadian Government offered to give preference to English goods by setting a lower tariff on them than on goods coming from foreign countries. Chamberlain persuaded the Cabinet to accept this, though it meant a breach with England's Free Trade traditions. Chamberlain had conceived a new commercial policy for England: he hoped for Free Trade between all the countries of the British Empire, with tariffs on all foreign countries. But the Dominions would not agree, so he compromised with the idea of Imperial Preference, or, as he preferred to call it, Tariff Reform, which meant that England and the Dominions would set high tariffs on foreign and low tariffs on imperial goods.

Free Trade *versus* Tariff Reform.   It was a dazzling idea. The Dominions had developed their natural resources beyond all expectations. The completion of the Canadian Pacific Railway in 1886 tapped the wealth of the prairies and more and more grain was flowing out of Canada every year. The invention of cold storage had brought the meat of Australia and New Zealand on to the tables of Europe. All this wealth could be England's, and in addition a steady sale for England's industrial products in the Dominions, if only the electorate would adopt Tariff Reform.

Chamberlain resigned from the Cabinet in 1903 in order to devote himself to a propaganda campaign. That autumn he addressed crowded meetings in Greenock, Newcastle, Tynemouth, Liverpool, Cardiff, Newport and Leeds, preaching the doctrine of Imperial Preference. He founded a Tariff Reform League on the lines of that Anti-Corn Law League which had been founded by the Manchester men half a century ago to urge the very opposite policy.

But Chamberlain found himself up against a formidable opposition. Habit, prudence and self-interest were against him. For fifty years Englishmen had pinned their faith to the doctrine of Free Trade; they were not prepared to abandon it for all the speechifying in the world. Liberals pointed out that Imperial Preference would be a gesture of defiance to foreign countries: if England started taxing foreign goods, foreigners would increase their taxes on English goods and so we would lose more than we would gain, for our trade with Germany and Belgium, for instance, was worth more than our trade with all the Empire. Nearly every class in the community agreed with the Liberals for reasons of self-interest. The shipowners and the 250,000 men employed in the shipping industry had nothing to gain by tariffs: why should they vote for anything which would not increase the volume of shipping? The landowners and the 1,000,000 men employed in agriculture had nothing to gain either: tariffs keeping out Russian and German wheat would merely help the Canadian growers and Canada was now able to supply all the wheat England needed at a price with which the English farmers could not compete. The industrial workers also were against tariffs for the simple reason that they would make their foreign food more expensive. Only the manufacturers were on Chamberlain's side. They knew that Free Trade had never worked because foreigners had persisted in tariffs and bounties—that is, in making Government grants to help manufacturers to sell their goods cheaply in England. Already the United States and Germany were " dumping " iron and steel and manufactured goods in the British Isles.

So England was divided. The older generation living to-day still remember the frenzied speeches of 1903–06 when "Joe" Chamberlain and a Liberal lawyer, Herbert Asquith, fought out on public platforms the issue between Free Trade and Tariff Reform; old men still say, "Of course, I'm a Free Trader," or, "Of course, I'm a Tariff Reformer," remembering that now dead issue. The Liberal papers, the *Daily News* and the *Daily Chronicle*, reduced their price to a halfpenny in the effort to reach a larger public. (The *Daily Mail* had come down to a halfpenny in 1898 and had won a million-a-day sale during the exciting years of the Boer War.) It is not surprising that at the General Election of 1906 Chamberlain was defeated. The Liberals came into power, to stay for ten years.

Although Free Trade won in 1906, a later generation recognized the wisdom of Disraeli and of Joseph Chamberlain. During the war of 1914–18 and afterwards England abandoned Free Trade. Probably she will never go back to it until the workers in each manufacturing country have adopted an equal standard of living, for so long as English workers need a few shillings a day to keep body and soul together and Japanese workers (for instance) need only a few pence, England cannot afford Free Trade because the Japanese, having less wages to pay, can always sell their goods at a cheaper rate than the English. England has abandoned Free Trade but she has not adopted Chamberlain's idea of Imperial Preference. The time for that was 1906; in the 1920's it was too late—the Dominions then were making their own manufactured goods and had no intention of abolishing the tariffs they had set on goods from England. By her decision in 1906 England had lost, for good or for evil, the opportunity of making the Empire a commercial unit.

The Passing of Victorianism. Chamberlain's campaign marked the end of the nineteenth century, the end of the Victorian age. The Queen had died in 1901 in her eighty-second year and had been succeeded by her sixty-year-old son, Edward VII.[1] At first she had not been popular—she had relied on her husband for everything and the British public disliked being ruled by that distant, unbending German. After Albert's death in 1861 she was even less popular for she went into severest mourning and rarely appeared in public, thus depriving the public of the spectacle that they demand from a monarch. This unpopularity was deserved for there was something morbid about her devotion to the memory of Albert; for forty years after his death she had his evening clothes laid out every day in his room and his basin filled with hot water. But towards the end of her reign, when with Disraeli's encouragement she relaxed her mourning and appeared again in public, all unpopularity was forgotten and her people made a heroine of her. The creed of the nation now was Imperialism, and Imperialism needs a figure-head; it was but natural that Englishmen should find that figurehead in the wilful, dignified little lady who had been Queen for as long as the vast majority of them could recollect. Historians remember her Golden Jubilee of 1887 as the occasion of the first conference of the leaders of the Dominions in London; Londoners remember it as the first time they discovered their affection for the Queen. Historians remember the Diamond Jubilee of 1897 as the time when Englishmen's pride in the Empire reached its most bombastic height; ordinary people remember it as the time when their pride in the Sovereign was at its most profound.

At the end of the old Queen's reign two inventions were beginning to change the face of England and of the whole industrialized world. The great scientific achievement of the nineteenth century had been the application to industry of steam-power; it was this invention which had made England's fortune because she was excellently endowed by nature with the coal from which this power was derived. At the end of the century two new sources of power were developed and in these England had no natural advantage

[1] The Queen had nine children. At the time of her death there were thirty-seven grandchildren.

over her rivals. The first was electricity: the electric lamp was perfected by Edison and Swan in 1888, the first electric trams ran in London in 1891 and the first underground railway in 1900. Already it could be foreseen that electric power might be applied to shipping and manufacturing as well as to lighting and to land transport. The second new source of power was the oil-fuelled internal combustion engine. The English were not prominent in the early history of motor-cars: the first Daimlers were made in France in 1887 and Benz cars in Germany in 1888. Not till 1896 was the law repealed which obliged every " horseless carriage " in Great Britain to be preceded by a man with a red flag. And if the men of 1896 could have foreseen that in the next generation these horseless carriages would be killing 120 people every week on the English roads they would doubtless have let the old law stand.

A great change was coming over the behaviour of the English people in the late Victorian age. They were " getting about " more, seeing more of strangers' ways of living and being shaken in their prejudices and conventions in consequence. The rich spent their winters in France instead of on their estates in the country. The less rich travelled from village to town and from town to country on the new " safety bicycles," which were invented in 1888 and soon superseded the old " penny-farthings." Free education was making society more gregarious, more inclined to be interested in the same things. The masses, who had just learned to read, took the same papers—the *Police Gazette*, the *Betting News* and the *Daily Mail*. They crowded to see the same spectacles: the first cinema was opened in 1892 and the first Wild West films followed a decade later. It was a great age for organized sport, an age when for the first time in England the spectators at games far outnumbered the players: the Cup Finals and the Rugby Football Internationals were first played in 1872, the County Cricket Championships date from the following year and all three gained rapidly in popularity during the next generation.

Behind this change in behaviour was a change in outlook. The complacency which characterized the Victorian age was weakening. The rich were beginning to take a rather less patronizing interest in the sufferings of the poor. " Slumming " became more than fashionable. Toynbee Hall, the first settlement of university men in the East End, was founded in 1886. William Booth's *Hallelujah Band* of converted criminals attracted members of all classes and took on the name of *The Salvation Army* (1878) and the dimensions of a religious revival.

In the arts public taste was as execrable as ever. The *Daily Telegraph* wrote of the Albert Memorial that it was " assuredly the most consummate and elegant piece of elegiac art which modern genius has produced." But there was an increasingly strong revolt against what Matthew Arnold called " Philistinism " among people of the younger generation. It was the time of the æsthetes who adored the pictures of Pre-Raphaelites and who believed that art was completely divorced from life—an attitude which W. S. Gilbert held to ridicule in a popular operetta, *Patience* (first produced in 1881). It was the time, too, of a new movement in the theatre. Pinero and Henry Arthur Jones wrote admirable drawing-room comedies on daring themes such as divorce. Oscar Wilde went further; the wit and cynicism of his plays shocked London and earned for him in Germany a reputation as the greatest British dramatist since Shakespeare. Altogether there was new blood running in the æsthetic veins of England at the end of the century. The art of the " naughty nineties " was insignificant compared with the Romantic movement of the beginning of the century; but it was important in that it showed a spirited disgust with the smug materialism of Victorian England.

The Emancipation of Women. Nothing shows so clearly the reaction against Victorianism—as well as the nature of Victorianism itself—as the movement for the emancipation of women. The Victorian idea was that " the Woman's place is in the home." It is true that the working-class woman was more often in the mill or in someone else's home, serving. But the middle-class woman was kept in her home as surely as in a prison. Girls were educated in their parents' house; they were not allowed to go out alone and they were debarred from every career except marriage. This system might have worked well enough if there had been enough men for the girls to marry; but there were not. For every ten marriageable women there were only nine men; at least one woman in ten was condemned to living on her family in the despised position of an " old maid."

The movement for the liberation of middle-class women began as a movement for education. The first schools for their higher education were set up when Miss Frances Buss founded the North London Collegiate School for Girls (1850) and Miss Dorothea Beale became Principal of Cheltenham Ladies' College (1858). Secondary education for girls became an established fact in 1872 with the foundation of the Girls' Public Day School Trust. In that same year a women's college, Girton, was founded at Cambridge and in 1878 Lady Margaret Hall was opened at Oxford. Slowly the professions opened their ranks to women, who towards the end of the century began to appear as doctors, lawyers and journalists and to take a part in local government.

The next stage in the emancipation movement was to give women a legal right to their property. Until 1870 a woman was not allowed to keep even her earnings. Until 1882, when Gladstone passed the *Married Women's Property Act*, a woman's income and possessions became the property of her husband on marriage. Gladstone's Act was the beginning of the end of the Victorian ideal of womanhood. Young women began to appear in public restaurants and a new type of resort, the tea-shop, was opened to cater for them.[1] They began to go out unchaperoned, to play gentle outdoor games and to wear less cumbersome clothes.

The next step towards emancipation was a movement to give women the vote. It had started in the mid-Victorian

[1] The Aerated Bread Company opened its first tea-shop in 1880.

age when John Stuart Mill tried to move an amendment to include women as well as men in the Reform Bill of 1867. The Queen was against it from the beginning: in 1870 she wrote of " this mad, wicked folly of ' Women's Rights,' with all its attendant horrors, on which her poor feeble sex is bent, forgetting every sense of womanly feeling and propriety . . . It is a subject which makes the Queen so furious that she cannot contain herself "—an attitude which may seem a trifle unreasonable in view of the fact that the Queen herself enjoyed a full share of " Women's Rights " without experiencing any of the attendant horrors.

Towards the end of the century the movement gathered way, but in 1897 the Tories turned down a Bill to give women the vote and the Liberals, whose democratic principles might have been expected to incline their ear to the claim of women, rejected a similar motion in 1904. Now the opposition was not to the emancipation of women as such but to the course which emancipation had taken. It was held that women had used their new right to education not to educate themselves as women but to ape the curriculum and ideals of men, and that the movement for Women's Suffrage was but another attempt to usurp masculine privileges.

One by one the pillars of the Victorian age were crumbling in the last two decades of the century and of the Queen's reign. The bonds of middle-class women were being broken, the strongholds of Philistinism were being stormed, the powers of steam and horse were being rivalled by those of electricity and the petrol engine. And if Imperialism had survived as the political creed and Free Trade as the economic principle, there were forces at work in the late Victorian age and the early twentieth century which were to change the whole political and economic outlook of Great Britain. It was the Working-Class Movement which drew the attention of the rulers to those forces.

Chapter XII: THE WORKING-CLASS MOVEMENT, 1880-1913

Co-operation and Trade Unionism – English Socialism – The New Unions – The I.L.P. – The Fabian Society – Conservative Reforms for the Workers – Liberals' Social Reforms – The Parliament Act – Strikes of 1911-12.

"Geography," according to a famous definition, "is about maps; History is about chaps." Yet most histories confine themselves to the doings of statesmen and soldiers and to the conquests and comforts of the ruling class. Of the real "chaps," of the working class which includes 90 per cent[1] of the population, little or nothing is said.

The working class in England experienced more changes in the nineteenth century than in any other period in history. In the first quarter of the century they suffered appallingly from the sudden change-over to machine industry which is called the Industrial Revolution. Here and there they rioted, but always in vain. It was the time of Peterloo and the Six Acts.

In the second quarter of the century they suffered still—it was the time of the Chartist insurrections and the Hungry Forties. Robert Owen gave workers and employers a lead and the Chartist leaders agitated to secure workers a voice in Parliament. Owenism and Chartism failed, yet there was some improvement in working-class conditions in that generation. The workers had a friend in high places in the handsome person of Antony Ashley Cooper, the seventh Earl of Shaftesbury. Shaftesbury was largely responsible for the Ten Hours' Act (1847) and for the long series of Factory Acts which forbade child labour, restricted

[1] If we call people with under £250 a year poor, people with between £250 and £2,000 a year middle class and people with over £2,000 rich, then to-day 90 per cent of the population are poor, 9·5 per cent middle class and 0·5 per cent rich.

woman labour and obliged employers to provide decent ventilation and accommodation for their employees. The whole of Shaftesbury's long life (1801–85) was devoted to the welfare of the poor; in addition to the above reforms he was responsible for changing the lunatic asylums of England from prisons to hospitals, for abolishing the practice of sending boys up chimneys as living brooms, for establishing schools for "ragged children," for looking after shoeblacks in his "shoeblacks' brigade," and for setting an example of decent housing for workers by building model estates in Battersea and in his native village in Dorset. To his memory the "Eros" monument in Piccadilly Circus was erected. Shaftesbury's was a golden example but the working class needed more than private charity: it needed public recognition of its right to decent conditions.

In the third quarter of the nineteenth century the condition of the workers improved. Thanks to Free Trade there was little unemployment. Wages, as we have said, rose by a third and the workers had some share in the general prosperity of the mid-Victorian age. Conservatives and Liberals alike passed measures of social reform and the credit for the Education Acts of 1870 and '80 and the Trade Union Acts of 1871 and '75 must be divided among them.

Co-operation and Trade Unionism.

In these years the workers effectively developed those three methods of peaceful combination (Co-operatives, Friendly Societies and Trade Unions) which they had evolved at the beginning of the century and which were to prove so much more efficacious than rioting or Chartism. Co-operation had begun in Robert Owen's time in a most realistic form. The idea was that workers should form a society and pool their savings until they had enough to build a Village of Co-operation in which they would be able to live free from employers and tradesmen alike. Soon the idea of villages dropped out and Co-operation began to develop along the lines of the Friendly Societies. Workers formed Building

Societies into which they put their savings and from which they borrowed money to build or to buy their own houses. The profits of the society went to the members, who were thus able to become householders with all the sense of security and responsibility which ownership brings. An even more important form of Co-operation was combination for retail trade. This movement was launched permanently in 1844 when twenty-eight working men calling themselves the Rochdale Equitable Pioneers paid a pound each into a common fund with which they bought groceries and household supplies and opened a little shop in the house of one of their members in Toad Lane in Rochdale. Members bought from the shop at market prices and the profits instead of going to a middleman were paid out to the members in the form of a dividend. From this humble beginning the movement spread prodigiously, Co-operative Retail Societies springing up all over the country. In 1864 the Co-operative Wholesale Society (C.W.S.) was formed to supply the retail societies, who became members of the C.W.S. on the same profit-sharing basis on which individuals were members of the retail societies. In 1869 a Co-operative Congress was formed as a sort of parliament to which the various societies sent representatives; it has met annually ever since. To-day the Co-operative Societies have over 6,000,000 members and £200,000,000 is paid into their tills every year.

The idea of a Trade Union, or associaton of workers in a trade to look after their common interests, was not new. The Printers had had a Union, which they call a chapel, since 1666, and Unions had been formed in many trades at the beginning of the nineteenth century. The spread of Trade Unions was slow, for two reasons. First, the Government, consisting of men of the employer class, was against it. Secondly, the workers themselves had to learn by long and painful experience the necessity of standing together. Hundreds of Unions sprang up in the early thirties but they withered away again through lack of discipline.

These two difficulties were overcome by what was known as the New Model in Unionism. The New Model was supplied by the formation in 1850 of the Amalgamated Society of Engineers (A.S.E.). This Union of skilled men organized itself in the sound tradition of the Friendly Societies. It levied a subscription of a shilling a week from its members and used the money to pay out insurance benefits. Thanks to this they were able to stand a lock-out of three whole months in 1852. In the end they had to give in and accept their employers' terms, but they had gained invaluable experience: the men had held together for once and had made the sacrifice of thirteen weeks' wages for the good of their common cause. Workers in other skilled trades followed their example and set up Unions on the New Model: the Carpenters, the London Tailors and Compositors and the Building Trades, for example, each organized a strong Union. The last named went on strike in 1859 and actually forced a draw with their employers. The workers were learning discipline and common sense. At the same time the Government was learning to respect these skilled men for their peaceful and dignified methods and for their steady perseverance. We have seen how the Liberals granted Trade Unions legal protection in 1871 and the Conservatives allowed them peacefully to picket in 1875. Thus by the end of the third quarter of the century the obstacles in the way of the growth of Unionism had been removed.

The Birth of English Socialism. It was in the fourth quarter of the nineteenth century that the workers began to make real progress. In that generation—and especially between 1880 and 1900—there was a real Working-Class Movement in England. It would be more accurate to say that there were *two* movements: one called Socialism, made for the workers by middle-class reformers, the other called Trade Unionism, made by the workers themselves.

English Socialism began in 1880 when a certain Henry Mayers Hyndman read and inwardly digested Marx's book on Capital. Hyndman was an Etonian who had led an adventurous life, playing cricket for Sussex, fighting with

Garibaldi's Thousand, travelling in Australia, Polynesia and the United States. Nothing in his life moved him like his reading of *Das Kapital*. The book had been published in German a dozen years before and was only just translated into English. Its picture of the misery and injustice caused by the capitalist system, under which all the means of production and all the profits were held by a few men in every country, and its conclusion that the toiling majority would be moved to demand and to seize their share in the ownership and the profits converted Hyndman to the cause which is called Communism or, in its less violent forms, Socialism. Already there had been a short and unsuccessful revolution in Paris where Marxists had set up a Commune for a few months in 1871. Already there was a powerful Socialist (Social-Democrat) party in the German Parliament. Now it became Hyndman's ambition to create a Socialist party in England. He called on the aged Disraeli and implored him to lead a movement for " peace with comfort," explaining that by comfort he meant " plenty to eat, enough to drink, good clothes, pleasant houses, thorough education and sufficient leisure for all." But Disraeli knew by experience how conservative the poor as well as the rich people of England were: " It is a very difficult country to move, Mr. Hyndman," he replied, " a very difficult country, and one in which there is more disappointment to be looked for than success."

A year later, when Disraeli was dead, Hyndman formed the first English Socialist party, which he called the Social Democratic Federation (S.D.F.). Hyndman was a strange leader for a popular movement. In his top-hat and yellow gloves and square-cut frock-coat he solemnly paraded the streets of London with a banner displaying the Socialist device—" Workers of the World, Unite "—or stood on a barrow in Hyde Park expounding the theories of Marx in a clipped and cultured accent. It is no wonder that he found little support among the working class. His followers were not workers, but intellectuals like himself. William Morris, the poet and craftsman, joined the S.D.F. and was seen—

a striking figure with his blond beard and rough blue suit—marching behind Hyndman or addressing listless audiences at a street corner in the slums. Edward Carpenter, the poet and ex-Fellow of Trinity Hall, supported Hyndman and gave him money to launch his paper, *Justice*. Bernard Shaw, then a young sandy-whiskered Irish journalist, joined the S.D.F. and spoke interminably to whomsoever would listen to him, on Clapham Common, in Hyde Park, at street corners with William Morris and in the coffee-shops of Bermondsey. But none of these idealists really wanted a bloody revolution of the Marxist type. Morris and Carpenter were poets; soon they left the movement, Morris to restore some of the fine craftsmanship of pre-industrial days by designing furniture and wallpaper and chintzes and books, Carpenter to retire to the moors above Sheffield, where he and his friends made sandals—the symbol of a simpler and more sentient age. As for Shaw, he soon realized that the workers were not ready for Socialism and left the S.D.F. to form a society—the Fabians—which was to prove more effective than Hyndman's.

Hyndman's career reached its height in February 1886 when a great meeting of workers was held in Trafalgar Square. The crowd was in an ugly mood and it looked as if a free fight with the police would ensue. This was the last thing Hyndman wanted. He led the crowd away towards Hyde Park, but their blood was up and there was no stopping them from smashing windows in Pall Mall and St. James's Street and from looting shops in Piccadilly. This outburst condemned the S.D.F. in everyone's eyes. The S.D.F. failed, but leaders of the working class learned one thing from its failure: they learned that Marxian methods would not do for England.

The New Unions. Englishmen did not want a revolution: they wanted shorter hours and higher wages. The English way of working for these was through the Trade Unions. So far, only the skilled workers who form the aristocracy of labour had learned to combine in Unions. Now the Union movement spread to the rank and file, to the unskilled workers. In March 1886 Will Thorne formed the Gas Workers' and General Labourers' Union; it was a model for the Unions of the future, for it had no sick funds but concentrated on winning the 8-hour day—by strikes if necessary. The first victory of the new Unionism was won in 1888 when the London Match Girls went on strike and their fortitude and the writings of Mrs. Annie Besant shamed the employers into making concessions. The second came in 1889 when the Gasworkers won the 8-hour day. The third was a much more auspicious affair.

Ben Tillett formed the beginnings of a Union among the London dockers. These men had a mighty grievance: they were obliged to go down to the docks in the small hours of the morning to wait for hours on end in the hope of being taken on by the shipowners' agents, and then, even if they were lucky, they got paid fivepence an hour and often were dismissed after an hour or two's work. Ben Tillett demanded a wage of sixpence an hour with a minimum shift of four hours. The shipowners refused. And then, on the morning of August 17, 1889, Tillett called a strike. It was a gamble: the Union's funds amounted to a total of 7s. 6d. and it could hardly be imagined that every docker in London would stay away from work on no pay, in the common cause. Yet it succeeded. The dockers were loyal to the Union; other workers came out on strike in sympathy with them till by the end of August there were 100,000 strikers in London; money flowed in for them from well-wishers all over the world—£30,000 was sent from Australia. Tillett and John Burns were the leaders: to them the credit must go for preventing any looting and disorder. Under their orders tens of thousands of men marched in procession through the streets of London every day, displaying their grievances on banners, until public opinion had come completely round to their side. On September 14 the shipowners gave in and the strike ended. The dockers got all they demanded.

The Trade Unions were now a powerful force in the

country. By 1895 they numbered a million and a half members—in other words, a fifth of all the adult male workers, or half the workers of the northern counties of Lancashire, Durham and Northumberland. They had a parliament of their own: ever since 1871 they have sent representatives to a Trades Union Congress which meets in one or other of the towns of England and discusses the grievances of the working class and the policy which organized Labour should pursue.

There was no doubt that the Trade Unions had power, but there was considerable doubt in which direction they would use it. The Unions were for the most part conservative in the sense that they accepted the capitalist system and the division of the population into employers and employed; they contented themselves with struggling for better conditions for the employed, within the existing system. But the new leaders, such as Tom Mann and John Burns, were Socialists and had been members of the S.D.F.; they wanted to replace the capitalist system by a Socialist system in which the State would be the only employer and all profits would be shared among workers of all classes. The next step was to convert the T.U.C. to Socialism.

The Independent Labour Party. In this endeavour two men did unforgettable work. Robert Blatchford gave up writing for middle-class papers, by which he had been earning £1,000 a year, and started a Socialist weekly called the *Clarion*. Soon the *Clarion* had gained a circulation of 60,000 a week. It was more than a paper, it was a movement; and it spread like a religion. Red Clarion vans toured the country preaching Socialism where the doctrine had never been heard of before; Clarion Clubs were formed here, there and everywhere—cycling clubs, camping clubs, cricket and football clubs. It became " the thing to do " for boys and girls of the working class to join a Clarion Club and cycle a hundred miles, maybe, on a Sunday to hear Blatchford or Bruce Glasier or young Ramsay MacDonald make a Socialist speech. It was the first fine careless rapture of the Socialist movement in England; the working class has never recaptured the enthusiasm of those days, but one still meets ageing folk in the North who treasure copies of Blatchford's *Merrie England* or speak with affection of what they call " The Movement."

The other man to spread the cause of Socialism was Keir Hardie, a Scot who at six years old worked as an errand boy and went down the mine at the age of nine. He had the Scotsman's pious temperament and tenacity. " I am a Socialist," he once said, " because Socialism means Fraternity founded on Justice, and the fact that in order to secure it it is necessary to transfer land and capital from private to public ownership is a mere incident in the Crusade." In 1892 Keir Hardie was elected to Parliament. He shocked the House by his dress—he wore a cloth cap and a coarse tweed suit—and by his straight speech. " Most members of this House," he said with shocking truth, " have a more direct interest in the Stock Exchange than they have in the sufferings of the poor."

Hardie's great work was to merge the Socialist and the Trade Union movements into a single stream. For this purpose he formed a small party of Socialists to be the leaven of the T.U.C. It was called the Independent Labour Party. Thanks to Hardie and the I.L.P., the Trades Union Congress, when it met at Bradford in 1893, passed a number of Socialist resolutions: it declared for national ownership of means of production, for an 8-hour day, for State provision for the aged, sick, disabled and widows.

This was the peak of Keir Hardie's success. The T.U.C. soon regretted its revolutionary mood of 1893. The last years of the nineteenth century were years of defeat for the working-class movement. Employers were alarmed and combined to resist the workers' demands, and the Conservative Government was on the side of the employers. In 1897 the engineers struck for an 8-hour day: they stayed out for thirteen weeks, which cost the Union £116,000 in strike pay: and then they had to give in and come back to work on the old terms. The South Wales miners struck, and their strike too was broken. There are two reasons for this falling off in the Labour movement. The first is that a new trade depression had set in and with it unemployment. Employers did not mind a strike now; they even were glad to close their works while there was no profit to be made by keeping them open. The second reason is that a wave of patriotic enthusiasm had overtaken the country and for the moment it seemed more important to cheer the heroes of the South African War than to continue the Labour struggle.

At this point the T.U.C. adopted a new policy. They decided to run their own candidates for Parliament. Hitherto they had had no party: the Union members voted Liberal or Conservative as they pleased. In 1908 the T.U.C. formed a Labour Representative Committee to win seats for Labour Members. " The Secretary of the Committee was a certain James Ramsay MacDonald, of whom, until this moment, hardly anyone had heard. He was a man of thirty-four, of a sombre and handsome countenance. The son of a Scotch peasant woman, he had attended an elementary school and had become a school teacher. He had gone to London to seek a livelihood where for some time he had lived the hand to mouth existence of the intellectual worker of humble origin. . . . He was one of the founders of the Independent Labour Party. Everything about his past, his obscure origin, the life of destitution he had lived for ten years in London, destined him, one might have imagined, to become a revolutionary. In reality he had the politician's temper and gifts, and the founders of the Labour Representation Committee could not have chosen a better secretary. He displayed that blend of moral austerity and practical shrewdness which composes the typical Scot."[1] Under MacDonald's guidance two Labour Members were returned at by-elections in 1902 and 1903. This was the beginning of the Parliamentary Labour Party as we know it.

[1] Halévy, *History of the English People*, published in 1929.

The Fabian Society. The reforms which the working class so ardently desired were not to be won by Labour Members. It was the Liberal party which, realizing the power of organized Labour, decided to win the workingman's vote by adopting a policy of social reform. The lines of this policy had been laid down for them by two very different authorities. The first was a small group of intellectuals which was formed in 1894 under the name of the Fabian Society. The name implied that they stood for reforms that were gradual (was not Fabius nicknamed *Cunctator*, the delayer?). The moving spirits in the society were Bernard Shaw, Sidney Webb, a clerk in the Foreign Office, and his wife Beatrice. They knew that it is the nature of English people to move slowly; their policy was to educate the middle classes in the doctrines of Socialism and to show how Socialist reforms would profit all classes. In books and pamphlets, in lectures and discussions they proved that Socialism need not be revolutionary. They showed that municipal governments in England were actually adopting Socialist methods with unquestionably good results: publicly owned gas-works, water and drainage systems, roads, tramways and libraries were all in a sense Socialist and no one would quarrel with them. The Fabians took the sting out of Socialism and made it acceptable in the eyes of the middle class.

The second model for the Liberals to copy was none other than Bismarck, the Iron Chancellor of the German Empire. " Give the working man the right to work as long as he is healthy, assure him care when he is sick, assure him maintenance when he is old," Bismarck had said in 1884, " if you do that and do not fear the sacrifice, or cry out against State Socialism—if the State will show a little more Christian solicitude for the working man, then I believe that the gentlemen of the Socialist party will sound their bird-calls in vain." Bismarck was as good as his word: he had actually introduced insurance against sickness and pensions for the aged and was at work on a scheme of unemployment insurance when he was dismissed in 1898.

Conservative Reforms for the Workers.

These measures were not applied in England until 1906 when the Liberals came into office for what was to be a run of ten years. The Conservatives under aristocratic Prime Ministers like Lord Salisbury (1886-92 and 1895-1902) and his nephew Arthur Balfour (1902-06) had not considered that it was the business of the State to pay out money to the working class; such a course they felt to be demoralizing: the workers should be encouraged to provide for their own old age out of their savings. The Conservatives were, however, alive to the need for social reform in other directions and their long term of office (1886-1906) is memorable for three important social measures.

First they passed in 1888 a *Local Government Act*. It will be remembered that three years after the Reform Bill of 1832 had given the vote to the urban householder an Act was passed setting up Town Councils to look after the local government of the towns. Now, four years after the Reform Bill of 1884 had given the vote to the agricultural workers, the Government led by Lord Salisbury set up County Councils elected by the ratepayers to be responsible for the duties which had previously been carried out in the counties by Justices of the Peace. In Tudor and Stuart days the duties of these country gentlemen had been numerous and their authority supreme in country places. Such a cheap and admirable body of voluntary public servants could be found in no other country. But when the field of local government was growing so rapidly it became necessary to relieve them of the greater part of their work and to give the people of each county a voice in local affairs. Roads and bridges, health and sanitation, education and police have largely come under the control of the new elected County Councils. (*See* Appendix II.) The J.P.s still perform useful functions as local magistrates and still receive no salary.

Secondly, the Conservatives passed, in 1897, a *Workman's Compensation Act*. This made employers responsible for accidents or illness brought on workmen as a result of their work and for damage done by workmen on duty. It was a most necessary measure. In the pre-machine days when men worked with simple tools or with their own bare hands they could be expected to look after themselves. But now that men worked with machines their lives depended on the precautions taken by their employer. A badly ventilated pit, an uninsulated wire, an ill-guarded machine might cost a worker his life. And there were now all manner of new and dangerous trades: steel-working which may cause blindness, stoking coke ovens where the fumes are poisonous, unloading grain ships which exposes the labourer to anthrax. The Act of 1897 was wise in putting the responsibility for loss of life and health on to the employers.

Thirdly, the Conservatives passed an important *Education Act* in 1902. We have seen how the first State grant for education was made to religious societies in 1833 and how Board Schools were first set up with public money in 1870, and how attendance at these or other schools was made compulsory in 1880. In 1899 Lord Salisbury set up a Board of Education, which was a Government department in Whitehall charged with looking after education. The new Act of 1902 abolished the School Boards and put their schools under the care of the Town Councils and County Councils, subject to the advice and approval of the Board in Whitehall. This was the beginning of a national system of education which has since developed enormously. In 1918 it was made compulsory for children to attend school from the age of five to fourteen, and scholarships were provided to enable a few intelligent pupils to go on to Secondary Schools and on again to the Universities. Thus at last a thorough education was possible for poor men's children. But there is still one system for the poor and another for the rich !

Liberals' Social Reforms. The Liberal Government of 1906 was pledged to bring in more sweeping social reforms.

The Prime Minister was Sir Henry Campbell-Bannerman (until he died in 1908 and was succeeded by Mr. Asquith), but the work of reform fell on the shoulders of the Chancellor of the Exchequer, Mr. Lloyd George, an able and eloquent Welsh solicitor. He understood the grievances of the workers and sympathized with them. In those days a labourer who lost his job and had no savings must go with his family to the workhouse, to be herded with beggars, tramps, pickpockets and ne'er-do-wells of every description. In those days a labourer who was ill or who grew old had to choose between starving or going to the workhouse. In many cases he preferred starvation. Mr. Lloyd George changed all that by a series of reforms which working folk in England will never forget.

Of these the Act providing *Old Age Pensions* was the first and possibly the most important. The State undertook to give five shillings a week to every poor man and woman over seventy years old. (The sum has since been raised and the age reduced.) It was not intended then, and is not intended now, that the aged should be kept entirely by these pensions, which were calculated to make up the savings of a decently thrifty person to a sum sufficient to live on.

In 1909 came a *Trade Boards Act*. This provided a means for regulating wages in four sweated trades (tailoring, lace-making, paper-bag-making and chain-making). In old days wages were fixed by the Justices of Peace, on the principle of a fair wage. In the nineteenth century they had been fixed by the employer, on the principle that the wage paid should be the minimum which workers could be found to accept. Trade Unions had provided for workers in many trades a means of bargaining for better wages. The Trade Boards Act provided a means also for workers who had no Union to protect themselves; it set up committees consisting of workers, employers and independent members to fix wages. Thus " sweating " was minimized, if it was not altogether abolished.

Another achievement of the Liberals in 1909 was the

setting up of a Royal Commission on the Poor Law. The Commission roundly condemned the Act of 1834 and suggested that outdoor relief should be given in some cases and that the children of paupers and aged and infirm persons should be looked after in special institutions instead of being herded with rascals into the general workhouses which had so richly earned the nickname of Bastilles. These recommendations were not adopted until later; it was 1919 before the Ministry of Health was given power to control and lend money to the Poor Law Guardians.

The year 1911 is famous for two social reforms of immeasurable importance. The *National Health Insurance Act* set up a system, based on that of Bismarck in Germany, by which workers could get the services of a doctor and of a hospital, together with a weekly grant while away from work through illness. To be eligible for this workers had to pay a premium of $4\frac{1}{2}d.$ a week (in the form of stamps bought at the Post Office and stuck on insurance cards), and their employers had to pay a further $4\frac{1}{2}d.$ and the State $1\frac{1}{2}d.$ a week. (The contributions were subsequently raised.) This National Health Insurance has removed a load of anxiety from the worker's mind and has perhaps done more than anything else to improve the health of the nation.

Finally, in 1911, the first measure was passed for *Unemployment Insurance*. It entitled insured workers to a " benefit " of 7s. a week for the first fifteen weeks of unemployment. As with the Health Insurance, the premiums were paid by workers, employers and State alike. We shall see how this Act saved England from chaos in the hard times which followed the war of 1914–18.

The Parliament Act of 1911.

It is obvious that all these social reforms would impose a heavy burden on the Treasury. Before the Bills could become law the money had to be found to pay for them. In his Budget of 1909 Mr. Lloyd George proposed to raise an extra fourteen millions by increasing income-tax, super-tax and death-duties and by a tax on undeveloped land. In other words, it was the landowners who were being asked to pay for the benefits of the poor. Now the landowners were most of them Conservatives and many of them members of the House of Lords; they realized that the proposed taxation would make it impossible for the old families to preserve their estates intact. So the House of Lords rejected the Budget.

The Liberals were determined to carry their Budget and the social reforms which depended on it, whether the Lords would agree or not. Mr. Asquith dissolved Parliament and appealed to the electorate, which returned him to power again, though with a smaller majority than before. He then brought in the *Parliament Bill* by which all control over Budgets and other Money Bills was to be taken out of the hands of the House of Lords and their power to reject other Bills confined to such as should be sent to them not more than twice in two years.

The difficulty lay in inducing the Lords to pass a measure which would abolish most of their political power. A second time in one year (1910) Mr. Asquith dissolved Parliament to make sure that the country was on his side, and this time the election gave him so small a margin of Liberal votes that only the support of the Irish Nationalists and the Labour Members would give him a majority. He persevered with his programme although public opinion was so evenly divided, and this it was that made Party politics unusually bitter in the years before the World War. In 1911 the Parliament Bill was brought before the Lords again, this time with the announcement that the new King, George V, had agreed to create new Liberal peers if necessary to pass the Bill. In 1911, as in 1832, this threat was enough to bring the Lords to heel. Most of the peers abstained from voting and the Bill became law by 131 votes to 114.

The Strikes of 1911 and 1912.

In a single generation many great victories had been won for the working class. The unskilled workers had learned to organize themselves;

the Trades Union Congress had carried the battle for better conditions into Parliament by creating the Labour party; the Liberals had yielded to this pressure by giving the poor insurance against sickness, accident and unemployment and pensions in old age; and finally the power of the House of Lords had been destroyed so that workers need never again fear resistance to the will of the majority from that quarter. On the other hand there was still great distress among the working class. Between 1900 and 1913 real wages fell by 6 per cent. In the nineties it was estimated by statisticians (Charles Booth and Robert Giffen) that five out of six labourers in London were earning less than 30s. a week and that one out of every three was living in a state of poverty.[1]

The working men, therefore, were not appeased by the Liberals' reforms; they still wanted shorter hours and higher wages. Three great strikes marked the years 1911 and 1912. First the Sailors' and Firemen's Union struck: they wanted a uniform scale of pay at all ports, and this the Port of London Authority refused to concede. The Transport Workers' Federation came out in sympathy with the sailors, and traffic in the Port of London was at a standstill. Winston Churchill urged that troops should be called out to break the strike, but the Cabinet intervened in time to prevent bloodshed and the Port Authority gave way.

Then in August the Railway Workers went on strike. Traffic on all lines was paralysed by the strike and the general public, finding no trains running to take them on their holidays, realized perhaps for the first time the force of organized labour. Again the Government intervened and set up a Royal Commission to inquire into the railwaymen's grievance.

In February of the following year, 1912, a third strike broke out. This time it was the Miners, who were out for a

[1] In the decade that followed prices rose, yet in 1911 five million out of the eight million adult male workers of Britain were still earning less than 30s. a week.

settled minimum wage in every pit in Great Britain. They complained that many men, paid for piece-work, were set to work on such difficult seams that they were simply not able to earn a living wage. Again, it was not the employers but the Government that ended the strike: a Minimum Wage Act was passed, giving the right of fixing minimum wages to joint committees of employers and workers in each coalfield.

Neither Transport Workers, nor Railwaymen, nor Miners had won a complete victory by their strikes, but each had shown that they were a force to be reckoned with. Employers in general and the Government in particular knew that they would have to pay their workers more and more in wages. This would mean putting up the price of the goods which England lived by selling. And to be able to go on selling these goods they would have to keep at all costs their markets in colonial and foreign countries and to prevent the further expansion of their rivals, the other industrial countries of Europe.

Chapter XIII: THE CAUSES OF THE GREAT WAR

Competing Empires – Germany's Industrial Revolution – Germany's Needs: Colonies and a Navy – *Pièces de Résistance*: Morocco and the Near East – Preparation for War – The Balkan Crisis.

WHILE THE MINDS of Englishmen were thus occupied with the exciting issues of industrial strife and social reforms and with the ever faster and ever more spectacular march of science, affairs on the continent were drifting towards war. The English people took no notice. Not for generations had they cared so little for what was happening in Europe.

Competing Empires. The reasons for this apathy are not far to seek. After the hard-fought South African War the public had been accustomed to regard England's proper attitude to Europe as one of " splendid isolation," in the phrase of Lord Salisbury, who from 1886 to 1902 was largely in control of England's foreign policy. Salisbury believed in keeping England free from all alliances, commitments and other entanglements on the continent. Englishmen at that time were passionately interested in the expansion of the Empire. They may have realized that other nations had similar imperial interests, but it was believed that those need not come into conflict with the interests of England, so long as statesmen like Salisbury were prepared to pursue a policy of prudent bargaining to share the spoils.

Salisbury's bargains were usually prudent, in the sense that both parties benefited by them. The trouble was that Empires became ever more powerful until most of the known world had been divided among them without any arrangement being made to keep the peace in the future. While the nineteenth century was merging into the twentieth imperial expansion was proceeding faster than ever in Asia, America and Africa. In the Far East of Asia Japan went to war with China in 1894 and seized Korea. The European Powers were grateful for this demonstration of the weakness of China: Germany occupied the Pacific peninsula of Kiaochou in 1898, Russia occupied Port Arthur and Britain took Wei-hai-wei, and there followed a bargain by which China was partitioned for commercial purposes between these four Powers and France. In this Great Britain got the lion's share—the trade of the immense Yangtze valley. China attempted to resist. An association of patriots, called " Boxers," made a valiant attempt to hurl the " foreign devils " into the sea, but they were powerless against modern fire-arms; the Powers looted the Summer Palace of Pekin, crushed the rising and presented the Chinese Government with a formidable indemnity bill to pay for their trouble.[1]

Meanwhile in the West, the U.S.A. had gone to war with Spain in 1898, seized Cuba and made herself mistress of the Caribbean and Central American Republics which became her " spheres of influence." This influence extended over the Republic of Panama through which she built the canal which is now the Suez of the West. At the same time in Africa Germany was claiming the hinterland of Zanzibar— Nyasaland and Uganda—where the British East Africa Company had valuable trading rights. Salisbury persuaded her to abandon this claim in return for the North Sea island of Heligoland. This meant that Nyasaland and Uganda became part of the British Empire while Germany gained a naval base which might one day be used against Britain.

Salisbury's policy kept Britain out of European entanglements while this imperial expansion was going on, but there

[1] The Western Powers later felt that they could afford to be generous with this indemnity and spent most of it on providing scholarships for giving Chinamen the blessings of a Western education.

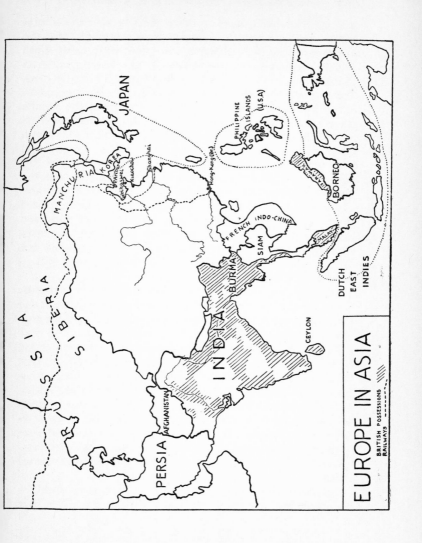

were three dangers in his refusal to commit himself. First, it left England unable to prevent the persecution of subject peoples in Europe. For example, in 1894 the Turks took to massacring their Armenian subjects; Salisbury attempted to exert some moral influence but refused to intervene by arms: the consequence was that in three years the Turks murdered a hundred thousand Armenians. Later, when Crete rebelled against Turkey, Salisbury actually sent a fleet to defend the island in 1897, but he could not prevent Turkey from defeating Greece who had taken the islanders' part. The result was that England lost prestige in the Near East, and what England lost another Western Power gained.

The second danger of refusing European alliances was that the imperial ambitions of the European Powers might clash. One clash did occur in Africa in 1899 when the French coming from the west met the English coming from the north at Fashoda on the Upper Nile. A French officer, Marchand, was building a French fort at Fashoda; Kitchener went out and obliged him to withdraw, but not before the Press in Paris and London had raised a clamour for war. The breeze died down in a few months; it should have been enough to show which way the wind would blow in the next century.

The third danger of refusing alliances was obvious. The other Powers of Europe were forming alliances and the Continent was being divided into two camps. Germany extended her treaty with Austria into a *Triple Alliance* by the inclusion of Italy in 1882. France retaliated by seeking the friendship of Russia: in 1888 she lent Russia 500 million francs to help her to set up factories and to complete the Trans-Siberian railway, and in 1894 these overtures were followed by a definite alliance, or *Entente*, by which France and Russia agreed to help each other if either were attacked by the Central Powers of the Triple Alliance. An armaments race began between the Central Powers on one hand and France and Russia on the other. It reached such a pitch that in 1899 Tsar Nicholas II called a conference at The Hague to put an end to this growth of armies and navies. The Hague Conference set up a Permanent Court of International Arbitration to settle legal disputes between nations. It also drew up a series of rules, agreed to by all civilized nations, for the humane treatment in future wars of wounded, prisoners of war and non-combatants and for the abolition of specially cruel weapons, such as air-raids and " projectiles the sole object of which is the diffusion of asphyxiating gases." But the International Court had no power to compel nations to abide by its decisions, and the rules of war have never been observed in practice. As for the armaments race, it went on as fast as before. In 1900 Germany doubled her navy.

Salisbury kept England out of both Triple Alliance and *Entente*. On the whole he favoured the Central Powers, though four times between 1879 and 1899 he refused to sign treaties proffered by Germany. But by the time of his resignation, in 1902, the policy of isolation could be continued no longer: trouble with France over colonies was continuous and trouble with Germany was increasing. England had to decide between France and Germany.

Germany's Industrial Revolution. The traditional enemy of England was France. We fought her in the Hundred Years War, we fought her when under Louis XIV she threatened to cut off our trade with the Netherlands, we fought her in the days of the French Revolution and Napoleon, and we stood by while Prussia defeated her in 1870. But after 1815 England had nothing to fear from France. From 1815 to 1870 we had no rival to our industrial power and there was no danger of friction. Then, after 1870, we had a new and formidable rival: Germany learned the tricks of the industrial trade in a single generation. In 1870 she was an agricultural country, exporting wheat and other food-stuffs and importing manufactured goods. In 1900 she was an industrial country, exporting coal and iron and machinery of all kinds, and importing food. By 1900 she was actually beating us at our own game. Her iron, which had been worth little in 1870, was turned into steel by the process invented by a Londoner, Gilchrist Thomas, and by 1910 her steel and iron exports were worth £100,000,000—which was more than those of Great Britain. Her coal, the output of which increased from 30 million tons in 1871 to 190 millions in 1913, was cheaper than ours and English ships actually went to German ports to fill their bunkers. Her chemical industry made ours seem parochial—in 1913 her export of dye-wares alone was worth £10,000,000. And in the electrical industry she led the world, supplying all countries with electrical furnaces, railways and appliances of every kind.

One simple secret was the cause of this astonishing success: combination. While British industrialists worked as individualists, fighting each other by keen commercial competition for profits, German industrialists worked as a team. The steel manufacturers combined in a colossal Steel Union, of which the mighty firm of Krupp's was but one among many. The coal producers combined in the Rhenish-Westphalian Coal Syndicate which controlled half the coal output of Germany. The thousands of chemical firms combined in a unit which controlled the production, distribution and price of dye-wares, fertilizers and most chemical products. And the electricity industry combined into two huge groups, Siemens and the A.E.G., which agreed not to compete with each other.

Against this remarkable work of organization the English firms were as little able to compete as the village shop against Woolworths. At last they began to copy German methods. The first Trust, or amalgamation of producers, was made in the salt industry when the Salt Union was founded in 1888, including some 65 firms. Other trusts and *Cartels* (or loose combinations for fixing prices between producers) followed. But the process was slow, and even to-day, though the chemical industry has combined in the I.C.I. (Imperial Chemical Industries) and electric power distribution is controlled by a central Board, the iron and steel and coal industries are still in the hands of a multitude of competing firms.

There was another side to the German genius for combination. The Germans welcomed State control. While the English industrialists insisted that the Government should leave them alone (*laisser-faire*) and feared Government interference, even in the form of Factory Acts, as a restriction of their individual liberty, the Germans looked to the Government as their leader. The State fostered the growth of German industries by means of tariffs and subsidies. Whereas England allowed foreign goods to come into England free of duty, a tariff of 25 per cent was charged on goods coming into Germany. This was nothing to the tariffs imposed by some countries—the Russian tariff was 130 per cent—but it was enough to give the German manufacturers a long start. State subsidies made the start still longer. Whereas in England the railways were owned by the shareholders of private companies, who expected them to earn high dividends and therefore had to charge high freights, in Germany all the railways (except some three thousand miles of line) were combined under State control and the State charged exceptionally low freights for industrial goods. At the same time merchant shipping lines were subsidized by State grants. Thus German exporters were able to get their goods conveyed cheaply to the ports and over the seas. Before long England was flooded with German goods; and the mark " Made in Germany " was on half the goods in the English kitchens and all the toys in the nurseries of pre-war days.

Germany's Needs: Colonies and a Navy. This industrial expansion was not without grave dangers for Germany. In the first place her population had increased so fast (from 40 millions in 1870 to 68 millions in 1914) that she could no longer grow enough food to feed it. By 1911 a third of the wheat consumed in Germany came from abroad, and more than a third of the sugar and fats. That meant that in the event of a war she would have to live on rye-bread and very short rations indeed. Secondly, she was dependent now on her trade in manufactured goods and this in turn depended on her ability to buy raw materials and sell finished products abroad. Therefore she needed a strong Navy to protect her merchant shipping, and colonies to provide her with raw materials and markets.

It was at this point that Germany came into conflict with England. For centuries the British Navy had been supreme and Britons had come to believe that the high seas were theirs by right: " Britannia *Rules* the Waves," they sang, although the real words of the song (" Britannia, *Rule* the Waves ") expressed a hope rather than a fact. For a century the British Empire had been the biggest colonial Power, and in the general scramble for colonies in the generation that followed 1874 this lead had been maintained: Britain acquired 5,000,000 square miles of colonies with 88 million inhabitants, France 3,500,000 square miles with 36 million inhabitants and Germany only 1,000,000 square miles and a paltry 17 million inhabitants. So when Wilhelm II, a young and ambitious man, became Kaiser (Emperor) of Germany and began to build up a German Navy and to connect the Baltic with the North Sea by cutting a canal through Kiel, Great Britain took it as a national insult. And when Wilhelm insisted that Germany should have a " place in the sun," by which he meant a larger colonial Empire, Great Britain took it as an unfriendly gesture towards herself, the greatest Empire in the world. Germany already had a few colonies—Togoland, Cameroons, South-West Africa, Tanganyika, and a peninsula in China and a few islands in the Pacific; it was felt in England that those were enough.

But Wilhelm was serious in his demand for a navy and for colonies. In 1890 he had dismissed Bismarck, who disliked the idea of both because they might mean trouble with England. Seven years later he put through his first Navy Bill and his second followed in 1900. Then he began his quest for an Empire.

Pièces de Résistance: **Morocco and the Near East.** There were two places which were commercially valuable and which had not yet been absorbed by the older imperial Powers. One was the Near East, valuable for the oil resources of Mosul and Persia, and as the junction of the trade routes between Europe, Asia and Africa. The other was Morocco, valuable for phosphates and for rumoured oil resources, and as the key to the western Mediterranean. The German Government had its eye on both, and round them the troubles of the next fourteen years were centred.

In 1903 Wilhelm began his penetration of the Near East by acquiring from the Turkish Sultan Abdul Hamid II (" Abdul the Damned ") the right to build a railway from Berlin to Baghdad. He suggested that England should co-operate in the venture, pointing out that it would give a quick passage for mails to India *via* Koweit on the Persian Gulf. But England refused. King Edward, who after Salisbury's resignation in 1902 played a large part in the conduct of English foreign policy, hated his German cousin. On the other hand he had the greatest affection for France and things French (did he not set the fashion for Englishmen to spend their holidays on the French Riviera ?). It was largely under his guidance that England made a treaty with France in 1904.

The first-fruit of the Anglo-French Entente was a joint agreement over Morocco. Openly, this was an understanding that England would leave France with a free hand in Morocco as France had left England with a free hand in that other province of the Turkish Empire, Egypt. Secretly, it was a treaty to partition Morocco between England, France and Spain. In 1905 the German Chancellor, von Bülow, got wind of this secret treaty and was justifiably indignant. The Kaiser arrived in a yacht at Tangier to assure the German trading community there that he would protect German trade and Moorish independence and demanded that the Powers should call an immediate conference to give both their guarantee. There was a tremendous storm in diplomatic tea-cups; England hated the idea of German warships in the Mediterranean and France was determined to have Morocco, if only for the soldiers it would provide for her Army. But none the less a conference was called at Algeciras, the Spanish holiday resort, and the Powers paid lip-service to the independence of Morocco. And there the Moroccan question rested—for a while.

There remained the question of the Near East. England's policy was always to prevent any major Power from getting a foothold there. For a hundred years the most serious threat had come from Russia, and against Russia British policy had accordingly been directed at the Crimean War and at the Congress of Berlin. But now Russia was a defeated nation. She was defeated, to the surprise and delight of contemporary Englishmen, by the Japanese in 1904—and the most serious threat to the Near East now came from Germany and Austria. So England reversed her policy and in 1907 made an alliance with Russia. A Triple *Entente* of France, England and Russia now faced the Triple Alliance of Germany, Austria and Italy.

The Central Powers felt that they were being encircled. It seemed that their new outlet, the Berlin-Baghdad railway, was being threatened by the Anglo-Russian alliance. To secure this outlet Austria in 1908 officially annexed Bosnia and Herzegovina. These provinces were nominally part of the Turkish Empire. Austria had in fact occupied them since 1878, but other Powers had hoped to have a hand in their future: Serbia, to whom the Bosnians were related, and Russia, who still regarded herself as the godmother of the Balkans. Both Powers protested against Austria's action as an infringement of the Treaty of Berlin (1878), but no action was taken. The cauldron of the Balkans was simmering but it had not yet reached boiling-point.

Meanwhile the armaments race was entering on a new lap. In 1908 a rumour reached the British Government that Germany was proposing to lay down new ships at such a rate that within six years their Navy would be larger than the British. Panic overtook the Cabinet, who demanded an additional £20,000,000 to spend on the Navy. Britain gained a long lead in all-big-gun ships, the first of which, the *Dreadnought*, had been built for Admiral Fisher in 1905.

Three years passed without international incident and then in 1911 the healing wound of Morocco was opened again by France, who sent out a military expedition in defiance of the Algeciras arrangement. Germany replied by sending a warship, the *Panther*, to the Moroccan harbour of Agadir. Her policy was to insist that if Germany gave up her trading rights in Morocco she should be compensated by a place in the sun somewhere else. Again the incident was smoothed over, but not before an ominous pronouncement had been made by Mr. Lloyd George who said in a speech at the Mansion House that " if a situation is forced upon us in which the peace could only be preserved by the surrender of the great and beneficent position which Britain has won by centuries of heroism and achievement, by allowing Britain to be threatened where her interests are vitally affected, as if she was of no account in the Cabinet of Nations, then I say emphatically that peace at that price would be a humiliation intolerable for a great country like ours to endure."

Preparation for War. The general public both in Germany and England were still utterly unconcerned by all this talk of war. They had heard the cry of " Wolf " from kings and politicians before and they were not moved by it now. In Germany the Socialists were the strongest parliamentary party, having one-third of the votes of the electorate behind them, and the Socialist party was pledged to peace, having undertaken never to fight against their fellow-workers of other nationalities. In England people were thinking, not of any European danger, but of the possibility of civil war in Ulster and of the disturbance of the peace which a group of women known as the Militant Suffragettes was perpetrating at home. These women, frustrated in all peaceable attempts to make good their claim to be allowed to vote, had embarked on a campaign of rowdyism which, under the vigorous leadership of Mrs.

Pankhurst, they kept up between 1909 and 1914. To draw attention to their cause, they broke windows and assaulted Cabinet Ministers with umbrellas, set fire to empty houses (including Lloyd George's villa at Walton), threw themselves under horses at the Derby, chained themselves to the grille in the House of Commons and when put into prison refused food and drink. The Liberals refused to be intimidated. It was 1918 before Lloyd George passed the fourth Reform Bill which gave the vote to women who were either married or over 30 years of age (and incidentally to all men over 21). Another ten years passed before Baldwin's Conservative Ministry gave the vote to all women over 21.[1]

The popular Press in England was still pro-German in 1913. "At this moment," said the *Evening News*, "we can honestly say that the peace of Europe has no better friend than the versatile monarch whose qualities have won him the respect of all nations. . . . We all acknowledge the Kaiser as a very gallant gentleman, whose word is better than many another's bond, a guest whom we are always glad to welcome and sorry to lose, a ruler whose ambitions for his own people are founded on as good right as are our own."

Yet preparations for war went on. The head of the German Navy, von Tirpitz, scouted a British suggestion for a truce in naval construction. The German Army chiefs had laid detailed plans for the invasion of France. The English First Lord of the Admiralty, Mr. Winston Churchill, went on building the British Navy up to the "Two Power standard"—that is, up to the strength of any two foreign navies combined. The Secretary of State for War, Lord Haldane, quietly reorganized the army for use in conjunction with the French against Germany. For service abroad he built up an Expeditionary Force, a small unit—only 150,000 strong—but excellently trained and

---

[1] In 1832 there were less than one million electors in England and Wales; in 1867 there were nearly two million; in 1885 over four million; in 1918 over seventeen million and in 1929 twenty-five million.

ready for immediate embarkation. For home defence he revived the old Volunteers, which had once been the delight of the Duke of Wellington, and turned them into a Territorial Army by giving them Government money, uniforms and equipment, and officers from the regular Army. For a reserve of officers he started Officers' Training Corps in schools and universities, again providing War Office assistance so that some thousands of young officers should be ready to take their places as subalterns in the event of war. The Royal Flying Corps (later to become the R.A.F.) also dates from Haldane's administration.

The Balkan Crisis. While these preparations were on foot the Balkan cauldron boiled over. Since 1908 most of the Balkan States had freed themselves from Turkish rule. Three of them, Greece, Bulgaria and Serbia, joined together in the Balkan League for the purpose of expelling the Turks from Europe. Russia favoured the Balkan League, but Germany and Austria favoured the Turkish Government, which was now in the hands of a body of reformers calling themselves the Young Turks, who had deposed Abdul Hamid. In 1912 the Balkan League went to war with Turkey and deprived her of all her European territory with the exception of Constantinople and Eastern Thrace. Then, in 1913, the victors quarrelled over their conquests and went to war with each other.

This was Austria's opportunity. A strong party in Austria wanted to annex Serbia and to establish a protectorate over all the Southern Slavs. A leader of this party, Conrad, was the friend of Franz Ferdinand, the heir to the Austrian throne. In the summer of 1914 the latter chose, most imprudently, to go to Bosnia for manœuvres, and on June 28, in the Bosnian village of Sarajevo, he was assassinated.

The British public was unmoved by the news—to them it meant nothing but another "Balkan atrocity." Besides, Europe at that moment seemed more disposed for peace than it had been for years past. Yet within five weeks of the

Sarajevo incident seven great nations were at each other's throats.

It happened like this. Austria was glad of an excuse to attack Serbia, so accused the Serbian Government of conniving at the murder and demanded impossible retribution, refusing Serbia's request that the matter should be laid before an international Congress. The Russian Government made it clear that they would fight for Serbia, and the German Government made it equally clear that they would fight for Austria. On July 30 orders went out for the mobilization of the Russian Army and on August 1 Germany declared war on Russia. On the following day Germany launched her attack on France (Russia's ally), sending troops over the Luxemburg frontier, and on August 3 war was declared between France and Germany.

There remained the problem of England: would she remain neutral or would she fight? The Cabinet was divided on this point. Sir Edward Grey, the Foreign Secretary, had offered to mediate between the combatants; his offer had been rejected and now he felt in honour bound to help France. Then something happened that brought public opinion in England round to this point of view: the German armies marched through Belgium, to attack France from an ill-defended quarter, the German Chancellor brushing aside the treaty of 1839 (guaranteeing Belgium's independence) as an " insignificant scrap of paper." A wave of indignation swept over England and there was rejoicing when it was known that at 11.30 p.m. on August 4 England had declared war against the German Empire.

The cause of the war was not Agadir or Sarajevo or the violation of Belgium; those incidents, like every other, were merely incidental. The cause of the war was the economic system which had been adopted by the industrial Powers, especially Britain and Germany, the United States and Japan. Each, to a greater or lesser extent, lived by manufacturing goods for export. Each lived by investing capital in " backward " countries. Each was, therefore, dependent for its living on winning and keeping colonial possessions which provided the materials, the markets and the dividends. England in 1913 bought £659,000,000 of raw materials from abroad, sold £525,000,000 of manufactured goods and had £4,000,000,000 invested overseas (twice the sum invested in 1900). Germany bought £530,000,000 worth of materials, sold £496,000,000 worth of goods and had £1,200,000,000 invested abroad. Each country had to increase its holdings abroad in order to keep up its standard of living. Since there were no longer enough " places in the sun " to provide for the needs of Germany and England, to say nothing of those of other countries, war was bound to come unless the Powers agreed to stop the system of competition.

The tragedy was that no one realized what was happening except the business men who were too intent on private profits to be aware of public dangers. The masses everywhere still thought in terms of pre-industrial days when countries had been more or less self-sufficient; they did not realize that industrialism had made the European countries economically interdependent and that a European war would mean an economic set-back for victors as well as for vanquished. Everywhere they still thought in terms of local wars with small arms between little professional armies; they did not realize that a European war would mean wholesale destruction of conscript armies and of civilians as well. Secure in their ignorance, the masses everywhere gave full rein to their spite and malice and mistrust, and when at last war came they welcomed it.

Chapter XIV: THE GREAT WAR, 1914-18

War in the Open – The War of Blockade – Jutland and the Somme – The Submarine Campaign and Nivelle's Offensive – The Russian Revolution – Germany *Contra Mundum* – The Cost.

The Government of every country was prepared for the war but none foresaw what manner of war it would turn out to be; otherwise it is unthinkable that it would ever have been fought. The Germans reckoned on a sudden dash on Paris which would encircle the French capital and the French Army within a brief five or six weeks. The French were confident that they could hold their well-fortified frontier until their Russian allies, who outnumbered the German and Austro-Hungarian forces by 3 to 1, could overrun the plains of Prussia and Hungary. The English were ready to join the war but doubted—until Belgium was actually invaded—whether it would be necessary for them to do so. All were agreed that the war would be short and the risk of defeat well worth taking.

1914: War in the Open. The German plan of campaign was simple. First a hurricane offensive in the west to wipe out the French Army, then an offensive in the east against the slow-moving Russian forces. The western campaign, as worked out by Schlieffen between 1891 and 1906 and modified later by Moltke, was to consist in a sweeping advance on Paris through Belgium. The French forces guarding the fortified frontier from the Vosges to Luxemburg were to be held, and no more than held, while the real offensive swept down upon them from the German right wing. " Strengthen the right wing," were the last words of Schlieffen on his death-bed in 1913.

THE GREAT WAR 233

The offensive began according to programme, the Germans advancing as regularly as clockwork and shattering the Belgian fortifications with the new 17-inch howitzers from the Skoda works. By August 14 they were in position on the Franco-Belgian frontier, and then began that Battle of the Frontiers which lasted until the 25th and cost France 300,000 men. The British Expeditionary Force landed in time to take part in this battle, which is known to Englishmen as the First Battle of Mons because it was there that their part of the action was fought. There their first casualties—1,656 dead—occurred.

The Allies lost the Battle of the Frontiers and a general retreat began. Day after day in the sweltering summer weather the Allied columns trudged back, crossing the Somme, crossing the Aisne and the Ailette, crossing the Marne. Day after day the German advance swept on until von Kluck, in command of the right wing, was within twenty miles of Paris.

And then, on September 6, the French turned and fought the Battle of the Marne. This time, in spite of exhaustion from the long retreat, they were in good position. Their units were in touch with each other, their left flank was strengthened by reserves rushed out from Paris in taxi-cabs. The Germans had advanced too fast, their troops were not in position, their supply organization was anything but complete. Moltke had forgotten Schlieffen's watchword and had weakened his right wing by sending two corps to the Russian front. His advance was checked by the Allied counter-attack. The Germans retreated to the line of the Aisne.

The Battle of the Marne changed the whole character of the war. The Germans settled down to trench warfare to defend their new line, which they were to hold almost intact for three and a half years. Their attempt to snatch a sudden victory had failed, but they were in possession of the industrial areas of France, including 80 per cent of her coalfields and nearly all her iron. The Germans were on the defensive, but on the defensive in the enemy's

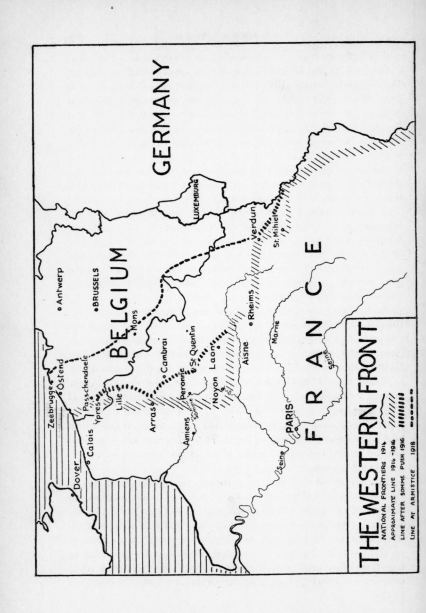

country. Only one hope of forcing a rapid victory remained: it might still be possible to push their right wing round the French flank, cutting them off from British reinforcements. But this attempt failed: the English held the enemy at Ypres, the French pushed their own trenches further and further to the west until the flanks of both forces rested on the sea. All hope of a flank attack was gone. It was stalemate.

Away in the east the Central Powers were also on the defensive. The Russian Army, fabulously strong in men and weak in organization, had advanced far into East Prussia and into Austrian Galicia. An old Prussian General, von Hindenburg, with the help of Ludendorff, his brilliant Chief-of-Staff, was able to defeat the Russians at the Battle of Tannenberg (August 27, 1914) and to roll the Russians back to within thirty-five miles of Warsaw, but he could not take Warsaw. Meanwhile the Austrian offensive had failed in Galicia and in the south the Serbs had risen against their traditional enemy and had routed an Austrian army, taking 40,000 prisoners. It appeared that the Government which had clamoured loudest for war was least able to conduct it: the Austro-Hungarian forces were more than half of them anti-Austrian and anti-Hungarian, consisting of Poles, Czechs and Slavs who were waiting for an opportunity to desert the Empire which had held them so long in subjection.

Christmas 1914 was a strange feast. It was not the birth of Christ but the birth of Mars that was celebrated. The people of England gave themselves up to the most misleading of all emotions, moral indignation. There was no sense of danger as yet, no fear that the island would be invaded or food supplies cut off, only a mass hatred against the "Huns" who had violated the neutrality of Belgium. Lord Haldane, the creator of the Expeditionary Force, the First Hundred Thousand, fell into disgrace because he had once been the friend of Germans. The hero of the nation was Kitchener, the new Secretary for War, who was calling upon the men of Britain to enlist, calling to such effect that by Christmas there were nineteen hundred thousand under arms—young men who thought the war a great adventure, idealists and men longing for an ideal who alike were happy to risk their lives in the cause which they felt to be just. Those who were not under arms competed to show their patriotism by hunting down their neighbours as spies.

1915: The War of Blockade. While winter held the armies frostbound each side sought desperately for new weapons. The French had used liquid fire in 1914 and were preparing to use it in greater quantities in the spring campaign; the Germans got ready to use cloud-gas (chlorine) for the first time; the British War Office possessed an even more effective weapon in the tank, but refused to make use of it, less through moral scruple than through lack of imagination. And each side sought desperately for new allies. The Germans had already found one in Turkey, where loans of German money and ships bore interest in bringing the Young Turks into war against Russia. The Allies were able to buy one more cheaply, by promises. Italy was committed to the Central Powers by the Triple Alliance, but Italians considered the Austrians to be their natural enemies and they were tempted by Lord Grey with the promise of part of the Austrian Tyrol (where 300,000 Austrians lived), most of the Dalmatian coast, and a share in Germany's colonies in Africa. They signed the Treaty of London in April 1915 and declared war on Austria, prudently postponing their declaration of war on Germany until August in the following year.

The war in 1915 was a war of blockade. The Germans began the year with an attempt to cut Britain's communications at sea. In January there was a naval encounter off the Dogger Bank, in which the Germans lost the *Blücher* and each side had one ship crippled. Then in February they launched their first submarine campaign. It was not a success, partly because they had not enough submarines and partly because they were anxious not to break with the United States of America. In May a submarine sank the

British liner *Lusitania* which was bringing munitions as well as passengers to England. A hundred American citizens were drowned and the outcry in the United States was so great that Germany promised not to sink liners in the future without due warning. Britain replied to these attempts by imposing a really effective blockade of Germany in the North Sea. All neutral ships were searched and cargoes intended for the Central Powers were diverted. This blockade, maintained until months after the Armistice was signed, is said to have caused the death of 750,000 people in Germany through under-nourishment or its consequent diseases.

Blockade is a slow weapon. If the war were not to degenerate into a war of exhaustion the enemy lines must be broken by a rapid offensive. The Allies attacked on every front in 1915, but everywhere their attacks failed. All attempts to break through on the Western Front were repelled with terrible losses: British attempts at Ypres in March and at Loos in September were unsuccessful, as were more costly French attempts at Neuve-Chapelle (March), Festubert (May) and in Champagne (September). On the Eastern Front the summer saw the Russians suffer no less than two million casualties and lose their hold on Poland and Galicia. It was necessary to find some new point of penetration.

Turkey seemed the weakest link in the enemy's chain, so against Turkey three offensives were launched in 1915. All three failed. The Russians were unable to penetrate into Anatolia by way of the Caucasus. The Indian Government planned an advance into Mesopotamia (Iraq) but its expeditionary force was besieged in Kut and surrendered in June 1916. By this time the most spectacular offensive of all had been launched and had failed in Gallipoli, where the British attempted to open the route to Constantinople by piercing the Dardanelles by a combined attack of fleet and army. The fleet bombarded the Turkish forts but failed to pierce the Narrows. The army landed on the east and south-east of the Gallipoli peninsula and tried to storm the central heights. At first they were within an ace of

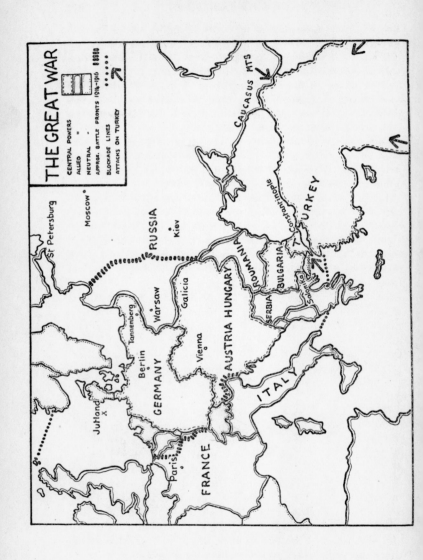

victory with a surprise attack, but the heights were held, against odds of three to one, by a young and unknown Turkish officer, by name Mustapha Kemal. After that, from March to December, English and Anzac[1] troops kept their footing on the coast, suffering from disease and frostbite as well as from Turkish guns, until at last, when their casualties had reached 130,000 dead, wounded and missing, the order came to evacuate Gallipoli.

Not only the Dardanelles campaign, but every other enterprise of the Allies in 1915 was a failure. The year ended with the overrunning of Serbia by the Central Powers, a victory which gave them open communications between Turkey and Central Europe. Bulgaria had joined the war in October and between them Bulgarian and Austrian forces, admirably led by the German Falkenhayn, drove the 200,000 Serbian troops over the Albanian mountains in a mad scramble for the sea. Only half of them succeeded in reaching the ports.

1916: Jutland and the Somme.

When the year 1916 began the German people were confident of victory. Their leaders were anything but confident: they knew that England and France were preparing a great offensive on the Western Front and that the real strength of England had not yet been brought to bear. Kitchener, the hero of Khartoum, had promised to raise a volunteer army of 2,000,000 men and to have them trained and brought into France by May 1916. To the astonishment of everyone outside England he was succeeding. And now he had plans for a new conscript army. In March the conscription law was passed in England and the new army might be expected in the field by the summer. To anticipate the Allied offensive the Germans launched a great attack on Verdun in February. But the French, fighting as they had fought at the Marne, with the certainty that defeat would mean the total conquest of France, held Verdun.

[1] Australian and New Zealand Army Corps. In the course of the years 1914–18 the British Dominions and colonies contributed a million and a half troops to the war and India another million and a half.

Three months later the Germans made an attempt of a very different nature to break the ring that encircled them. The North Sea blockade maintained by the British Fleet was leaving them short of necessary food supplies and of the materials of war. For their fleet to engage the British Grand Fleet was out of the question, the odds were too heavily against them. But they might hope to engage successfully isolated detachments of the fleet. On May 31 they nearly succeeded. About noon Hipper, commanding the German light forces, ran into Beatty who, with two squadrons of battle-cruisers and one of fast battleships, was steaming southward, off the coast of Jutland. Turning south, to join von Scheer and the German High Seas Fleet, he engaged Beatty in a running fight at 15,000 yards range and sank two of the English ships. But Beatty, warned in time of the trap into which he was running, turned and raced north to join Jellicoe and the Grand Fleet. The Germans followed, firing jubilantly and confident of victory, and then about six o'clock Beatty made contact with Jellicoe and the Germans realized that the thing they most dreaded was upon them: an open fight with the overwhelming force of the British Grand Fleet. Von Scheer turned and made for his coast, fighting hard. Jellicoe followed but he guessed wrongly at Von Scheer's destination on the coast and in the darkness the High Seas Fleet got safely to port.

Both sides have claimed victory in the Battle of Jutland, the Germans because they sustained only half the British losses, in men and in tonnage, the British because they retained mastery of the seas and were able to maintain the blockade. In reality the only result of the battle was to convince both sides that an open fight at sea was not to be risked.

By the end of June the Allies' preparations for their great offensive in the west were complete. Every weapon in modern warfare had now been forged and the ensuing Battle of the Somme was without precedent in its severity. It lasted five months, five appalling months of artillery barrage, infantry rushes, counter-barrage and counter-attack. In the end the Allies had advanced their line by five to seven miles over a front thirty miles long. This would have been a considerable gain if the Germans had not an infinitely superior line, marvellously fortified by Ludendorff,[1] to fall back upon. The cost of that battle of the Somme was over half a million casualties on either side.

In the east too the Allies' offensive was unsuccessful. They had been joined by Roumania in August, but that disorganized nation, for all the careful timing of her entry into the war on the part of her wily Prime Minister Bratianu, was knocked out almost instantly and by Christmas had lost her capital and three-quarters of her territory. The Allies made up for this failure by forcing Greece to take part in the war. There had been an Allied base at Salonika since 1915; now King Constantine was deposed and the pro-Ally Venizelos established in power. The Germans claimed that the Allies' violation of Greek neutrality deprived them of any right to criticize Germany's violation of Belgium.

In December 1916 the position stood much where it had been in December 1914. The war had lasted two and a half years and the losses had far exceeded what anyone in 1914 could have imagined as the limit of endurance. Yet neither side had gained anything. This surely was the time for peace. The soldiers on both sides had failed to force a conclusion: now was the politicians' opportunity to end the war by negotiation.

The obvious mediator was President Wilson of the United States, the leader of the greatest of the neutral Powers. He sent his friend, Colonel House, to London to state the terms of a settlement which the United States were prepared to support. To us to-day they seem reasonable terms[2] but the British Government would not hear of

[1] The English called it the Hindenburg Line.
[2] They included the restoration of Belgium, Alsace-Lorraine and Serbia; the cession of Constantinople to Russia, the Trentino to Italy and Poland to the Poles; the compensation of Germany by territory outside Europe; and the abolition of competitive armaments.

them: they held that it was for Germany to sue for peace. On December 16 Germany sent her note to the Allies. It was a grandiloquent document in which the Germans offered no definite concessions; they offered to surrender a portion of Alsace but said nothing about evacuating Belgium. This made the Allies harden their hearts. They rejected the German note as " empty and insincere." Two and a half years of intense war propaganda on either side had achieved its purpose: it had inoculated the masses everywhere with war-fever and with the conviction that their cause was just in the eyes of God. Only the soldiers in the trenches doubted the divine purpose behind the slaughter to which they were subjected.

1917: The Submarine Campaign and Nivelle's Offensive.

The war went on. The rulers of the combatant Powers laid plans for a new onslaught in 1917. In England, Mr. Lloyd George, who had won admiration for his vigorous conduct as the first Minister of Munitions, preached the doctrine of the knock-out blow and succeeded in displacing Mr. Asquith as Prime Minister of a non-party Government. He formed a small War Cabinet in which the most active movers were Sir Maurice Hankey, Lord Milner and the South African General Smuts, and he persuaded the French Government to replace the cautious Joffre—*le père Joffre* as the *poilus* called him—by the eager and plausible Nivelle, who prepared for a spring offensive which he intended to be a veritable knock-out blow on the Aisne. The British commander, Haig, whom Lloyd George distrusted, was made partially subordinate to Nivelle.

As in 1916, the Germans forestalled this attack by an offensive of their own, this time on the sea. They launched their great submarine campaign against all ships, enemy or neutral, bringing cargoes to Allied ports, which they proclaimed to be in a state of blockade. They knew that they stood to lose the neutrality of the United States, but the risk was worth taking for they had a chance of bringing

Great Britain to her knees through starvation. And in this they very nearly succeeded. The British public were not told how near they were to defeat: in the month of April the German U-boats sank one ship out of every four that left British ports—a total of 875,000 tons of shipping—and there was only six-weeks' supply of corn left in the United Kingdom.

The submarine campaign failed. It brought America into the war: on April 6 the United States pledged her help to the Allies as an Associated Power. And gradually Britain fought down the U-boat menace, providing convoys of warships to accompany cargo-boats so that the death-roll from enemy torpedoes dropped. Yet 1917 was a dark year for England: the U-boats sank 2,439 ships in all and it needed a system of strict rationing of meat, sugar and butter to prevent the food shortage from turning to starvation.

On the Western Front the French offensive failed. The Germans retreated five miles or so to the impregnable Hindenburg Line and there met and repelled Nivelle's attacks. Mutiny now spread like fire among the despairing French troops. To divert German attention from what might well have turned into a total collapse Haig's troops were rushed into a counter-attack beyond Ypres. That diversion, the Battle of Passchendaele, lasted from July to October and cost England 300,000 of her young men, killed and wounded. It was some consolation that in November, when Haig struck at Cambrai, the new British weapon, the tank, proved successful. Used properly now for the first time, the tanks showed that the Allies had at last found a weapon which could penetrate the German defence.

Before the end of the year there was bad news for the Allies from other fronts. In the South the Italians who had been fighting somewhat listlessly on Austrian territory were routed at Caporetto and were driven in disorder down the mountain passes into the heart of their own country. In the East there was a disaster beside which Caporetto faded into insignificance. Russia was out of the war.

The Russian Revolution.

The Tsarist Empire had cracked under the strain. In 1905 when the Tsarist despotism had showed its incompetence by allowing its forces to be defeated by Japan there had been revolutionary risings in Moscow and Petrograd which were put down only with the greatest difficulty. Now in 1917 when the Tsarist despotism had showed not only incompetence but criminal negligence in leaving millions of men not only defeated but starving and freezing to death in the trenches, now when the Tsar was weak to the point of inanity and the Tsarina, who dominated him, was hysterical and incidentally a Prussian, there were revolutionary risings which were not put down at all. In March the workers of Petrograd, aghast at the prospect of famine which misgovernment had brought upon them, went on strike. They were joined by the garrison. They prevented the Tsar from returning to his capital by pulling up the rails in front of his train. A Provisional Government of Liberals was set up. Englishmen were delighted at the news, preferring Liberals to a despotic Tsar and believing that now the Russians would play a more telling part in the war. There was never a greater mistake. The Russians responded to the Provisional Government's plans for a great offensive by deserting in hundreds of thousands: the soldiers simply dropped their arms and made off eastward for their villages.

The failure of the planned offensive meant the failure of the Liberal Government. The soldiers and workers had formed committees (called Soviets) for local government and gradually more and more of the Soviets were turning away from the Liberals and towards the Communists, especially towards the group of Communists led by Lenin and Trotsky (and known as the Bolsheviks, or Majority, because once at a party conference in 1903 they had out-voted the less extreme sections). In November the Communists seized the capital. It was an almost bloodless revolution: there was no resistance because the Bolsheviks were so obviously the only organized group that meant business.

Then came the task of winning the rest of Russia to the Communist revolution. Lenin announced his policy in a few simple words: " Bread to the starving, Land to the peasants, Power to the Soviets and Peace to all People." Lenin's revolution succeeded because he promised the people what they wanted and was able to keep his promise. The peasants, many of them deserters just back from the war, got the land which their ancestors had coveted through generations of serfdom. The workers, under the direction of the Bolshevik party, confiscated all stores, factories and machinery to be henceforth the property of the State. And the Bolshevik Commissars, while preparing for a civil war against the landowning and capitalist class in Russia, asked the Central Powers for peace.

Germany could now have overrun Russia but she was anxious for an immediate peace so as to be able to get at the food supplies of the fertile Russian Ukraine, without which her own people would starve. She wanted to free her troops from the Eastern Front, for without them Germany could not hold out in the west. A peace conference met at Brest-Litovsk in December and after months of delay, during which Trotsky argued interminably and the Germans applied the screw by advancing to within a hundred miles of Petrograd, a treaty was signed between Russia and the Central Powers. Russia was to give up Poland, the Baltic Provinces, the Ukraine, Kars and Batum, and was to grant Germany an immense indemnity and all the trade privileges she wanted.

Germany *Contra Mundum*. Whether the terms of Brest-Litovsk could ever be carried out depended on Germany's ability to win the war on other points. She stood almost alone now. The Allies had lost Russia and also Roumania, which caved in as soon as Russia's support was removed, but Germany was about to lose the help of Turkey and Austria-Hungary. Those Empires were on the point of foundering like the Russian under the strain of war. Already in 1917 the Turks had been swept out of Baghdad by the army of Sir Stanley Maude and out of Palestine by the forces of Lord Allenby who had advanced from Egypt with his eastern flank covered by hosts of Arabs which Colonel Lawrence had brought into the war on the promise of independence when victory was assured. Already the Austrian strength was sapped by the wholesale desertion of Czechs and Poles, Croats and Slovenes from her armies. Everything now depended on Germany. And Germany put her whole strength into one great offensive on the Western Front, which, Germans prayed, might crush the Allies before their American auxiliaries could be brought into action.

On March 21, eighteen days after the signing of the Treaty of Brest-Litovsk, General Ludendorff delivered his first blow. It took the form of a smashing surprise attack on the British Fifth Army (under General Gough) on the Somme. The British line bent, broke: the British lost 100,000 men in a week and retreated thirty miles before another stand could be made in front of Amiens. Then Ludendorff launched his second blow, this time at Armentières where the Allied line was feebly held by Portuguese troops. A third blow followed, against the French, who retreated as far as the Marne, as they had retreated in the dark days of 1914. To the Allies it seemed that all was lost. Agonized they waited for Ludendorff's next blow, which would surely mean defeat to their cause.

Ludendorff's next blow never came. He had no reserves. The stricken people of Germany had no reserves to send him. Weakened by the blockade (the winter of 1917–18 was known as the Turnip Winter), exhausted by the ceaseless demands for men and supplies, disheartened by the news that a million Americans had already landed in France, the German people were on the point of revolution. The people of the Allied countries did not know this; they expected defeat. But Foch, who in March had been appointed Generalissimo of the Allied forces, discerned the weakness behind the apparent triumph of the Germans and ordered an offensive to begin on July 18. All along the line the Allies were victorious now: on from the Marne the

French advanced and the English fought their way back to the Somme. In September the Hindenburg Line was broken. Away to the north the Belgians were sweeping onward. In the south of the line the Americans took St. Mihiel.

It was not the end. The Germans had retired in good order. Their military machine was still intact. But Ludendorff knew that the end was in sight and on September 29 he had a paralytic seizure, showing on his own body the stigmata of the agony into which the Central Powers were plunged. The following day Bulgaria surrendered. Next month Turkey surrendered and let the British Fleet sail through the Dardanelles to take possession of Constantinople. By this time the Austria-Hungarian Empire had fallen to pieces: the Czechs in Prague, the Hungarians at Buda-Pest, the Slavs in the South were proclaiming themselves independent Republics, while the last Austrian army in Italy was letting itself be beaten by the British and Italian troops at Vittorio Veneto. In Germany the masses had turned against the Kaiser's Government. Only the abdication of the Kaiser could avert a revolution, and the Kaiser refused to abdicate. Not until the Navy mutinied and hoisted the Red Flag in the ports rather than put to sea against the victorious enemy, not until Communism had spread to Munich, not until the crowds were out in the streets of Berlin did the Kaiser sign a deed of abdication and take to flight, on November 9, 1918. A mildly Socialist Government—we should call it Liberal—came into power in Germany with the ex-saddler Ebert as President. Then, while Berlin writhed in the influenza epidemic (1,722 had died of it in that city alone by October 15) and Communists fought for a social revolution on Bolshevik lines, the new Government consented to an Armistice.

The terms of Armistice were dictated by Foch. On November 7 a German delegation had made its way through the lines and had been received by him in his railway-coach headquarters near Compiègne. The terms he laid down were terrible and humiliating: complete surrender of all German fleet, artillery and air force and

Allied occupation of the right bank of the Rhine. Yet the Germans felt they had no alternative but to accept. At the eleventh hour of the eleventh day of the eleventh month of 1918 Armistice was signed.

The Cost. It was ended, the greatest war in the world's history. The people of England gave themselves up to hysterical rejoicing. They rejoiced because the war was over and also because they thought that it had been worth while. Prophets for thousands of years had taught that violence settles nothing, that its only result is to hasten the processes of material growth and to slow down the spiritual growth which underlies material change. But people still believed that the convulsion they had gone through was "the war to end war," "the war that would make the world safe for democracy."

They had not yet counted the cost. Nearly all the able-bodied men of England had joined the forces and of these one in nine was killed. Only one in nine, but the rest—the wounded, the prisoners, and the men who had come through intact—had undergone an experience so terrible that the mark would be on them for the rest of their lives. This was the loss that Britain sustained: three-quarters of a million dead, twice that number wounded and the heart of a whole generation of men and women ravaged by four years of terror.[1]

[1] Only four nations suffered more severely. Exact figures will never be obtainable, but the casualties among armed forces have been estimated as follows:

Germany	1,800,000	dead	4,000,000	wounded
Russia	1,700,000	,,	5,000,000	,,
France	1,400,000	,,	2,000,000	,,
Austria-Hungary	1,200,000	,,	3,600,000	,,
British Empire	900,000	,,	2,000,000	,,
United States	100,000	,,	200,000	,,
Total for all belligerents	13,000,000	,,		

These figures do not include prisoners of war or losses sustained by civilian populations as the result of war. The influenza epidemic, starting in the belligerent countries in 1918 among populations weakened by the strain of war, spread all over the world and killed many millions of people.

The bill of the war was reckoned at ten thousand million pounds, to which must be added seven hundred and fifty million pounds' worth of lost shipping. The National Debt had been increased ten-fold—from £700 million to £7,700 million, and of this £1,000 million was owed not to British lenders but to America. This economic loss might seem crippling, especially when it is realized that most of the sum of human effort during these four years had been bent upon destroying things rather than upon making them. Yet strangely enough the feverish destructive efforts of the war years had led to economic gain rather than to loss. Necessity had produced in four years inventions which might have needed four decades of gestation in peace time. It had produced new methods of working, new armies of workers—women-workers—and a new spirit of co-operation and corporate exertion. Industry had become for a time no longer private, but national, no longer a profit-making activity but a social service for the benefit of the nation. The Government had taken over mines and railways and had bought the supplies of raw material which it handed over to the industrialists to manufacture in return for a commission. At the end of the war, in spite of the infernal waste of men and materials, England found herself richer than ever, richer in the sense that she was capable, with her reorganized industries and replenished labour force, of producing more goods than ever before.

This was England's gain from the Great War of 1914–18. This, and the opportunity of redrawing the map of Europe at the Peace Conference. What use would she make of these opportunities?

Chapter XV: THE VERSAILLES SETTLEMENT AND AFTER, 1919-35

The Peace Treaties – The League of Nations – The Mandate System – The New Europe – The Years of Plenty – The World Depression – The Versailles Settlement Fails.

GERMANY SIGNED the Armistice on the understanding that the subsequent treaties of peace should be based on the Fourteen Points of President Wilson. Of all the plans which had been put forward in the last year of war the Points alone were based on a clear and acceptable principle. The principle was "self-determination," or the right of every people to decide for themselves the State to which they would belong: "Every territorial settlement must be made in the interests of the population concerned; and not as part of any mere adjustment of claims among rival States." As part of this principle the President insisted that there should be no victimization of the vanquished: he demanded "open covenants of peace openly arrived at," and in his fourteenth point he stipulated that a League of Nations should be set up "for the purpose of affording mutual guarantees of political independence and territorial integrity to great and small nations alike."

The Peace Treaties.   At first it was not doubted that a just and lasting Peace would be made on those lines. After all, Wilson was President of the strongest nation in the world: the Allies were dependent on America for money and the distressed countries of Europe were being kept from starvation by American food. When he came to Europe for the Peace Conference Wilson was greeted as a saviour by Allies, enemies and neutrals alike.

But by the time that the Conference met in Paris on January 18, 1919, a change had come over public opinion. It was obvious now that the victors wanted not so much peace as revenge. Lloyd George had held a General Election in the previous December; his Coalition Ministry was returned to power with a huge majority, but the slogans which had won the election were " Make Germany Pay ! " and " Hang the Kaiser ! " Someone described the new House of Commons as " the wealthiest, the least intelligent and the least representative since Waterloo." In France the war fever was running even higher. The French people were behind Clemenceau in his determination to crush Germany beyond the possibility of recovery. In Italy the spirit was the same: Orlando was sent to Paris to exact his pound of flesh with interest—the pound being the territories promised at the Treaty of London and the interest being the old port of Fiume. When Wilson reached Paris he found the Points forgotten and the Central Powers absent: Germany and her friends had been forbidden by the Allied Powers to take part in the peacemaking.

So the Peace Conference resolved itself into a wrangle between Wilson and the small nations on one side and the great Allied Powers on the other. If there had been no hurry about concluding the settlement a decent compromise might have been reached; but there was a desperate hurry. Europe was in the throes of revolution and it seemed that Communism must inevitably spread over the Continent if peace were not imposed quickly from Paris. Three European Empires had crumbled in the earthquake of war and Red flames were breaking out among the ruins. In Germany the Republican Government of moderate Social Democrats and Liberals which had overthrown the Kaiser was now fighting a civil war against German Communists. In Austria-Hungary four states had established themselves as heirs to the old Dual Monarchy, and in one of these, Hungary, a Communist régime was in power. In Russia the Bolsheviks were holding out against the Whites and the detachments which France and Great

Britain had sent to try to save the old régime. Among these troops themselves, Communism was spreading. There were minor mutinies in England where soldiers were tired of waiting for demobilization. It was obvious that not for anything would the Allied soldiers go on fighting. The peacemakers had not a moment to lose: famine as well as revolution was stalking the land in those days, famine in Belgium and famine in Germany and in Austria which were still cut off by the Allied blockade.

In the interests of a quick settlement the Paris negotiations were left to a committee of four—Wilson, Clemenceau, Lloyd George and Orlando—and in this committee Wilson was easily out-manœuvred. Though he stood out against Orlando's demand for Fiume, so that the Italian delegate went home in a huff, he had to give in to most of Clemenceau's demands. Lloyd George would have come to Wilson's help but he was tied by his election promises to " make Germany pay." So in May 1919 the German Government was horrified by the news that they must sign a treaty which bore no resemblance to the Fourteen Points. They protested, but there was no alternative: on June 28 they signed the Treaty of Versailles in the very hall where Germany had celebrated her triumph over France in 1871.

The treaty was designed to deprive Germany of her resources as an industrial Power. She lost much of her coal and iron: Alsace and Lorraine went back to France, the Upper Silesian mines went largely to Poland (after a plebiscite[1] in 1921) and the coal of the Saar went to France, until the plebiscite of 1935. She lost all her ships: the treaty gave her merchant fleet to the Allies and the splendid German liners appeared under new names, the *Leviathan*, the *Berengaria*, the *Homeric* and the *Majestic*, sailing for American and British shipping firms. She lost

[1] A plebiscite is a vote of the whole people on a given point. In accordance with the principle of self-determination, the treaties provided that plebiscites should be held in a number of districts of mixed nationality so that the inhabitants might choose to which State they would belong.

her arms: her Navy was scuttled in the Scapa Flow, her Army was limited to 100,000 men and her aircraft destroyed. She lost control of her rivers: these valuable means of transport were put under international control and the Rhineland under occupation by Allied troops for fifteen years. She had her land cut in two by the " Polish Corridor " —a tract of land 260 miles long by 80 miles wide. Altogether she lost one-eighth of her territory and one-tenth of her people. She lost her colonies, which were to be divided among the Allies under the League of Nations. She was obliged to admit sole responsibility for making the war. And as if this was not enough, she was forced to undertake to pay to the Allies an unlimited sum in Reparations: by May 1921 she was to pay £1,000 million towards a total to be determined later.

The treaties presented to the other Central Powers were scarcely less vindictive. In September 1919 Austria signed the Treaty of St. Germain-en-Laye which left her a tiny landlocked state of 6,500,000 inhabitants. Two millions of these lived in the capital, Vienna; the countryside was too small and too poor to provide the food the townsmen needed or to buy the goods the townsmen made. Thus there was no future for Austria but to become part either of Germany or of Hungary; and these eventualities were explicitly forbidden her by the treaty. Hungary signed the Treaty of Trianon in June 1920 (when her Communists had been safely driven out), which reduced her from 125,000 square miles to 35,000, from 21 million inhabitants to 8 million. Her losses included four-fifths of her iron ore. She was left a small agricultural kingdom without a king—the Hapsburg Monarchy was excluded from succession by the treaty; a small patriotic nation without a third of her nationals—the treaty put over two million Magyars under Roumanian and Czech rule.

There remained Turkey. The Ottoman Empire, like that of Hapsburg, Hohenzollern and Romanov, had crumbled in the wars; all that was left to the Turks was Anatolia and Thrace and this remnant the Allies proposed

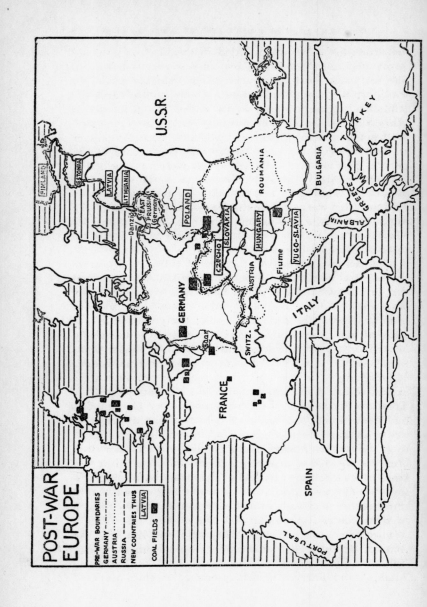

to petition by the Treaty of Sèvres, which three so-called representatives of Turkey had been induced to sign in August 1920. This almost incredible treaty gave Thrace and Smyrna to Greece, Eastern Anatolia to the Armenians and the Kurds, the cotton and corn-growing country of Adalia to Italy, and Constantinople to an Allied Commission. The awards to the Armenians and Kurds and some of the award to the Greeks were in accordance with the principle of self-determination; but nothing except the directly contrary principle of Imperialism could justify the awards to Italy and to the Allied Commission. When the Turkish Nationalists under Mustapha Kemal repudiated the treaty Greece was encouraged to attack Turkey with 80,000 men and with some British supplies from Salonika. After a bitter war the Turks drove the Greeks into the sea. It became necessary to offer a new treaty to the Turks. Lord Curzon went to Lausanne to negotiate with them but the concessions they demanded were too much for him and it was left to Sir Horace Rumbold to conclude the Treaty of Lausanne in July 1923, by which Turkey was left in full possession of Anatolia and of Constantinople and Eastern Thrace. The Sick Man had taken a new lease of life; and his bag and baggage were still in Europe.

The League of Nations.   In Wilson's mind there had been one hope that the Paris treaties might soon be modified into something that would savour more of peace. That hope was the League of Nations. Included in every treaty was a Covenant prescribing the machinery and procedure and hinting at the purpose of the League. The purpose was to prevent war. The machinery consisted of a permanent Secretariat at Geneva, an Assembly of two delegates from every Member-State meeting annually in September, and a Cabinet or Council of eight, four being representatives of the Great Powers and four being elected from the smaller nations. There was also an International Labour Office at Geneva to look after the interests of the working class throughout the world, and a Permanent Court of

International Justice at The Hague to decide legal points arising in the interpretation of treaties. The procedure by which this machinery was to achieve its purpose was, briefly, as follows: " The Members of the League agree that if there should arise between them any dispute likely to lead to a rupture they will submit the matter either to arbitration or to enquiry by the Council and they agree in no case to go to war until three months after the award of the report . . . " (Article 12). " Should any member of the League resort to war in disregard of its Covenants . . . it shall *ipso facto* be deemed to have committed an act of war against all the other members of the League, which shall hereby undertake immediately to subject it to the severance of all trade and financial relations . . . and the prevention of all intercourse between the nationals of the Covenant-breaking State and the nationals of any other State, whether a Member of the League or not. It shall be the duty of the Council in such case to recommend to the several Governments concerned what effective military, naval or air force the members of the League shall severally contribute to the armed forces to be used for the protection of the covenants of the League . . . " (Article 16).

Whether this League would fill Liberal expectations depended not on the Covenant but on the degree of support which public opinion would give it. More than fifty States joined the League but three of the Great Powers did not. The United States had lost all faith in their President by July 1919 and refused to join the League or to sign the Versailles Treaty: Americans were determined never again to be dragged into war outside their own continent. Germany was regarded as an enemy and was not admitted to the League until 1926. Soviet Russia was thought beyond the pale of capitalist society and was not admitted to the League until 1934. For many years the League was dominated by its Council[1] and the Council was dominated

[1] The Council consisted at first of four major Allied Powers with permanent seats (Great Britain, France, Italy and Japan), and of two minor Allied Powers (Belgium and Greece) and only two others (Brazil and Spain) with temporary seats.

THE VERSAILLES SETTLEMENT AND AFTER 257

by the Allied Powers who were determined to use the League machinery in order to enforce in their strictest interpretation the Paris treaties. Germany, Austria and Hungary complained, with some justice, that though the League refused to consider any modification of their boundaries as laid down by the treaties, it did nothing but register a mild protest when Lithuania extended her boundaries in 1923 by seizing Memel, which, though taken from Germany by the treaties, was administered by Germans under the control of an Allied Commission. Germany further complained that the plebiscites by which Eupen-Malmédy was given to Belgium and the best parts of Upper Silesia to Poland were unfairly conducted by the League. (In the latter case the complexity of the problem might be held to excuse the League.) This suspicion that the new League was but the old *Entente* writ large overshadowed much of the good work which was being done from Geneva in the League's early years—work such as the loan made to Austria in 1922 and the protection given to national minorities in many countries of Europe.

The Mandate System. The most important task accomplished through the League in its early years was the division of the colonies of Germany and Turkey among the Allied Powers. The principle adopted was that these colonies should become " mandated territories " for whose well-being the Powers should be responsible to the League until they should be thought fit to govern themselves. " To those colonies and territories which as a consequence of the late war have ceased to be under the sovereignty of the States which formerly governed them and which are inhabited by peoples not yet able to stand by themselves under the strenuous conditions of the modern world, there should be applied the principle that the well-being and development of such peoples form a sacred trust of civilization. . . . The best method of giving practical effect to this principle is that the tutelage of such peoples should be entrusted to advanced nations who by reason of their resources, their experience or their geographical position can best undertake this responsibility, and who are willing to accept it, and that this tutelage should be exercised by them as Mandatories on behalf of the League. . . . In every case of mandate the Mandatory shall render to the Council an annual report in reference to the territory committed to its charge." Under this 22nd Article of the League Covenant, Palestine, Transjordan and Iraq (Mesopotamia), Tanganyika, and a small part of Togoland and the Cameroons became mandated territories of Great Britain; Syria and the remainder of Togoland and the Cameroons went to France; the German Pacific islands were divided between Japan and Australia, and German South-West Africa became a mandated territory of the Union of South Africa. Of the great Allied Powers only Italy was denied a share in the colonial spoils—an omission which the League was to regret in 1935 when Italy determined to extend her empire by war and overran Abyssinia, one of the few self-governing negro States left in the world.

The treaties which we may call the Versailles Settlement were an improvement upon the Vienna Settlement of 1815 only in so far as the principle of self-determination may be said to be an improvement on the principle of legitimacy, and democracy an improvement upon despotism. The League of Nations had in practice something in common with the Congress System. The League Council was as bitterly opposed to Socialism and to treaty-revision as the Holy Alliance had been opposed to Liberalism and to Nationalist risings. In one important respect Versailles sinned where Vienna did not: Versailles victimized the vanquished, whereas Vienna had left the vanquished intact. The reason for this is that the men who made the Versailles Settlement had to consider the wishes of the masses who elected them, whereas the men of Vienna were responsible only to themselves. It must be admitted that the masses in 1919 got the peace that they deserved.

The New Europe: Communism and Fascism.

Its punitive clauses apart, the Versailles Settlement was a triumph of Nationalism and Liberalism. The revolutions which had failed in 1830 and 1848 succeeded in 1918–19. Germany became a Republic under a constitution made at Weimar which was the most liberal the world had ever seen. Austria, mutilated as she was, tasted the first, and somewhat unripe, fruits of liberal democracy under a new federal constitution. The Czechs of Bohemia gained independence at last in the new Republic of Czecho-Slovakia. The Slav subjects of the old Austro-Hungarian Monarchy were joined with the Slavs of Serbia and Montenegro in the new and, it was hoped, democratic kingdom of Yugo-Slavia. Even the Baltic subjects of the old Russian Empire gained self-government in the four new States of Finland, Estonia, Latvia and Lithuania. Poland, which had been wiped off the map at the end of the eighteenth century, became a self-governing nation again—and more than a nation, for the treaties gave her a million German subjects in West Prussia and after the treaties she seized Vilna from Lithuania and vast tracts of West Russia and of the Ukraine from the Soviets.

Liberal Nationalism was not, however, to have all its own way in the new Europe. Two new political systems which were quite different from anything that had been known in 1830 and 1848 established themselves in Italy and Russia. The Soviet régime in Russia was founded on the principles of Karl Marx. Lenin, the leader of the revolutionaries, gave the control of the factories and local government to councils (Soviets) of workers, putting all under the supreme authority of the Communist (Bolshevik) party. The Bolsheviks repudiated the three ideals which had made modern European civilization what it is—the Christian Religion, Private Property and Individual Liberty; for a decade after the Revolution the word " Bolshevism " inspired the same hatred and fear that " Popery " had inspired in Englishmen in Stuart days. At the same time the Bolsheviks repudiated the debts of the Tsarist Empire: they refused to pay interest on the hundreds of millions of pounds which France and England, among other Western Powers, had invested in the industries and railways of Russia. To prevent the spread of Communism and to recover their investments England and France fought the Bolsheviks—until they realized that the task was hopeless and withdrew their troops, the French in the spring, the English in the autumn of 1919.

Very different was the revolution which transformed Italy. A hundred years ago Italy was merely a " geographical expression." Cavour and Garibaldi had made it a nation. By the wars of 1866, 1870 and 1914 Italy skilfully enlarged her frontiers, taking care always to join the winning side. In 1918 she succeeded in bringing about the ruin of her enemy, the Austrian Empire. But something was missing. Victory brought no glory—the Italian Army had scarcely won a battle and their Government's claim to Fiume had been rejected by the peacemakers. Peace brought no prosperity—everywhere in Italy there were strikes and Anarchist outrages in the three years after the war. Liberalism brought no orderly government—the politicians were venal as well as feeble and commanded no respect whatever. Italians needed a new ideal to bind them together as rods were bound round an axe in the *fasces* of Imperial Rome. The new ideal was given her by Benito Mussolini who marched his black-shirted Fascists to Rome in 1922, turned out the Parliament men and made himself Chief Minister under King Victor Emanuel III. Such contempt had he for the old Liberal ideals that he said " the corpse of Liberty is not only dead but stinking." This violent adventurer, caring for nothing but energy and efficiency, was to give stability and strength and pride to the Italians, who within the next decade became a powerful military and industrial nation.

The Years of Plenty. The history of Europe since the war falls into three periods: the years of transition (1918–23), when the victors were busy punishing the vanquished; the years of plenty (1924–29), when the victors lent money to the vanquished in the hope of restoring the pre-war economic system, and the lean years (1929–36), when that system broke down and the greatest economic depression ever known spread over Europe and the whole civilized world.

In the first period the policy of England and France was aimed at making Germany pay. The question was *what* could Germany pay? Conference after conference was held to determine the amount and the manner of Reparation payments but no solution could be reached. French politicians wanted to demand an impossible amount so that Germany would default and France would have an excuse to seize her remaining industrial districts. English politicians preferred not to cripple Germany in a way which would make her unable to buy English goods. At last the French and Belgians got impatient and making a pretext of a minor German default marched into the great industrial district of the Ruhr and established martial law. The first result of this was that the German Government went bankrupt, issuing more and more notes to pay its debts— until the *mark* became valueless. The second result was that England and the United States hit upon another method for extracting Reparations from Germany.

The new method was set out in the report of an international committee presided over by an American banker called Dawes. The Dawes Plan proposed to lend money to Germany so that she could set up industries out of the profits of which Reparations could be paid. First the German Government established a new currency called the Gold Mark. Then in August 1924 it was agreed that a foreign loan of 800,000,000 gold marks should be made to Germany immediately, with which to reconstruct her industries. Reparations were fixed at 1,000,000,000 gold marks for the first year, rising in increased instalments in future years to the standard annuity of 250,000,000,000 gold marks in 1929.

The Dawes Plan inaugurated a more peaceful period of

European history. In England anti-German feeling had largely died down and it was a popular move when at the Locarno Conference of 1925 Germany was allowed to apply for membership of the League of Nations. But France was still uneasy. Twice within living memory her land had been invaded by Germans; she was desperately anxious to have the fullest security against a third invasion. At Locarno England agreed to guarantee one of her frontiers, undertaking to make war against Germany or France if either should attack the other over the Franco-German boundary as laid down at Versailles. This was not enough for France who wanted the whole Versailles Treaty to be guaranteed. She made treaties with Belgium, Poland and the Powers of the Little Entente (Czecho-Slovakia, Jugo-Slavia and Roumania), lending them money to arm themselves against possible attacks from Germany.

On the whole Europe was prosperous in the five years after 1924. The new nations were getting on their feet at last, thanks to foreign money and their own efforts: Poland and Czecho-Slovakia were developing their coal and iron resources, and were on their way to becoming considerable industrial powers; Austria and Hungary enjoyed little economic prosperity, but achieved a momentary political balance between the equal and opposite extremes of Hapsburg restoration and Socialist revolution; and even the kingdom of the Serbs, Croats and Slovenes (Yugo-Slavia) seemed to be surviving the dissensions of her varied peoples and the disapproval of her Italian neighbour. French industry was flourishing, thanks to a financial reconstruction which fixed the franc at a fifth of its former value, and thus enabled France to pay her debts cheaply and to sell her goods cheaply abroad. The German people were basking in the sun of a world which seemed anxious only to lend them money. Under the Dawes Plan money was lent for industrial development, but private American bankers went further: loaded with money which was useless to them unless they could let it out on interest, they lent to Germany and Austria not only for industrial development, but for building town halls, swimming-baths, sports stadiums and for all manner of purposes which could not hope to yield a profit out of which interest could be paid. Between 1924 and 1928 Germany borrowed £720,000,000 from foreign investors.

The World Depression. The world was living in a fool's paradise. The whole economic structure depended on borrowed money which could be paid back only on the assumption that the world would consume rapidly increasing quantities of goods of every sort. If the increase were not rapid interest could not be paid. If interest were not paid more loans would not be made and half the world would go bankrupt.

This is what happened in the World Depression which followed 1929. In the years of plenty the agricultural countries had put so much land under cultivation that the output exceeded the amount the world could afford to buy, so prices dropped, ruining the agriculturists. At the same time American investors got frightened and in October 1929 stocks on the New York Exchange slumped and investors lost most of the money they had paid for their shares. This meant that Americans stopped lending money to Germany—only $550,000,000 was lent in 1929 against $1,000,000,000 in 1928. It also meant that America could not afford to buy goods in the old lavish way, and since America was the richest nation in the post-war world this caused prices to drop still further.

World prices sank to half the level of 1924. Every debtor had therefore to make twice the previous amount of goods in order to pay his old debts. In May 1931 Austria went bankrupt. In July bankruptcy spread to Germany. We shall see in the next chapter how the crisis spread to England; here our immediate concern is with the effect on Europe as a whole.

The effect of bankruptcy and of the ensuing business chaos was that democratic Governments were unable to keep order. In the crisis the bankrupt countries turned to despotism. In Austria, in Poland, in Hungary, in Yugo-Slavia despots ruled. In Germany the Liberal Constitution of Weimar was suspended and Chancellors ruled by absolute decree. The decrees got Germany nowhere and a new revolution prepared itself. Goaded to desperation by the exactions of the Allied Powers under the Versailles Treaty, shamed by the weak Liberalism of the Weimar Republic, Germans turned to a new prophet who preached defiance of Versailles, denounced foreigners and Jews and insisted on the necessity of the rearmament and resurrection of Germany under a National-Socialist Government. The prophet was Adolf Hitler, who in his soaring ideals and humble person (he was the son of a minor Austrian Customs official and had been a house-painter until he joined the Army as a private soldier and was invalided out of the war) seemed to the suffering millions of Germany typical of themselves. In January 1933 Hitler became Chancellor and within two years he had succeeded, as Mussolini had succeeded in Italy, in restoring by threats and violence the strength and self-esteem of Germans and in reinstating Germany as an armed nation in Europe, in spite of the League of Nations.

Failure of the Versailles Settlement. The Versailles Settlement had collapsed. By 1935 the principles of Liberal democracy were preserved in Great Britain, France and the United States alone among the Great Powers. As for Nationalism, it had everywhere run to seed, and in two ways: military and economic. In the League Covenant the Members had recognized that " the maintenance of peace requires the reduction of national armaments to the lowest point consistent with national safety and the enforcement by common action of international obligations." Yet by 1935 every nation was spending more on its armaments than it had spent in 1913; Great Britain's military expenditure, which had been £80 millions in 1913, was estimated

THE VERSAILLES SETTLEMENT AND AFTER 265

at £188 millions for 1936,[1] and Great Britain was by no means the worst offender in this respect. Military barriers between nation and nation were paralleled by economic barriers: after the war every nation had increased tariffs to keep out foreign goods, and after 1929 these tariff walls were built higher and higher as nations strove to become more and more independent of goods from abroad.

The pre-war economic system had been built on two assumptions: the first that a few industrial States should sell manufactured goods to the rest of the world in exchange for food and raw materials; the second that there would always be an increasing demand for goods of all sorts. Both these assumptions had been proved false. Already before the war industrialism had been spreading outside the ring of Great Powers—India, Canada, Australia and Italy, for example, were setting up their own industries; after the war this process was accelerated and other countries such as Poland and Czecho-Slovakia joined the race. Then after 1928 the demand for goods ceased to increase, so that between 1929 and 1934 the total industrial output of the world dropped by 24 per cent. Only the smallest fraction of the distress caused by this can be imagined: food-producers, unable to sell their goods at a profitable price, destroyed them—corn was burned on the Canadian prairies, coffee was thrown into the sea in Brazil; industrialists, unable to sell their goods at all, closed down their factories and dismissed their workers.

According to League of Nations statisticians, 2,821,000 men were unemployed in Great Britain in 1933, over 1,000,000 in Italy and 5,599,000 in Germany.

Statesmen made desperate efforts to put the clock back. A Reparations Conference sitting at Lausanne in 1932 virtually cancelled Reparations, but it was too late to save Germany from Hitlerism. A British Imperial Conference meeting at Ottawa in the same year made trade agreements

[1] These like all other statistics must be taken with a pinch of salt: the £ no longer buys as much as it did, and the pay of soldiers and sailors is much higher in these days.

between Great Britain and the Dominions, but it was too late to think of establishing Empire Free Trade—by the agreements the Dominions did not reduce tariffs on British goods, they merely raised the tariffs on foreign goods. A World Economic Conference meeting in London in 1933 tried to stop the fall of prices and the rise of tariffs and to restore international trade, but it failed utterly because each nation was too busy trying to rescue itself from the Depression to look ahead to an international system. A World Disarmament Conference sat at Geneva from 1933 to 1935, but it had nothing but negative results: while it was sitting Germany increased her armaments and left the League of Nations, Japan invaded Manchuria and left the League of Nations, Mussolini planned to invade Abyssinia and threatened to leave the League of Nations. Conferences could not put the clock back; the hands of time were travelling beyond the nineteenth century and beyond the nineteenth-century ideals which had inspired the peacemakers at Versailles.

Chapter XVI: YEARS OF TRANSFORMATION, 1918-35

The Post-War Slump – The Gold Standard – The " General " Strike – The Crisis of 1931 – The End of *Laisser-faire* – The New British Empire – Conclusion: the Second Industrial Revolution.

WHEN THE WAR ENDED England found herself in an enviable position. People everywhere were anxious to buy the goods which they had denied themselves during the four long years of war-time privation, and they naturally turned to England for clothes and coal and iron and machinery and for money. So England's trade boomed: coalowners and shipowners made fantastic fortunes and the money merchants of the City of London did rousing business. The boom enabled nearly 4,000,000 demobilized soldiers to find jobs in industry as well as hundreds of thousands of women who had signed on for employment during the war. For a time it seemed that the politicians were not exaggerating when they boasted of building " a land fit for heroes to live in."

The Post-War Slump. Then suddenly the boom ended. In two years the emergency post-war demand for goods was satisfied and England found to her astonishment that her three great sources of income were drying up. She was no longer the workshop of the world for other nations had learned the manufacturing game and during the war every State had lent money to its industrialists to set up factories at home. Also the world had found new fuel in oil and a new motive power in electricity and was no longer dependent on British coal. With the decline in the export trade came a decline in English shipping, for less trade meant fewer cargoes to carry. And the investment business was suffering, partly because all the money invested in Russia was lost now the Bolsheviks were in power, and partly—and this was much more important—because American bankers had learned the trick of lending money overseas and had taken advantage of England's pre-occupation in war to make New York instead of London the centre of the world's money-lending transactions.

The end of the boom in England showed itself in a terrifying increase in unemployment. By 1921 a large proportion of the men engaged in coal-mining and in shipbuilding were out of work. The total number of unemployed reached a million in January and had risen to two and a half million by July. It was the most serious crisis England had known since the years after Waterloo.

Lloyd George met the crisis by giving a "dole" of Government money to the unemployed. This was done by an *Unemployment Act* of 1920 which enabled the Unemployment Insurance Fund to borrow money from the Exchequer (a power which was increased by subsequent Acts until the debt of the Fund to the Exchequer in 1931 reached £115,000,000). The dole saved the unemployed from starvation and England from riots but it did nothing to put an end to the slump. Somehow England's industries had to be put on their feet again. Lloyd George tried to do something by his *Safeguarding of Industries Act* of 1921 which protected "industries indispensable in the event of another war" and by putting a tax on foreign goods which were being "dumped" in England, that is, offered for sale at less than the cost of production. But that was only nibbling at the real problem, which was to find a way of making English goods cheap enough for other countries to buy. English goods were expensive because English industries, being the first in the world, were organized on lines which were now out of date, and because English workers, having won a comparatively high standard of living, were anxious to retain if not to increase it. During the war the major industries had been taken over by the Government; the Government might have taken the opportunity to reorganize them after the war, but this would have savoured too much of Socialism, and Lloyd George preferred to return mines and railways to their private owners. The workers persistently demanded State ownership of these industries, especially of the mines where the innumerable private owners were much harder task-masters than the half-dozen great companies who between them controlled all the railways. They believed that State ownership, by cutting out private profits, would make it possible for them to be better paid. The three great Unions of Railwaymen, Transport Workers and Miners reverted to their policy of 1911–12 and carried out strikes on a big scale during the years 1919–21. The result was that the Railwaymen won higher wages (£3 a week) and the Miners shorter hours (7 hours a day), but the reorganization of industry was postponed. So England's goods remained too expensive for foreigners to buy in the old way.

The depression deepened. In 1922 Lloyd George resigned and his Coalition Government was followed by a Ministry of Conservatives under first Bonar Law and then Stanley Baldwin. The Conservatives had a quite definite policy based on two planks: the first was to protect English industries at home by putting tariffs on cheap foreign imports, the second was to win back for the City of London its position as the banker of the world. Before they could impose additional tariffs they felt bound to ask the country's consent and that consent, in 1923 as in 1906, was not forthcoming. The elections returned 257 Conservatives, 158 Liberals and 191 Labour members; and since the Liberals were prepared to combine with Labour to defend their traditional policy of Free Trade it was a Labour Government under Ramsay MacDonald which came into power.

It was the first Labour Government England had ever known, and the electorate, considerably surprised at the Labour victory, was not prepared to let it go far in a Socialist direction. Ramsay MacDonald was anxious to secure the revival of trade with Germany and gave his support to the Dawes Plan and the Locarno Pact. Then he proposed to assist a similar revival of trade with Russia by lending the Soviets money to enable them to buy British goods. The people of England did not trust the Labour politicians much and they did not trust the Soviets at all. A terror of Bolshevism swept the country and MacDonald, obliged to appeal to the electorate, was defeated at the election of 1924 which returned 413 Conservatives, 118 Liberals and only 151 Labour members.

The Gold Standard.

Mr. Baldwin was now able to go on, not with his tariff policy, but with his plan to restore the banking business of the City of London. Now, a banker depends on his reputation for reliability: a customer will deposit a pound with him only if he is sure of being able to get a pound back. But pounds may vary in value (if for example a country chooses to print millions of paper notes its currency will become less valuable): how were customers to be sure that the pound they got back would be of the same value as the pound they deposited? This assurance was given them by Peel's Act of 1819 which obliged the Bank of England to give gold of a definite weight in return for every pound-note presented for exchange, and by Peel's Bank Charter Act of 1844 which obliged the Bank to keep a reserve of gold for all but a few million pounds of its note issue. The Bank Charter Act had been suspended in time of crisis, but on the whole the Gold Standard was maintained. Other countries made their currencies exchangeable for gold and in pre-war days everyone knew how much a pound and a dollar and a franc and a mark and so on were worth in terms of gold. This meant that they knew how much their currencies were worth in terms of other currencies: a Frenchman, for instance, sending 25 francs to England knew that they would buy one pound's worth of goods and therefore he felt safe in trading with England. During the war the Gold Standard had to be suspended because the belligerent countries were spending their gold reserves on military expenses. The pound sank in value and the franc sank still further (consequently Frenchmen had to send more francs than before to buy a pound's worth of English goods and therefore preferred not to buy English goods at all). Only the United States dollar kept its value fairly stable and therefore it was to New York that the world began to send its banking business.

The policy of the Conservatives was to return to the Gold Standard. They expected that this would give foreigners confidence in England and bring the banking business back to London. They also expected that other countries would return to the Gold Standard and that international trade would begin to flow confidently as before. The first move was made in 1923 when Mr. Baldwin promised that England would pay her debt to America in full—£2,200 million in all. The second move was made in 1925 when Winston Churchill, then Chancellor of the Exchequer, announced that the Bank of England would give in exchange for notes gold at the old rate.

This was all very well for the City financiers, to whom financial business duly flowed back to London. But it was hard on the industrialists. England had agreed to pay twenty shillings for every pound she owed and the money had to be found. The burden fell largely on the industrialists who were selling goods to foreigners; these goods now stood at a high price, thanks to the re-valued pound sterling—often at a higher price than foreigners could afford. To make it worse, other countries had no such burden: the French Government paid only a fifth of the money it owed its creditors and the German Government nothing at all.

The " General " Strike. It is not surprising in these circumstances that English industrialists tried to cut down their costs by cutting down the wages they paid their employees. Nor is it surprising that the employees, who cared nothing for the Gold Standards of City financiers, resisted. The mineowners announced that a cut in miners' wages would begin in July 1925. The miners replied that they would strike rather than accept reduced wages. To postpone the evil day the Government gave the coal industry a subsidy (amounting in the end to £24,000,000) to carry it over until April 1926. Meanwhile a Royal Commission reported that the coal industry should be taken over by the State and that the mineowners should lose most of their royalties and the miners some of their wages. The Conservative Government ignored the first parts of the recommendation but insisted that the miners' wages should be cut by over half a crown in the pound. The miners refused, and the Trades Union Congress supported the miners and threatened a General Strike unless the suggested cuts were withdrawn by May 3.

On the morning of May 4 the strike began. It was not really a general strike, for the T.U.C. insisted that workers engaged in essential services such as lighting and sanitation should stay at work. But two and a half million workers—nearly a sixth of the entire working population—were on strike.

Now, if ever, was the time for the Socialist Revolution, for the Class War which Marx had said would take place in England: the industrial workers were united in sympathy with the strike, the middle class was united against it—providing embarrassing numbers of volunteers to unload ships at the docks, drive trains and trams and enroll as Special Constables. But nothing of the kind occurred. The strikers preserved the utmost good-humour; the volunteers had no animosity except for Mr. A. J. Cook, the miners' leader. Never was that respect for law, inbred in Englishmen since the Roman invasion, so remarkably shown. When a great lawyer, Sir John Simon, had given his opinion that every striker was liable to be sued for damages and every strike leader liable to damages " to the utmost farthing of his personal possessions," when Mr. Justice Astbury had declared from the Bench that the strike was " illegal and contrary to the law," the Trades Union Council surrendered unconditionally. The " General " Strike ended on May 12, nine days after it had begun.

A great opportunity had been lost. The Government had lost its chance of reorganizing the mining industry, the miners lost $13\frac{1}{2}$ per cent of their wages—for after staying out on strike for another seven months they had to accept the cuts. The greatest loss fell on the Trades Union Congress which had put its hand to the plough of direct action and had turned back. In 1927 a *Trades Union Act* was passed which limited the right of workmen to strike: any strike calculated to coerce the Government indirectly was declared illegal, any picketing which could be construed as intimidation was declared a crime, and all participation in party politics by Trade Unions composed of Civil Servants was forbidden. Largely as a result of the General Strike's failure and of the Act's restrictions Trade Unionism declined rapidly in the following years. In 1920 there had been 8,334,362 members of Trade Unions; in 1935 there were 3,500,000.

The Crisis of 1931. The years 1927 to 1929 were outwardly calm. The unemployment figure was still over a million and the depression still hung over the great exporting industries (exports for 1924 had been worth £940 millions, in 1929 they were worth £839 millions), but Englishmen still had an average standard of living twice as high as Germans, Frenchmen and Belgians and three times as high as Italians.[1] The Conservative Government sat undisturbed until 1929 when the elections returned 260 Conservatives, 59 Liberals and 287 Labour members. Labour came into office again under Ramsay MacDonald, with their power again confined to what they could do without provoking a union of the two capitalist parties against them.

The calm was giving way now to gathering clouds and distant thunder. Unemployment was rising steadily from 1,200,000 to the two million mark and beyond. There was a nasty scandal in the City over frauds perpetrated by a certain group of financiers. Then came the slump on the New York Stock Exchange which sent the stock exchange quotations of the world jumping and trembling like a barometer before a storm. The storm burst in the summer

[1] According to the calculations of Professor J. W. Angell.

of 1931. On July 14 the Government published the report of the Macmillan Committee on Finance and Industry which had been sitting for the last twenty months. This report exposed to the world the weakness of British finance. It showed that the City had taken to lending money for long periods and borrowing for short periods: thus if foreigners should choose to call back their loans the City would have no means for paying them for a considerable period. The alarm caused by this was increased by the report of the May Committee on National Expenditure (published on July 31) which pointed out that for years Britain had been spending more than her income and that the next Budget would be likely to find the Government £120,000,000 in arrears. To reduce this deficit the May Committee suggested that unemployment pay and wages of Government employees should be immediately cut to save £96,000,000.

The confidence in British finance which politicians had been trying ever since the war to build up was suddenly shattered. Foreigners rushed to withdraw their deposits from London. The gold reserves of the Bank of England were sinking fast. Earlier in July the Governor of the Bank had asked leave of the Government to borrow £50 million from Paris and New York. The £50 million soon disappeared and early in August the Governor was asking leave to borrow another £80 million. Mr. MacDonald was willing but the New York bankers were not: they wanted some assurance that Britain would balance her Budget. This would mean cutting down wages and the dole—a course which the Labour Government was pledged not to take. On August 23 Mr. MacDonald resigned.

A day later he was in office again, but no longer as the head of a Labour Ministry. He had interviewed the King at Buckingham Palace and had returned with the royal assent to a plan for a new coalition. Mr. MacDonald formed an Emergency Cabinet of four Conservatives, two Liberals and four Labour men. It was called a National Government, but it was not national for the Labour party repudiated it and disowned MacDonald and his National

Labour Cabinet Ministers. It was pledged to keep England on the Gold Standard, but it failed to keep its promise. Foreigners were unimpressed by the cuts which it made in the wages of public servants and in unemployment relief: they continued to withdraw their money from England. On September 15 there was a mutiny of sailors at Invergordon in protest against the cuts. Predicting a revolution in Britain, foreigners withdrew their money faster than ever. The Governor of the Bank asked for legislation to permit him to stop paying out gold, and on September 21 the Bill was rushed through Parliament. Britain was off the Gold Standard.

The pound sterling was no longer worth its weight in gold. It became merely a promise to pay. It dropped in value and after a few months settled at about 13s. This meant that for every £ England owed to foreigners she paid only 13s. and thus relieved herself of $\frac{7}{20}$ of her existing foreign debt. It also meant that foreigners were better able to buy English goods, for now they need only send $\frac{13}{20}$ of the former price. This should have meant a big revival of our exporting industries, but the revival was checked by two things: first foreign countries increased their tariffs on English goods, and secondly many nations (chiefly the Scandinavian States, the South American Republics, the British Dominions and Japan) followed us off the Gold Standard and fixed their currencies at about the same level as ours. But on the whole going off the Gold Standard helped English debtors (at the expense of foreign creditors), helped English exporters and did not harm our banking business, for other nations were in worse difficulties than England so that by comparison London still stood out as a model of financial security.

The End of *Laisser-faire*. A General Election held in October 1931, when Englishmen were still in a panic over the crisis, showed that public opinion was behind the National Government. The National group, consisting of many Conservatives, a few Liberals and a handful of MacDonald-Labour men, won 554 seats; the Labour party won 52. The National Government was in power with every prospect of a long term of office. The problems before it were staggering: there were three million unemployed.

The policy the new Government adopted was a complete reversal of the principles on which the economic policy of England had been based for the last hundred years. Free Trade and *laisser-faire*, which had been advocated by Adam Smith in 1776 and put into practice in the early Victorian age, which had made us fabulously rich when we were the first industrial nation in the world and which had been retained in a modified form when our supremacy was threatened by new industrial Powers, were now abandoned. The years 1931–35 marked the end of an epoch in the history of England.

First, the National Government suspended free imports. An *Import Duties Bill* which became law on February 29, 1932, put a tariff of 10 per cent on foreign goods and set up a committee to impose additional tariffs wherever foreign imports should threaten to swamp home products. Thus we turned our backs on Adam Smith's famous dictum that " if a foreign country can supply us with a commodity cheaper than we can make it, better buy it of them with some part of our own industry employed in a way in which we have some advantage."

Secondly, the National Government, to help English exporters, made agreements with a dozen countries (including Denmark, Sweden and the Argentine) by which they were allowed to send a quota of goods to England on condition that they took a certain amount of English goods in exchange. A new principle of planned economy was thus adopted in place of *laisser-faire*.

Thirdly, the principle of planning was extended to industry in two ways. The first of these was the development of a new type of organization known as the Public Utility Company. The private Joint Stock Company, which was the

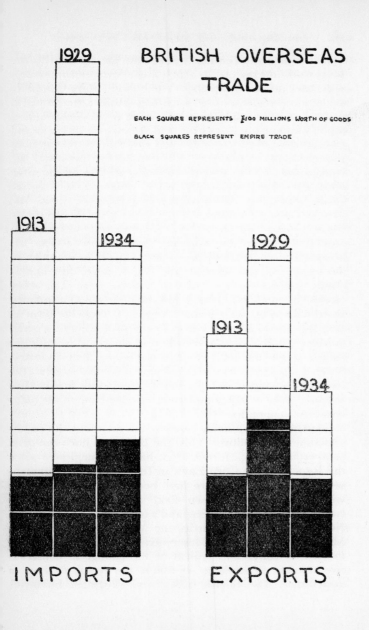

typical nineteenth-century instrument for getting things done, works for the profit of its stock-holders in competition with other private companies. The Public Utility Company works, as its name implies, for public utility; the profits, if any, go to the people who buy what it produces, and it enjoys a monopoly in its own field. In essence this is an old English idea; Peel had chartered the Railway Companies and the Bank of England on public utility lines, and the Universities and the British Museum were run on the same principle. The twentieth century extended the public utility idea to the Metropolitan Water Board (1902), the Port of London Authority (1909), the Central Electricity Board (1926) and the British Broadcasting Corporation (1927). To these the National Government added the London Passenger Transport Board (1933) to organize in the interest of travellers all the trams, buses and underground railways of the Greater London area. The other method of public planning in industry was still in its infancy when this book was being written. It took the form of *Enabling Acts* to allow the majority of producers in a given industry (shipbuilding and cotton-weaving, for example) to submit a scheme for the organization of their industry, which if approved by the Government would be given the force of law and made binding on competing firms. Thus the old system of free competition was reverting to the older system of monoplies.

Fourthly, the National Government set about the reconstruction of agriculture. This, the basic and once the most prosperous of English industries, had been neglected since the Repeal of the Corn Laws in 1846. Since the eighteen-seventies English farmers had been unable to compete with cheap foreign-grown food and by the nineteen-twenties 60 per cent of England's food came from abroad. Now in the nineteen-thirties the Minister of Agriculture, Major Walter Elliot (a Conservative who had once been a Fabian—a conversion typical of the change in conservative opinion generally), set about the reorganization of agriculture. The British farmer was protected by tariffs on foreign food, by subsidies to help him to grow wheat and sugar-beet and by monopolies to allow him to fix the price of such things as milk, pigs, bacon, herrings, hops and beef. The monopolies were legalized by a number of *Marketing Acts* enabling two-thirds of the producers of any one commodity to plan the quantity, quality and price of their products and giving this plan (once it had received official approval) the force of law.

By this reversal of nineteenth-century policy the National Government restored the self-confidence of England which had been badly shaken by the post-war slump and by the crisis of 1931. It succeeded in balancing the Budget—with the aid of a reduction of the interest on £2,000,000,000 of War Loan from 5 per cent to $3\frac{1}{2}$ per cent and by a refusal to pay the war debts owed to America. And if it had failed to solve the problem of unemployment—nearly 2,000,000 men were still idle in the North of England and South Wales, where industry had once been most flourishing—it showed at least that England was still capable of making by methods of peaceful evolution the adaptations which other countries could only achieve by bloody revolution.

The New British Empire.

Meanwhile changes equally fast and far-reaching had been taking place in the Empire. The ideals which divided the Committee of Four who made the Versailles Settlement were the ideals which had divided Gladstone and Disraeli. Wilson stood for an almost Gladstonian Liberalism: " Remember that the sanctity of life in the hill villages of Afghanistan, among the winter snows, is as inviolable in the eye of Almighty God as can be your own. Remember that He who has united you as human beings in the same flesh and blood, has bound you by the law of mutual love "—Wilson would have echoed this. Lloyd George stood for a more-than-Disraelian Imperialism: we have seen how he sent armies to collect British debts from Soviet Russia and spread the British net over the Near East by accepting Mandates for Palestine and Iraq. But Lloyd George fell in 1922 and his Liberal Imperialism did not reflect the real trend of British postwar policy. The imperialist spirit of late Victorian England had vanished; Englishmen no longer believed in their mission to administer the world, and the few politicians like Winston Churchill who still held that faith were regarded as reactionaries. Englishmen now held, subject to one provision, the nationalist creed. They believed in the right of every people to govern itself. The provision was that the people concerned should show itself able and willing to safeguard English commerce and English investments.

Thus when nationalist risings broke out all over the Near and Far East in the post-war years England bowed to them, provisionally. When Persia rose under Riza Khan in 1921 and repudiated the treaty of 1907 which had divided her country in " spheres of influence " for Russia and for Great Britain, England recognized Riza, who was willing for the Anglo-Persian Oil Company to remain the greatest industrial concern in his kingdom. When Iraq under Feisal demanded independence, England granted it and surrendered her Mandate in 1925, the English Oil Companies in Mosul remained the greatest industry in Iraq. When Egypt made similar claims through the mouth of Zaglul and the Wafd, or Nationalist Party, England by a treaty of 1922 declared Egypt to be a " sovereign, independent State," but, because she feared that no Egyptian Government could safeguard the Suez Canal (for which England together with France and Italy was responsible by treaty), she kept her garrison in Cairo. It was the same in the Far East. When the Chinese Nationalist party (Kuomintang) marched north from Canton to Pekin in 1926, England surrendered many of her " treaty ports " to the Kuomintang, and when that party split she gave support in the form of money and expert advice to the strongest faction, which set up a Government at Nanking under Chiang-Kai-Shek.

In India the problem was more complicated. There

were £1,000,000,000 of British money invested there. Besides, England had undertaken serious responsibility for the good government of the huge country. In 1917 she announced her policy to be that of " the increasing association of Indians in every branch of the administration, and the gradual development of self-governing institutions with a view to the progressive realization of responsible government in India as an integral part of the British Empire." To this policy of gradual development England kept. In 1919 a series of reforms were inaugurated (known from the names of the Secretary for India and the Viceroy as the Montagu–Chelmsford Reforms) which gave to Indians in the Councils of the provinces the control of certain transferred subjects, such as agriculture, education and public health. But the key subject, finance, was kept in British hands. This system of divided rule was known as dyarchy. In the Central Government there was no dyarchy: the central power remained with the British, though there was an Indian Legislative Assembly with power to debate but not to legislate.

The Indian National party (Congress) refused to cooperate in the constitution. The Mahatma Gandhi, a man of great spiritual influence, joined the Nationalists and taught them how to resist the British by soul-force, or passive resistance. The movement spread like a religion; the British imprisoned Nationalists till the gaols of India were full, but there were always new passive-resisters to take the place of the prisoners.

In 1927 the British Government sent out a Commission under the chairmanship of Sir John Simon to report on the working of the Montagu–Chelmsford Reforms. The Commission reported that dyarchy had failed. It was time to frame a new Constitution. The advice of the leading princes and people of India was sought at two Round Table Conferences and at last, in 1935, a new Constitution of India was passed by Parliament. This made a further step in the direction of Indian self-government. British India and the India of the Princes were joined in a federated State which was to have a Government elected by Indians. The Federation was, however, bound to accept British control over finance, foreign policy and military defence.

With her African colonies, where the people were of a much lower standard of civilization, England went much more slowly in the direction of self-government. As Governor of Nigeria, Lord Lugard had inaugurated a policy known as Indirect Rule by which the British made the laws and the natives were left to carry them out, subject to supervision by British administrators. After the war " Indirect Rule " was extended to Uganda and to the Mandated Territory of Tanganyika. It was not extended to Kenya where 17,000 British settlers continued to hold the only cultivatable land and to use the labour of the natives to work it.

Meanwhile in the self-governing Dominions changes in a similar direction were being made. Canada, Australia, New Zealand, South Africa and the Irish Free State became members of the League as fully-fledged States. At the Imperial Conference of 1926 a new formula was found to describe the relations between Great Britain and the Dominions: they were declared to be " autonomous communities within the British Empire, equal in status, in no way subordinate one to another in any aspect of their domestic or external affairs, though united by a common allegiance to the Crown and freely associated as members of the British Commonwealth of Nations." This declaration was given the force of law by the Statute of Westminster (1931): the Dominions were declared to be as independent of the " Mother " country as they were of each other, and there was no legal bond between them but the Crown. Whether a Dominion might secede at will from the Commonwealth, and whether it might remain neutral if Great Britain declared war, were left moot points.

The members of the British Empire were moving steadily towards self-government. Only in two countries was there a movement in the opposite direction. In Malta, which had been a British Colony since 1814 and had been granted control over its local affairs in 1921, a quarrel arose between the British party and the Maltese Nationalists who wanted a closer connection with the Roman Church and with Fascist Italy; the result was that in 1933 the British Colonial Office took over all control of Maltese affairs. In Newfoundland, which was the oldest British colony and had been given self-government in 1855, a shocking state of bankruptcy and corruption developed which obliged the Newfoundland Government to surrender its powers and to accept the control of commissions appointed by England.

The British Empire was one of the few to survive the Great War of 1914. It survived because it let itself move in accordance with the spirit of the age.

Conclusion: the Second Industrial Revolution.

When the Great War of 1792–1815 ended Englishmen found themselves, as we said in the first sentence of this book, living in a new world. When the Great War of 1914–18 ended Englishmen found that their world had changed again. It was not a change back to pre-1815 conditions (history never repeats itself, though human nature is always the same), but neither was it a change along the lines laid down between 1815 and 1914.

The changes which dislocated English life with the coming of the Machine at the beginning of the nineteenth century were: first a rapid increase in population, secondly a shift of population from the South to the North of England, thirdly the growth of the great coal, iron and cotton industries, and fourthly the emergence of a new principle known as *laisser-faire*. By the end of the first third of the twentieth century progress in each of these directions was seen to be coming to an end.

First, the pace of the increase of the population was slowing down. It is true that the 1931 census showed more people in Great Britain than ever before, but the increase was caused not by more children being born but by old people being kept alive for a longer period, thanks to medical science and better living conditions. In 1921 there were in Great Britain twelve million children under fifteen years of age. In 1931 there were less than eleven million. As these children come to the age for rearing families themselves the birth-rate must decline still further, and since old people cannot be kept alive for ever the total population must soon decline. It has been estimated that the population which in 1931 was 44,833,500 will sink to 42,671,900 by 1951, and that after 1951 the decrease will be more rapid.

Secondly, the population is shifting from the North and the industrial areas of South Wales to the Midlands and South of England. Between 1921 and 1931, when the population of England itself increased by 1,600,000, that of Wales and Scotland decreased by 90,000. Within England the counties of Durham and Northumberland lost 10 per cent of their population by migration while in the counties round London migration added 10 per cent to Buckinghamshire, 12 per cent to Essex, 15 per cent to Hertfordshire, 22 per cent to Sussex and actually 24 per cent to Middlesex. In the Midlands the population of the cities of Coventry and Birmingham increased by 200,000 between 1921 and 1931.

Thirdly—and this explains the second point—the great exporting industries of coal- and iron-mining, cotton- and wool-weaving and shipbuilding which had brought the population to the North in the nineteenth century were almost at a standstill. In the South Durham coalfield, where only a hundred and ten years ago the first railway had been laid to carry coal to the sea and where the opening of the pits had in a century sent the population up from 13,000 to 135,000, nearly all the pits were now closed and three-quarters of the working population was unemployed: the district was derelict. In industrial Scotland one-fifth, in South Wales one-quarter of the workers were unemployed. In Lancashire the conditions were as bad, in the West Riding they were not much better. The world

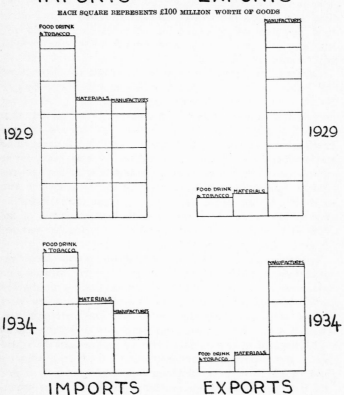

no longer wanted the old quantities of the old manufactures from England.

Faced with the loss of her export markets, England fell back on her markets at home and began to concentrate on supplying her own people with the goods which they had got into the habit of buying from overseas. Also England fell back on the skill of her craftsmen—that traditional skill which since the invention of machinery had made English machines the soundest in the world—and began to concentrate on turning it into new channels so that, in spite of tariffs and nationalist prejudices, people in foreign countries insisted on having their aircraft and warships and luxury cars made in England. New industries were growing up in the Midlands and the South to take the place of the old heavy industries of the North. In a generation the vast motor-car industry had grown up from nothing. Similar development was taking place in radio, rayon, and in a hundred smaller industries producing light domestic appliances and products of skilled engineering. Whether Great Britain would be able to change the whole balance of economy from heavy to light industry and find work of the new type for the people of her distressed areas was still an open question in 1935.

Finally, the principle behind Britain's policy changed from free competition (*laisser-faire*) to State Socialism. In 1815 the *laisser-faire* had done its work. It had let private individuals make unhampered use of their wits to develop the new machines and to use them to produce goods in quantities hitherto undreamed of, till mankind who for æons had lived in scarcity now lived in an age of plenty. Two million people—a sixth of the working population—were now unemployed: the necessary work of the world could be done without them. *Laisser-faire* had solved the problem of production; the time had come for public control to solve the problem of distribution and to turn unemployment into leisure. In 1815 the people were left to struggle for existence and the devil was allowed to take the hindmost. By 1935 the State had made itself responsible for educating the young, maintaining the unemployed and aged and for tending the sick. (*See* Appendix I.) At the same time the State was beginning to limit free competition in transport, manufacturing, food-production and in an increasing number of other activities.

This did not mean that England was becoming a Socialist State. Profits still went to private shareholders and the means of production were owned by a small majority of the people: nine-tenths of the people—those with less than £5 a week—were getting little more than half of the national income. But it did mean that the principles which the nineteenth century had called *laisser-faire*, or the Iron Laws of Political Economy, had gone. England had abandoned

> *The good old rule,*
> *The simple plan,*
> *That they should take who have the power*
> *And they should keep who can.*

APPENDICES

Appendix I: The Social Services.

No Government action has affected the lives of the majority of the people of England more than the increase in Social Services—that is, in services provided for the needy out of the public purse. In the early nineteenth century, in the heyday of *laisser-faire*, there were scarcely any Social Services except the Poor Law. Even in 1890 there were not many: education, housing and the treatment of certain diseases were, with poor-relief, almost the only forms of public service. To-day there is some form of Social Service provided for the citizen at every stage of his life if he is poor enough to need it. The child may be born in a public maternity home, vaccinated by a public official, cared for at infant welfare centres till he is five and educated at public elementary schools till he is at least fourteen. He has measles in a public hospital, swims in a public pool, plays in a public park. At the age of sixteen if he can get work and pays his weekly contributions the lad is insured against sickness, disablement and unemployment. If he cannot get work or loses his job and exhausts his unemployment insurance benefit he is kept in the necessities (though not in the comforts) of life by the Public Assistance Committee. When he marries he may live in a Council house, part of the cost of which is paid out of public money. When he grows old he receives a public pension, and when he dies he may be buried at public expense in a public cemetery. And then, as Sydney Smith would have said, he will be gathered to his fathers to be socially served no more.

The chief services and the cost in the years 1890 and 1933 are as follows:

APPENDICES

	1890 million pounds	1933 million pounds
Education	12	102·3
Hospitals, Mental Treatment, and Maternity and Child Welfare	1.4	22·6
Housing	0.2	44·8
Poor Relief	9	46
Unemployment Insurance	none	101·5
Health Insurance	none	36
Contributory Pensions for Widows, Orphans and the Aged	none	42
Old Age Pensions	none	41
War Pensions	none	43

The cost of all this was therefore about £480 million in 1933—over twenty times the cost of the Social Services in 1890—and this sum is certain to be increased in the near future. Of the whole expenditure of the Government (central and local) one-third goes on the Social Services. Where does the money come from? It is paid very largely by the same class of people who benefit by the services. A Government Committee (under Lord Colwyn) came to the conclusion in 1925 that the man earning £100 a year paid (particularly in indirect taxes on tea, sugar, tobacco, matches, beer, etc.) a larger proportion of his income than the man earning £1,000 a year.

Appendix II: Local Government.

AT THE BEGINNING of the period dealt with in this book the local government of England and Wales was carried on by Justices of the Peace—unpaid country gentlemen numbering about 5,000 in all, of whom one in four was a parson. In addition there were in 178 " boroughs," or towns which had once been granted a royal charter, Municipal Corporations—exclusive groups of local magnates. Local government then consisted in licensing public-houses, administering the law and looking after roads, paupers and prisons. That was all, or nearly all, though the Corporations sometimes provided police for their borough and regulated markets and maintained harbours.

To-day local government is carried on by Councils of men and women who are elected by the ratepayers. The chief organ of local government, except in the big towns, is the County Council (of which there are 59). Below the County Councils are Borough Councils (278) for medium-sized towns, Urban District Councils (697) for small towns and Rural District Councils (538) for country areas. Below the latter are Parish Councils (7,200), the duties of which are rapidly diminishing. The big towns are administered by County Borough Councils (83), with the exception of London for which there is the London County Council having under it 28 Municipal Boroughs and the City of London itself. This complicated system is illustrated diagrammatically on page 293.

Local government performs a vast number of functions in addition to those performed a century ago. Some of the more important of these are:

HEALTH

    including the provision of:

        Drainage and Sewage and Pure Water Supply.
        Mental Hospitals and Maternity Hospitals.
        Playgrounds and Swimming-pools.
        Food Inspection.
        Treatment for certain diseases.

EDUCATION

    including the provision of :

        Elementary Schools
            for children under 14. There are roughly 20,000 elementary schools with a total of 5,000,000 pupils.
        Secondary Schools
            for children from 11 to 18. There are about 1,700 Secondary Schools, with 450,000 pupils.

Central Schools, Day Continuation Schools, Junior Technical Schools, Evening Institutes, University Grants, etc.

Museums and Libraries
(There were 190,000,000 books borrowed from public libraries in 1934.)

TRANSPORT
including the provision of:
Roads and Paving, Lighting, Marking and Bridge-building.
Trams and Buses
(Over 4,000,000,000 journeys were made on these in 1933.)

PUBLIC ASSISTANCE
including the provision of:
Institutions (Workhouses).
Hospitals (Infirmaries).
Domiciliary Relief (Outdoor Relief).

HOUSING
including
Slum clearance.
Building of new houses (between 1923 and 1933 new houses built by local authorities numbered 704,000).
Town planning and Country planning.

POLICE
(There are nearly 60,000 police in England and Wales, costing over £20,000,000 a year.)

A hundred years ago the cost of local government was £10 million per annum; to-day it is £500 million. About half of the money is raised by the local Councils, largely in the form of rates—rates being so much in every pound of the value of houses and other property. The other half is made up by grants from the Central Government.

The local Councils derive their powers from Acts of Parliament, but the Central Government does not interfere directly in local affairs. The English system is to leave the conduct of local affairs to local authorities and to rely on inspection, advice and financial control to keep them up to the mark. A few of the Acts which applied new principles to local government are listed below:

Poor Law Amendment Act, 1834
   putting the administration of poor-relief under elected Boards of Guardians (in the Unions) and the Guardians under Central Commissioners.

Municipal Reform Act, 1835
   establishing Councils elected by ratepayers in certain towns.

Public Health Act, 1848
   setting up Central Board of Health and authorizing appointment of local Medical Officers of Health.

Public Health Act, 1875
   making the Board of Guardians authorities for sanitation as well as poor-relief.

Local Government Act, 1888
   establishing Councils elected by ratepayers in counties (including London).

Local Government Act, 1929
   abolishing Boards of Guardians and giving their power over Health and Poor-Relief to the County Councils who appoint Public Assistance Committees to look after the able-bodied poor.

Town-Planning Act, 1932
   giving Councils power to plan built-up areas (by an Act of 1909 they had power to plan undeveloped areas). The rebuilding of England's cities and the abolition of slums should result from this Act.

A century of progress in local government has achieved some remarkable things. The death-rate has been reduced by half and the rate of infant mortality by three-quarters. Diseases such as typhus, cholera, small-pox and typhoid fever, which were general a hundred years ago, have been almost wiped out. Illiteracy has been abolished. It is a fact that local government affects the life of the average citizen much more closely than Central Government—which seems odd when we consider that some 75 per cent of the electorate vote at General Elections, while only 30 per cent to 50 per cent trouble to vote at local elections.

Counties		
Rural Districts	Urban Districts	Municipal Boroughs
Parishes		

County Boroughs

London County	
Metropolitan Boroughs	City of London

Appendix III: Overseas Investment.

AT THE BEGINNING of the twentieth century, Englishmen were investing abroad half their annual savings. Of the whole wealth of England about one-quarter was invested in overseas countries in 1914. Yet in 1815 the proportion invested overseas was insignificant. Foreign investment on a large scale is of comparatively new development.

It began when England became the first industrial country and London financiers lent money to foreigners to help them to buy English goods. First they lent to the war-stricken states of Europe, then to the South American Republics, then to any countries that wanted to build railways. In the 1870's there was a lull in lending: foreigners could not repay—it was the time of the Great Depression. But in the 80's money began to flow out of England again, this time to develop the Colonies and Dominions. In the twentieth century a new wave of foreign lending began.

Englishmen were buying shares in the oil-fields of Persia and Turkey and in the new industries of the Far East.

The following table shows roughly how much British money was invested abroad annually between 1860 and 1929:

Annual average for the period	*Millions of Pounds*
1860–64	30
1865–69	39
1870–74	61
1875–79	1
1880–84	24
1885–89	61
1890–94	46
1894–99	27
1900–04	21
1904–09	109
1910–13	185
–	–
1920–24	115
1925–29	99
1930–34	53

What would have happened if this money had been spent at home? That cannot be discussed here; there are no " ifs " in history.

INDEX

ABDUL HAMID II, Sultan of Turkey, 225, 229
Aberdeen, Lord, 122
Abolition of Slavery Bill, 67
Abyssinia, Italy's attack on, 258, 266
Acre, British capture of, 116
Act of Union, 167
Acts of Parliament:
    Abolition of Slavery, 36, 67, 99
    Artisans' Dwellings, 149
    Bank Holidays, 25
    Banks Charter, 89, 90, 97, 270
    British North American, 191
    Catholic Emancipation, 60, 88
    Coercion Bill, 173
    Combination Acts, 42, 43
    Corn Laws, 30, 90
    Crown Colonies, 190
    Disestablishment of the Irish Church, 171
    during reign of George III, 14
    Education, 1870, 140, 200
        1880, 200
        1902, 211
    Enabling, 278
    Factory, 67, 142, 199
    Friendly Societies, 150
    Game Laws, 15
    Habeas Corpus suspended, 40
    Import Duties, 276
    Joint-Stock Banks, 56
        Companies, 136
    Land Act 1870, 172
        1881, 173
    Land Purchase, 174
    Legalization of Trade Unions, 43
    Licensing, 142
    Local Government, 1888, 210, 292
        1929, 292
    Marketing, 279
    Married Women's Property, 197
    Mines, 142
    Minimum Wage, 216
    Municipal Reform, 71, 72, 73, 292
    National Health Insurance, 213
    Navigation, 51
    Old Age Pensions, 212
        ament, 213
        Law, 79
        mendment, 69, 70, 73, 292
        ohibition of truck, 86

Acts of Parliament—*contd.*
    Public Health, 1848, 292
        1875, 292
    Reform Bill, 65, 66
        Second, 139
        Third, 164
        Fourth, 228
    Restriction of Child Labour, 25
    Roman Catholic Emancipation, 60, 88, 169
    Safeguarding of Industries, 268
    Secret Ballot, 141
    Settlement Acts, 16
    Six Acts of 1819, 41
    Ten-Hour Day, 93, 199
    Town-Planning, 292
    Trade Boards, 212
    Trade Union Acts, 200, 273
    Unemployment Act, 268
        Insurance, 213
    Workman's Compensation, 210
    Wyndham Act, 173
Adelaide, colony founded at, 103
Advertisements, tax on, abolished, 138
Aerated Bread Company formed, 197
Afghanistan, Kandahar province seized by British, 155
    national independence regained, 160
    war in, 108
Africa, British and French clash in, 220
    Europe in (map), 189
    exploration of, 155
    grab for territory in, 187
    Indirect rule policy in, 282
    See also South Africa
Agadir incident, 227
Agricultural workers, hardships of, 16
    riots of, 43
    wages of, 14, 16, 24
Agriculture and Tariff Reform, 192
    development of, 15, 16
    neglect of, 147
    reconstruction of, 278
Albert of Saxe-Coburg, Prince Consort, 77, 94, 119, 120, 194
Albert Memorial built, 196
Alexander I, Tsar of Russia, 45, 48, 50, 51

INDEX

Alexander II, Tsar of Russia, and war with Turkey, 123
 despotic rule of, 124
Algeciras, Conference of, 226
Allenby, Lord, 246
Allgemeine Elektrizitäts Gesellschaft (A.E.G.), 222
Alsace annexed by Prussia, 128
 returned to France, 252
America. *See* United States of America
Anatolia, 255
Ancient Order of Foresters, 150
Angell, Professor J. W., 273
Anglo-Persian Oil Company, 280
Anti-Corn Law League, 91
Anti-Slavery Society formed, 36
Apprentice-children, 26
Arabi Pasha, 161
Arabs in the Great War, 246
Architecture in Regency Period, 37
Argentine Republic, exports to, 57
Arkwright, Sir Richard, invents spinning machine, 19
Armaments, post-war expenditure on, 264
 race in, 220, 221, 226
Armenians given Eastern Anatolia, 255
 massacred in Turkey, 220
Armistice, 1918, 247, 248, 250
Army, commissions in, 141
Arnold, Matthew, 145, 196
Asia, Europe in (map), 219
Asquith, Herbert H., 175, 193, 212, 214, 242
Astbury, Mr. Justice, on the General Strike, 272
Attwood, Thomas, demands currency reform, 75, 76
Auckland, Lord, Governor-General of India, 108
Austen, Jane, 37
Austin, Alfred, Poet Laureate, 185
Australia, an independent member of League of Nations, 282
 becomes a Dominion, 191
 given German Pacific Islands, 258
 gold discovered in, 89, 113
 in 1815, 100
 industrial growth of, 265
 meat trade with, 191
 self-governing colonies in, 105
 supports dock-workers' strike, 205
 trade with, 113
 troops of, in Gallipoli, 239
Austria, alliance proposed between Prussia, Russia and, 48
 alliance with Germany and Italy, 220

Austria, annexes Bosnia and Herzegovina, 226
 collapse of, 247
 defeats Serbia, 239
 Italian revolt against, 118
 Italy breaks free from, 124
 declares war on, 236
 obtains Lombardy and Venetia, 46
 Republic of, 253, 259, 262-4
 risings of 1848, 118
 sends troops to suppress Naples revolt, 50
 tries to annex Serbia, 229
 war with Prussia, 127

BADEN-POWELL, COLONEL, 186
Bakewell, William, 15
Baldwin, Stanley, 228, 269, 270, 271
Balfour, Lord, and social reform, 210
 rule of in Ireland, 174
Balkan League formed, 229
Balkans, Christians in revolt in, 152
 crisis of 1913 in, 229
 proposed (1853) division of, 121
 Turks in, 57
 settlement (1878) of war in, 154
Ballot, secret, 75
Baluchistan taken by British, 155
Bananas introduced into England, 144, 190
Bank Holiday Act, 25
Bank of England, 30, 87, 89, 274
Bankers and Spanish revolts, 54
Banking, 30, 56, 87, 89, 270, 275
Bantu race of South Africa, 158, 187
Barbary pirates, 49
Barclays Bank, 56
Baring, banking house of, 55
Baring, Sir Evelyn. *See* Cromer, Lord
Barnato, Barney, 184
Battles:
 Alma, 122
 Balaclava, 122
 Cambrai, 243
 Caporetto, 243
 Chilianwala, 108
 Colenso, 186
 Dogger Bank, 236
 El Obeid, 163
 Festubert, 237
 Gujerat, 108
 Inkerman, 122
 Isandhlwana, 159
 Jutland, 240
 Kimberley, 186
 Ladysmith, 186

INDEX

Battles—*contd.*
  Mafeking, 186
  Magdala, 156
  Magenta, 124
  Majuba Hill, 161
  Marne, 233
  Mons, 233
  Navarino Bay, 60
  Neuve-Chapelle, 237
  Omdurman, 188
  Paardeburg, 186
  Passchendaele, 243
  Pieter's Mill, 186
  Plevna, 152
  Rorke's Drift, 159
  St. Mihiel, 247
  Sedan, 128
  Sinope, 121
  Solferino, 124
  Somme, 240, 246
  Spion Kop, 186
  Tannenberg, 235
  Tel-el-Kebir, 161
  Vaalkranz, 186
  Verdun, 239
  Vittorio Veneto, 247
  Ypres, 235
Beaconsfield, Lord, and the Russo-Turkish War, 152, 154
  and Chartism, 77
  and Socialism, 203
  becomes Prime Minister, 148
  books of, 82, 83
  career of, 82
  death of, 160
  fall of Ministry of, 159
  Imperial policy of, 149, 159
  negotiates purchase of Suez Canal shares, 151
  on colonial independence, 106
  on Peel, 87, 92
  opposition to Gladstone, 139
  social reforms of, 149
  South African policy of, 158
Beale, Dorothy, 197
Beatty, Earl, in Battle of Jutland, 240
Beer Bill, 63
Beit, Alfred, 183
Belgium, African possessions of, 188
  Eupen-Malmédy given to, 257
  first king of, 62
  independence of, 62
    violated by Germany, 230, 241
  industrialization of, 182
  revolution of 1830, 61
  treaty with France, 262
Bell, Dr., 68
Bentham, Jeremy, 80
Bentinck, Lord William, 107
Benz motor-cars, 195

Berkshire, agricultural riots in, 43
Berlin, Congress of, 154, 226
  Treaty of, 226
Berlin-Baghdad Railway, 225, 226
Besant, Mrs. Annie, 205
Bessemer process of steel production, 132, 145
Beyrout, British capture of, 116
Bicycles invented, 195
Birkbeck, George, founds Mechanics' Institute, 68
Birmingham, 18, 21, 65, 71, 72, 76
Bismarck, Prince Otto von, 118, 126–8, 188, 209, 213, 224, 226
Blake, William, 31
Blanc, Louis, 118
Blanketeers, March of the, 40
Blatchford, Robert, 206
Board of Education established, 68
Board of Guardians established, 70
Board Schools started, 140, 211
Boer War, the first, 160
  the second, 185
Boers, hatred of British rule, 99, 158
Bohemia, 118, 259
Bokhara captured by Russia, 124
Bolivia, independence of, 54
Bolsheviks in Russia, 244, 251, 259
Booth, Charles, 215
Booth, William, founds the Salvation Army, 196
Borough Councils, 290
  elections, 71
Borrow, George Henry, 23
Botha, General, 187
Boulton, Matthew, 20
Bourbons, revolt against, 50
Boxer rising, 218
Boycott, Captain, 173
Bradford, 22, 71, 72
Brandreth, Captain, 40
Brassey, Thomas, 136
Bratianu, Ion, 241
Brazil, Cochrane commands fleet of, 54
Bridge-building, 291
Bridgewater, Duke of, 23
Bright, John, and the Corn Laws, 90
Brindley, James, 23
Bristol riots, 66
British Colonies:
  convicts transported as slaves to, 100, 103
  cost of defending, 106
  development of, 190
  emigration to, 101
  fever in, 190
  forced to trade with England, 51

British Colonies—*contd.*
  Government apathy towards, 106
  in South Africa, 158
  self-government for, 104 *et seq.*
  trade with, 112, 190
    in 1846, 106
    restrictions on, 51, 53
  troops contributed to the war by, 239
Dominions:
  first conference of leaders of, 194
  independent membership of League of Nations, 282
  new relations with Great Britain, 282
  troops contributed to the war, 239
Empire:
  Chamberlain's work for, 183, 190
  contingents in South African War, 186
  extension of, necessary for economic supremacy, 183
  in 1815, 98
  newness of, 98
  not a commercial unit, 193
  Nyasaland and Uganda become part of, 218
  principles of government of, 104
  Rhodes's work for, 183 *et seq.*
  South Africa added to, 187
  the new, 279
Mandated Territories, 258
ports in China, 112
settlers in the colonies, 102 *et seq.*, 114
British and Foreign Bible Society, 68
British Broadcasting Corporation, 278
British East Africa Company, 188
British North American Act, 191
British South Africa Company formed, 184
Brontë, Charlotte, 84
Brougham, Lord, 38, 56, 69
Browning, Robert, 145
Bruce, James, exploration of, 155
Brunel, I. K., 132
Buckingham Palace rebuilt, 37
Buenos Aires, independence of, 55
Builders' Union, 202
Building Societies, 200
Bulawayo, capture of, 184
Bulgaria, 152, 154, 229, 247
Buller, Charles, 104

Burgers, President of the Boers, 158
Burns, John, Socialist leader, 205, 206
Buss, Frances, 197
Byron, Lord, 32, 39, 55, 59

CABLES, FIRST, across the Atlantic, 114
  from Dover to Calais, 145
Cambridge University, improved education at, 69
  women's colleges in, 197
Cameroons under British and French Mandate, 258
Campbell-Bannerman, Sir Henry, 213
Canada as independent member of League of Nations, 282
  becomes a Dominion, 191
  self-governing, 105
  Free Trade treaty with America, 105
  grain trade with, 191
  in 1815, 98
  industrial growth of, 265
  Lord Elgin's work in, 105
  preferential treatment on corn from, 53
  rebellions of 1837, 104
  shipbuilding industry in, 99, 112
  tax on timber from, 53
  trade with, 113
  union of French and English, 105
Canadian Pacific Railway, 191
Canal construction, 23
Canning, George, commercial policy of, 51
  death of, 60
  Eastern policy of, 57 *et seq.*
  foreign policy of, 53
  on South American republics, 55
Canning, Lord, Governor-General of India, 109
Canterbury, N.Z., British colony at, 103
Cape Colony in 1815, 99
  Rhodes, Prime Minister of, 184
Capital in industry, 134
  invested abroad, 136, 293, 294
Capitalism accepted by Trade Unions, 206
  and neglect of workers, 24
  and the trade cycle, 90
  Cobbett's indictment of, 33
  introduced into manufacture, 20
  Marx on, 129
Carlyle, Thomas, 70, 81, 85
Caroline, Queen, 38
Carpenter, Edward, 204
Carpenters' Union, 202

INDEX

Carson, Sir Edward, forms private army in Ireland, 175
Cartels, 222
Cartwright, Edward, invents weaving-loom, 19
Casement, Sir Roger, 176
Castlereagh, Lord, 39
 and the Congress system, 49
 at the Vienna Congress, 45
 on Tsar Alexander I, 48
 passes the Six Acts, 41
 refuses to interfere in foreign internal politics, 50
Catholic Association in Ireland, 169
 Emancipation, 60, 88
  Bill passed, 169
  O'Connell and, 169
  Pitt and, 167
Cavendish, Lord Frederick, murder of, 173
Cavour, Count Camillo di, 124, 260
Cawnpore, massacres in, 111
 mutiny in, 110
Central Electricity Board, 278
Cetewayo, Zulu King, 158
Ceylon retained by England, 49
Chaka, Zulu Chief, 158
Chamberlain, Joseph, commercial policy of, 191
 founds Tariff Reform League, 192
 Imperial policy of, 190
 on development of markets, 183
Charles X, King of France, 61
Chartism, 76–7, 81, 93, 141, 199
Chateaubriand, 54
Chelmsford, Lord, in the Zulu War, 159
Cheltenham Ladies' College, 197
Cheques introduced, 89
Children as chimney-sweeps, 27, 200
 in industry, 26
 restricted employment of, 67
Chile, Cochrane commands fleet of, 54
China, 112, 218, 280
Church of England, Oxford Movement in, 78
Church Schools, Bible classes in, 36
Churches, Radicals' opposition to, 35
Churchill, Winston, 215, 228, 271
Cinema, first opened, 195
Civil Service, 141, 274, 275
Clapham Sect, 35
Clare, John, on village evils, 31
Clarence, Duke of, becomes William IV, 38
Clarion, the, 206
Clarkson, Thomas, as reformer, 36

Clemenceau, M., and peace terms, 251
Coaching, 23
Coal, 21, 23, 135, 222, 269, 271, 272
Coalition Government of 1931, 274
Cobbett, William, 14, 24, 32, 65
Cobden, Richard, 90, 91, 109, 139
Cochrane, Thomas. See Dundonald, Lord
Coercion Bill, 173
Coffee, reduction of tax on, 52
Coke, Thomas, 15
Cold storage invented, 191
Coleridge, Samuel Taylor, 32
Colley, Sir George, 160
Collins, Michael, 178, 179
Colombia, independence of, 55
Colonies, foreign as mandated territories, 257
 British. See British Colonies
 German, divided among Allies, 253, 257
Colonization, Wakefield's principles of, 102
Colwyn, Lord, 289
Combination Acts, 42–3
Common land, 13, 14, 37, 149
Commune in Paris, 203
Communication, development in means of, 22
Communism:
 in France, 129
 in Germany, 247
 in Hungary, 251
 in Russia, 244
 See also Marx
Communist Party, Manifesto of the, 129
Conference:
 Disarmament, 266
 Economic, 266
Congress System to prevent war, 48
 Castlereagh and the, 49
Congress:
 Aix-la-Chapelle, 49
 Berlin, 154
 Co-operative, 201
 Laibach, 50
 Troppau, 50
 Verona, 51
 Vienna, 45
Conscription, 177, 239
Consolidated Trades Union, foundation of, 73
Constantine, King of Greece, 241
Convicts transported to colonies, 100
Conway, River, suspension bridge over, 22
Cook, A. J., 272

Cook, Captain, claims Australia for England, 100
Co-operative Movement, 35, 41, 200, 201, 210
Corn Laws, 30, 53, 90
Cosgrave, William, 179, 180
Cotton, 19, 21, 22, 34, 126, 135, 284
Crabbe, George, on the workhouse, 16
Crete rebels against Turkey, 220
seized by Egypt, 59
Crimea, campaign in the, 122
Criminal Code, reforms in, 88
Cromer, Lord, work in Egypt, 162, 188
Crompton, Samuel, invents spinning mule, 19
Crystal Palace built, 131
Cuba seized by America, 218
Cunard Line founded, 132
Curzon, Lord, and Turkish peace terms, 255
Czecho-Slovakia, 247, 259, 262, 265

DAIMLER MOTOR-CARS, 195
Dalhousie, Lord, Governor-General of India, 108
Dardanelles, attack on, 237
Darwin, Charles, theory of the origin of species, 145
Davis, Thomas, 179
Davitt, Michael, organizes the Land League, 172
Dawes Plan for reparations, 261, 262
Death penalty reduced, 88
De Beers Diamond Company, 183
de Lesseps, Ferdinand, builds Suez Canal, 150
Derbyshire insurrection, 40
de Valera, Eamonn, 177, 179, 180
Diamonds, 158, 183
Dickens, Charles, 145
Disarmament Conference at Geneva, 266
Disestablishment of the Irish Church, 171
Disraeli, Benjamin. *See* Beaconsfield, Lord
Disraeli, Isaac, 82
Dreadnought type of battleship, 227
Duffy, Gavan, Jun., 178
Duffy, Gavan, Sen., 170
Dundonald, Lord, 54, 59
Dunedin, N.Z., Scottish colony at, 103
Durham, Lord, 104, 106

EAST INDIA COMPANY, 106 *et seq.*
Eastern question, 57 *et seq.*, 120, 152

Ebert, President, 247
Education:
  cost of, 289
  elementary, in 1833, 67–8
    in 1870, 140
    in 1880, 141
    in 1891, 141
    in 1902, 211
  higher, 68–9, 197
  in Ireland, 170
Educational reforms, 140
Edward VII, King of England, 194, 225
Edward VIII, King of England, 190
Edwards, Government spy, 41
Egypt, bankruptcy of, 151
  British garrison in, 280
  campaign against Greece, 59
  end of dual control in, 161
  independence of, 280
  modernization of, under Mehemet Ali, 59
  national revolt in, 161
  under British rule, 162, 188
Elder Dempster Shipping Company, 144
Eldon, Lord, Chancellor, 39
Electricity applied to industry, 195
  to telephone and lighting, 145
Elgin, Lord, Governor-General of Canada, 105, 109
Elliot, Major Walter, 278
Emigration to the colonies, 101
  to the United States, 114
Engels, Friedrich, and Communism, 129
  on Irishmen, 85
Engineers, Amalgamated Society of, 202, 207
Entente between France and Russia, 220
  Triple, 226
Epping Forest, 149
Eros statue in Piccadilly Circus, 100
Estonia, new State of, 259
Evangelicals, 35, 103
Exports from United Kingdom, 133, 135
  in George III's reign, 18
  nature of British, 285

FABIAN SOCIETY, 204, 209
Farmers, post-war distress among, 28, 30
Fascist régime in Italy, 260
Fashoda incident, 220
Feisal, King of Iraq, 280
Fenian Society formed, 171
Ferdinand VII, King of Spain, 51

INDEX

Financial crisis of 1931, 273
  reforms of Peel, 86
  weakness in England, 274
Finland, new State of, 259
Fisher, Admiral, 227
Fitzgerald, Vesey, 169
Fitzherbert, Mrs., married to George IV, 37
Foch, Marshal, 246, 247
France:
  and Eastern Question, 59, 60, 121–2, 151, 220
  and England, 139, 225–6
  and Empire, 100, 119, 188, 258
  in 1815, 46, 224
  in 1830, 61
  in 1848, 117
  in 1870, 128–9
  industries of, 182, 262
  Spanish succession for, 117
  supports Belgian rising, 61
Francis II, Emperor of Austria, supports France, 51
Franz Ferdinand, Archduke, assassinated at Sarajevo, 229
Frederick, Duke of York, 38
Frederick William III, King of Prussia, 45, 51
Free Trade, abandoned in England, 193, 276
  Gladstone an advocate of, 138
  introduced in England, 52, 92
  not adopted by Colonies, 191
  policy of, 91
  versus Tariff Reform, 191
French, General Sir John, and the Irish question, 175
Frere, Sir Bartle, 158
Friendly Societies, 41, 150, 200
Frost, John, Chartist, 77

GALLIPOLI, campaign in, 237
Game Laws, 15
Gas in warfare, 236
Gas Workers' and General Labourers' Union, 205
Gaskell, Mrs., 84
Genoa given to Sardinia, 46
George III, King of England, 13, 14, 18, 37, 100
George IV, King of England, 37, 38, 169
George V, King of England, 175, 214
Germany and the League of Nations, 256, 262, 266
  African possessions of, 188
  after the Vienna Settlement, 46
  alliance with Austria and Italy, 220

Germany—*contd.*
  and the Great War, 232–49
  civil war in, 251
  declares war on Russia and France, 230
  defeats Serbia, 239
  dumping of goods in England by, 192
  fight for national unity, 126
  France's demands on, for peace terms, 251
  health insurance system in, 213
  Heligoland ceded to, 218
  Hitler's National-Socialist régime in, 264
  industrial development, 182, 221, 222, 223
  losses under peace terms, 252, 258
  need for navy and colonies, 221, 223, 224, 227
  occupies Kiaochou, 218
  population of, 223
  post-war unemployment in, 265
  risings of 1830, 62
  Weimar Republic, 259, 261, 263
Giffen, Robert, 215
Gilbert, W. S., 196
Girls' Public Day School Trust, 197
Girton College founded, 197
Gladstone, William Ewart:
  career of, 137–9
  death of, 188
  first Ministry (1868–74), 140–2, 148
  second Ministry (1880–85), 159–64
  Irish policy of, 164–5, 172–4
  Married Women's Property Act, 197
Gold discovered in Australia, 89, 113
  in California, 89
  in South Africa, 89, 184
  Standard, explanation of, 270
    England abandons, 275
    in 1821, 87
  world-supply increased, 89
Goldschmidt banking house, 55
Goldsmith, Oliver, 31
Good Hope, Cape of, retained by England, 49
Gordon, General, in Sudan Expedition, 163
Gough, General, 175, 246
Grand Junction Canal, 23
Grant, Captain, discovery of, 156
Grattan and Catholic Emancipation in Ireland, 169
Great Eastern built, 132

INDEX

Great War:
  Allied offensive in, 240
  (1914–18), causes of, 217 *et seq.*
  cost of, 248
  course of, 232 *et seq.*
Great Western Railway, 132
Greece, alliance with Bulgaria and Serbia, 229
  given Thrace and Smyrna, 255
  independence of, 57 *et seq.*
  joins the Allies, 241
  war against Turkish Nationalists, 255
Grey, Earl, Whig Prime Minister, 63–6
Grey, Sir Edward, 230, 236
Griffith, Arthur, 178, 179

HAGUE, Conference at, 220
  Permanent Court of International Justice at, 256
Haig, Earl, 242, 243
Haldane, Lord, 235
Halévy, Elie, on the National Debt, 29
  on Ramsay MacDonald, 208
Hankey, Sir Maurice, 242
Hardie, Keir, on Socialism, 207
Hardinge, Lord, Governor-General of India, 108
Hargreaves, Richard, invents spinning-machine, 19
Haynau, General, 118, 120
Health Insurance, cost of, 289
  Services, 290
Heligoland, 49, 218
Hicks, Colonel, 163
Hill, Rowland, introduces Penny Postage, 72
Hitler, Adolf, 264
Holy Alliance, 48
Holy Sepulchre, 121
Holland refuses to remove restrictions on shipping, 52
  sells the Cape to England, 99
Home Rule for Ireland, 164, 173 *et seq.*
Hong Kong, acquisition of, 112
House, Colonel, 241
House of Lords deprived of control over Budgets, etc., 214
  powers of, curtailed, 175
Housing, cost of, 289
  municipal, 291
Hudson, George, the "railway king," 95
Hungary, Communism in, 251
  depotism in, 264
  post-war prosperity in, 262

Hungary—*contd.*
  risings of 1848, 118
  signs Treaty of Trianon, 253
Hunt, Henry (Orator), 40, 65
Hunt, Leigh, on George IV, 37
Huskisson, William, 52, 53, 60, 88
Hyndman, Henry Mayers, an apostle of Socialism, 202

IBRAHIM PASHA, campaign against Greece, 59
Immigration, Irish, 84
Imperial Chemical Industries, 222
Imperial Conference of 1926, 282
Imperial Preference. *See* Tariff Reform
Income Tax, abolished in 1816, 29
  reduced by Gladstone, 138
  restored in 1841, 88
Independent Labour Party formed, 206 *et seq.*
India, 106 *et seq.*
  industrial growth of, 265
  Montagu-Chelmsford reforms in, 281
  Mutiny in, 109
  Nationalist Party in, 281
  new Constitution of, 281
  safeguarding route to, 150 *et seq.*
Industry and Tariff Reform, 192
  and death rate, 84
  and the *laisser-faire* policy, 83
  benefit of railways to, 94
  child labour in, 26
  decline in exporting, 284
  development of new types of, 286
  electricity applied to, 195
  Government control of, during the war, 268
  investment in, 134
  Irish peasant labour in, 85
  Macmillan Committee on, 274
  mid-Victorian depression in, 146
  output in mid-Victorian age, 132, 135
  policy of planning in, 276
  State ownership of, 269
  steam-power applied to, 194
  subsidies for, 223
  working hours in, 25
Insurance against sickness, 209, 213
  against unemployment, 209, 213
Inventions, agricultural machinery, 15
  application of electricity to industry, 195
  of steam-power to industry, 194
  Bessemer steel process, 145
  bicycles, 195

INDEX

Inventions—*contd.*
  cold-storage, 191
  conversion of iron into steel, 132, 222
  electric lighting, 145
  internal combustion engine, 195
  locomotive engine, 23, 95
  macadam road surface, 23
  screw propeller, 132
  Singer's sewing-machine, 145
  spinning-machines, 19
  steam engines, 20
  telephones, 145
  war tanks, 236
  weaving-machines, 19
Investment of capital, 134, 136, 293
Ionian Islands retained by England, 49
Iraq, independence of, 280
  under British Mandate, 258
Ireland, 166–81
  emancipation of Catholics, 60, 167, 169
  potato blight in, 85, 92
Irish, effects of the, on England, 86
  journalists support Chartists, 76
Irish Free State, set up, 179
  in 1935, 180
Iron, 21, 22, 132, 145, 148, 222
Isaacs, Barney, 184
Ishmail, Khedive of Egypt, 150, 151
Italy after the Vienna Settlement, 46
  alliance with Germany and Austria, 220
  and the Peace terms, 251
  claims Fiume, 251, 260
  declares war on Austria, 236
  Fascism in, 260
  given Adalia, 255
  industrial growth of, 265
  nationalism in, 46
  post-war unemployment in, 265
  risings of 1830, 62
    of 1848, 118, 124
    of 1859, 124

JAMESON, DR., 184, 185
Japan at war with China, 218
  at war with Russia, 226
  cheap labour in, 193
  first commercial treaty with, 112
  given German Pacific Islands, 258
  invades Manchuria, 266
  Lord Elgin on, 112
Jellicoe, Earl, in battle of Jutland, 240
Jews, 62, 264
Jhansi, Ranee of, 111

Joffre, Marshal, 242
Jones, Sir Alfred, 144, 190
Jones, Henry Arthur, 196

KABUL, military expedition to, 108
Kandahar restored to Afghanistan, 160
  seized by Britain, 155
Kapital, Das (Marx), 129, 203
Kay, John, invents weaving shuttle, 19
Keats, John, 32
Keble, John, and the Oxford Movement, 78
Kenya becomes a Crown Colony, 188
Khartoum, siege of, 163
Khiva captured by Russia, 124
Kiaochou occupied by Germany, 218
Kiel Canal built, 224
Kimberley diamond mines, 158, 183
King's College founded, 69
Kingsley, Charles, 84
Kipling, Rudyard, 182
Kitchener, Earl, and the Fashoda incident, 220
  campaign in the Sudan, 188
  in South African War, 186
  Secretary for War, 235, 239
Korea seized by Japan, 218
Kossuth, Lajos, 118, 120
Krüger, President Paul, 160, 185
Krupp's steel works, 222
Kurds given Eastern Anatolia, 255
Kut, siege of, 237

LABOUR PARTY, 208, 269, 273
Lady Margaret Hall opened, 197
Ladysmith, relief of, 186
Laing, Alexander Gordon, 155
Laisser-faire, policy of, 80, 81, 91, 92
  Beaconsfield on results of, 83
  end of, 275, 286
Lamartine and the French Revolution, 117
Lancashire:
  Egyptian cotton exported to, 188
  fustian manufacture in, 18
  machinery wrecking in, 39
  See Cotton
Lamb, Charles, on George IV, 37
Lancaster, Joseph, 68
Land League of Irish Farmers, 172
Latvia, new State of, 259
Lausanne, Treaty of, 1923, 255
Law, Andrew Bonar, 269
Lawrence, Colonel, 246

INDEX

League of Nations, 255–8, 262, 282
Lecky, Wm. E. H., on invasion of Ireland, 166
Lenin, 244, 259
Leopold I, King of the Belgians, 62, 188
Liberalism fails in Italy, 260
    Gladstone the leader of, 165
    Holy Alliance opposition to, 258
    ideal of, 50
    in Versailles Settlement, 259
    triumphant in England, 209, 211
Light Brigade, charge of the, 122
Ligne, Prince de, 45
Lincoln, Abraham, President of the United States, 125
Lithuania, new State of, 257, 259
Liverpool, Lord, Prime Minister, 38
Livingstone, David, explorations of, 156
Lloyd George, David:
    and the Irish question, 178
    Chancellor of the Exchequer, 212
    Fourth Reform Bill of, 228
    Minister of Munitions, 242
    on the Agadir incident, 227
    Prime Minister, 251, 252, 268
Lloyds Bank, 56
Lo Bengula, Matebele King, 184
Local Government, 71, 210, 289
    cost of, 291
    functions of, 290, 292
Locarno Conference, 1925, 262
London County Council, 290
London Match Girls' strike, 205
London Passenger Transport Board, 278
London School of Tropical Medicine, 190
London Tailors' Union, 202
London Working Men's Association, 75
Londonderry, Lord, attack on, 66
Lorraine annexed by Prussia, 128
    returned to France, 252
Louis XVIII, King of France, 46, 61
Louis Philippe, King of France, 61, 115–17
Lovett, William, founds London Working Men's Association, 75
Lower Burma annexed, 108
Luddites, risings of, 39
Ludendorff, General, 231, 246
Lugard, Lord, 282
Lusitania sunk by submarine, 237
Lytton, Bulwer, 155
Lytton, Lord, Viceroy of India, 155

MACADAM, JOHN, inventor of road surface, 22
MacArthur, John, 113
Macaulay, Thomas, *History of England*, 146
Macaulay, Zachary, as reformer, 36
Macclesfield silk industry, 52
MacDonald, Ramsay:
    in early days of Socialism, 206, 207
    leads Labour Government of 1923, 269
    National Prime Minister, 274
McDonough, Thomas, 176
Mackenzie, William Lyon, 104
Macmillan Committee on Finance and Industry, 274
MacNeill, Eoin, 176
Mafeking, siege of, 186
Magyar risings, 118
Malta controlled by British Colonial Office, 283
    retained by England, 49
Malthus, Robert, economic theories of, 80
Manchester, death rate in, 84
    industrial quarters in, 25
    Massacre, 41
    School of reformers, 91, 139
Manchuria invaded by Japan, 266
Mandate system, 257
Mann, Tom, Socialist leader, 206
Manners, Lord John, 82
Manning, Cardinal, 78, 79
Maoris of New Zealand, 103
Marketing Acts, 279
Marx, Karl, *Das Kapital* of, 129, 203, 204, 259
Matabeleland, capital of, captured, 184
Maude, General Sir Stanley, 246
May Committee on National Expenditure, 274
Mazzini, Giuseppi, 118
Mechanic's Institute founded, 68
Meerut, Indian Mutiny begins at, 110
Mehemet Ali, Pasha of Egypt, 59, 116, 162
Melbourne, Lord, Prime Minister, 72
    action against agricultural rioters, 43
    and Queen Victoria, 77
    and the Tolpuddle Martyrs, 74
Memel-land seized by Lithuania, 257
Menai Straits, suspension bridge over, 22

INDEX

Mental hospitals, 290
  treatment, cost of, 289
Mercantilism, theory of, 51
Mesopotamia, campaign in, 237. *See* Iraq
Methodism, progress of, 35
Metropolitan Water Board, 278
Metternich, Prince, 45, 46, 61, 115, 118
Mexico, independence of, 55
Middle-classes, desire Liberalism and Nationalism, 50, 61 *et seq.*, 118, 142, 197, 209
Midland Bank, 56
Mid-Victorian era, 131 *et seq.*
Mill, John Stuart, 145, 198
Milner, Lord, 185, 242
Miners, cut in wages of, 272
  strike of, 215
  Union of, 269
Missionary work, 36, 103, 107
Moldavia, Russian army in, 121
Moltke, General, 233
Monroe Doctrine, 54
Montagu-Chelmsford reforms in India, 281
Montenegro, risings in, 57
Morea overrun by Egyptians, 59
  Egyptians driven out of, 60
Morocco, 225, 226, 227
Morris, William, 203
Mosul, oil companies in, 280
Motor-car industry, 286
Motor-cars, early types of, 195
Murray, John, publisher, 82
Murray River, exploration of, 101
Mussolini, Benito, sets up Fascism in Italy, 260
Mustapha Kemal, 239, 255

NAGPORE comes under British rule, 109
Nana Sahib, conqueror of Cawnpore, 110
Napier, Sir Charles, conquers Scinde, 108
  on the Chartists, 76
Napier, Sir Robert, 156
Naples, revolt against Bourbons in, 50
Napoleon I, Emperor of France, 119
  and sale of wheat, 30
  Hundred Days return of, 46
Napoleon III, Emperor of France, 119
  and Italian nationalism, 46, 124
  and nationalization of schools, 67
  and the Franco-Prussian War, 128, 129

Napoleon III—*contd.*
  and the Holy Sepulchre, 121
  and the Suez Canal, 150
Nash, John, architect, 37, 84
National Debt, Cobbett on, 33
  in 1815, 28
  post-war increase in, 249
National Government of 1931, 274
  policy of, 276
  trade agreements of, 276
National Provincial Bank, 56
Nationalists, aims of, 50
New Brunswick becomes self-governing, 105
New Harmony Village, 35
New South Wales, 103, 105
New World, creation of new republics in, 53
New Zealand becomes self-governing, 105
  commercial development of, 114
  first British settlement in, 103
  meat trade with, 191
New Zealand Company founded, 103
Newcastle, Duke of, 66
Newfoundland controlled by British Commissions, 283
  fishing rights off, 46
Newman, Cardinal, 78, 79
Nicholas I, Tsar of Russia, 34, 61, 114, 115
  and the Eastern question, 120
  death of, 123
Nicholas II, Tsar of Russia, calls Hague Conference, 220
Nicolson, Sir John, on Indian mutineers, 110
Niger, River, exploration of, 155
Nigeria becomes a Crown Colony, 188
  Indirect Rule in, 282
Nightingale, Florence, 123
Nile, River, damming of, 188
  exploration of, 155, 156
Nivelle, Marshal, 242
North London Collegiate School for Girls, 197
Northern Ireland, counties of, 179
Nova Scotia becomes self-governing, 105
Nyasaland becomes part of British Empire, 218

OASTLER denounces Poor Law, 75
O'Brien, Bronterre, 76
O'Brien, Smith, 170

INDEX

O'Connell, Daniel, and repeal of the Union Act, 170
    fights for Catholic Emancipation, 169
O'Connor, Feargus, 76, 93
Officers' Training Corps started, 229
Oil, 195, 280
Old Age Pensions, 212, 289
Oliver, Government spy, 40
Opium War of 1842, 112
Orlando, Signor, and Peace terms, 251, 252
Orphans' Pensions, 289
O'Shea, Mrs. Kitty, 174
Ottawa, Imperial Conference at, 265
Owen, Robert, as reformer, 34, 36, 74, 199
    champions Co-operative Societies, 42
    founder of Consolidated Trades Union, 73
Oxford Movement, 78
Oxford University, improved education at, 69
    women's colleges at, 197

PACIFICO, DON, 120
Palestine under British Mandate, 258
Palmerston, Lord, and Belgian independence, 61, 62
    and the American Civil War, 126
    and the Eastern question, 121, 122
    and the Schleswig-Holstein question, 127
    career of, 116
    dismissal of, 120
    foreign policy of, 116, 117, 119, 124
    Home Secretary, 122
    Prime Minister, 123
    resignation of, 60
Panama Canal, 218
Pankhurst, Mrs., 228
Paper, import duty on, abolished, 138
Papineau, Louis Joseph, 104
Paris, barricades in, 117
    Commune, 129 et seq., 203
    Peace of, 124
Parish Councils, 290
    relief, 16
Park, Mungo, explorations of, 155
Parma given to Empress Marie Louise, 46
Parnell, Charles Stuart, 172, 173, 174
Paxton, Joseph, 131
Pearse, Patrick, 176

Peel, Sir Robert, 60
    and Ireland, 60, 170
    and the Corn Laws, 92
    becomes Prime Minister, 77
    death of, 97, 131
    financial reforms of, 86 et seq.
    police force created by, 88
    reform of the Criminal Code, 88
Pensions for aged, 212
    for orphans, 289
    for widows, 289
People's Charter, six points of, 75
Persia, independence of, 280
Peterloo (Manchester Massacre), 41, 199
Phillip, Captain, reaches Botany Bay, 100
Philosophical Radicals, 79
Phœnix Park murder, 173
Piacenza given to Empress Marie Louise, 46
Picketing, legality of peaceful, 150
Piedmont combined with Savoy, 48
Pieter's Mill, battle of, 186
Pinero, Sir Arthur, 196
Pitt, William, the Elder, 51
Pitt, William, the Younger, and Catholic Emancipation, 167
    efforts for industrial reform, 52
Place, Francis, 42, 43, 65, 75, 101
Plebiscite, definition of, 252
Plimsoll, Samuel, 150
Poaching, penalties for, 15
Poland annexed by Russia, 46
    invaded by Russia, 62
    nationalist revolt in, 62
    new State of, 257, 259, 262, 264, 265
    Upper Silesia given to, 257
Police force in London, 88
    services, 291
Polish Corridor, 253
Political Economists, aims of, 79 et seq., 88
Political Register produced by Cobbett, 33
Poor Law Amendment Act, 69, 70, 73, 79, 292
    Commission, 70, 213
    Guardians, loans to, 213
    Oastler's denunciation of, 85
Poor Relief, cost of, 289
    municipal provision of, 291
    reforms in, 69
Popes, and educational reform, 61
    and temporal power, 62, 128
Population, Malthus's Essay on, 80
    of Great Britain, 16, 79, 283
Port Arthur occupied by Russia, 218
Port of London Authority, 278

INDEX

Portugal, colonies of, 53
  despotism in, 115
  fleet defeated, 54
Postage, penny, 72, 73
Prester John, 155
Printers' Union, 201
Punjab, British control of, 108
Pusey, Edward, and the Oxford Movement, 78

QUEEN'S UNIVERSITY, Ireland, 170
Queensland becomes self-governing, 105

RADICALS, 32 *et seq.*, 65, 79
Radio industry, 286
Raglan, Lord, 122
Rahman, Abdur, 160
Railway Companies and public utility, 278
Railwaymen's Union, 269
  strike of, 215
Railways, Berlin to Baghdad, 225
  built in Europe, 136
  built in India, 108
  early days of, 23, 94, 95
  first underground, 195
  in South Africa, 190
  State control of, in Germany, 223
Rates, 18, 291
Rayon industry, 286
Redcliffe, Lord Stratford de, 121
Reform Bill, 1832, 65, 66
  Second, 139
  Third, 164
  Fourth, 228
Regency Period in England, 37
Religion, need for organized, 35
  versus science, 145, 146
Reparations, 253, 261, 265
Rhenish–Westphalian Coal Syndicate, 222
Rhodes, Cecil, and diamond mining, 183
  and gold mining, 184
  becomes Prime Minister of Cape Colony, 184
  encourages Uitlanders to revolt, 185
  imperial projects of, 184, 187
  on the British race, 182
Ricardo, David, economic theories of, 80
Riza Khan, 280
Roads, development of, 22
  macadamization of, 23
  maintenance of, 291
Roberts, Lord, in South African War, 186

Rochdale Equitable Pioneers, 41, 201
Romantics, the, 31
Roman Catholics in Ireland, 167
  in the Holy Land, 121
Rosebery, Lord, leads Liberal Imperialists, 165
Ross, Sir Ronald, discovers malaria germ, 190
Rossa, O'Donovan, 171
Rothschild banking house, 55
Roumania joins the Allies, 241
  risings in, 57
  treaty with France, 262
  withdraws from Great War, 245
Royal Niger Company, 188
Rugby School, 69
Rumbold, Sir Horace, 255
Russell, Lord John, 72
  and Palmerston's policy, 119
  and the American Civil War, 126
  and the Corn Laws, 92
Russia and the Great War, 230, 244 *et seq.*
  alliance proposed between Austria, Prussia and, 48
  with France, 220
  annexes Poland, 46
  anxious to promote Greek independence, 59
  at war with Japan, 226
  Bolsheviks in, 244, 251, 259
  builds Trans-Siberian railway, 160, 220
  campaign against Turkey, 60
  declares war on Turkey, 152
  Entente with France and England, 226
  extends her frontiers towards India, 124
  France declares war on, 122
  import tariffs in, 223
  invades Poland, 62
  liberation of serfs in, 124
  need for checking extension of, 152
  not admitted to League of Nations, 256
  occupies Port Arthur, 218
Russo-Turkish War, 1853, 120

SAAR COALFIELDS, 252
Sailors' mutiny at Invergordon, 275
Sailors' and Firemen's Union strike, 215
St. Arnaud, Marshal J. L. de, 122
St. Germain-en-Laye, Treaty of, 253
St. Lucia retained by England, 49

INDEX

Salisbury, Lord, and Armenian massacres, 220
  and social reforms, 210
  refuses treaties with Germany, 221
  resignation of, 281
  sets up Board of Education, 211
  "splendid isolation," policy of, 183, 217
Salonika, Allied base at, 241
Salt Union founded, 222
Salvation Army, founded, 196
Samarkand, captured by Russia, 124
San Stefano, Treaty of, 154
Sarajevo, incident, 229
Sardinia, formation of Kingdom of, 48
  King of, leads revolt against Austria, 118
  obtains Genoa, 46
Schleswig-Holstein question, 127
Schlieffen, General, 232
School Boards established, 140
  abolished, 211
Science *versus* religion, 145
Scinde, conquest of, 108
Scotland, representation in Parliament, 64
Scotsmen, in Ireland, 166
Scott, Sir Walter, 32, 37, 82
Secret Ballot Act, 141
Seeley, Colonel, and the Irish question, 175
Senior, Prof. Wm. Nassau, 25
Serbia, alliance with Greece and Bulgaria, 229
  Austria tries to annex, 229
  defeated in the Great War, 239
  independent, 57
Shaftesbury, Lord, and Ten-Hour Day Bill, 93
  work for the poor, 199, 200
Shaw, George Bernard, 167, 204
Shelley, Percy Bysshe, 31
Shepstone, Sir Theophilus, 158
Shipbuilding, in Canada, 99, 112
  mid-Victorian slump in, 147
Shipping, decline in British, 267
  industry and tariffs, 192
  growth of, 132, 135
  restrictions removed, 52
Shipwrights, strike of, 43
Sicilies, the Two, given to Ferdinand IV, 46
Siemens, electrical works, 222
Silk, preferential treatment for Indian, 53
Simon, Sir John, on the General Strike, 272
  sent to India, 281

Singer, Isaac Merritt, invents sewing-machine, 145
Slavery, abolition of, 36, 67, 99
Slaves, trade in, 49
Slums, 25, 83, 84, 149, 196, 291
Small-holders, decline of, 14
Smith, Adam, economic theories of, 52
  policy of *laisser-faire*, 276
  Ricardo develops economics of, 80
  Wealth of Nations, 91
Smith, Sydney, 52, 288
  on taxation, 29
  on the Beer Bill, 63
Smuts, General, in South Africa, 187
  in War Cabinet, 242
Smyrna, given to Greece, 255
Soap, import tax on, abolished, 138
Social Democratic Federation formed, 203
  Democrats in Germany, 251
  reforms, Liberal, 209
    of Bismarck, 209
    of Disraeli, 149
  services in England, 289
Socialism, as propounded by the Fabians, 209
  birth of, in England, 202
  first use of the term, 42
  Keir Hardie on, 207
Socialist Party, first English, 203
  in Germany, 203
  resolutions of 1893, 207
South Africa, an independent member of League of Nations, 282
  becomes a Union with Dominion status, 187
  diamond mines in, 184
  gold discovered in, 89
  railways in, 190
  self-governing colonies in, 105
  trade with, 113
  Uitlanders in, 184, 185
  white settlements in, 158
South African War, 1899, 185
South American republics, British money invested in, 137, 293
  British trade with, 55, 56
  founded, 54, 55
  United States trade with, 57
South Australia, becomes self-governing, 105
  colony founded in, 103
Soviet régime in Russia, 244, 259
Spain, at war with America, 218
  colonies of, 53, 54
  despotism in, 115
  Louis Philippe interferes in, 117
  revolt against monarchy, 50, 51

INDEX

Speenhamland scale of relief, 16, 70
Speke, Captain, 156
Spence, Thomas, 40
Spinners, Union of, 42
Spinning, 13, 14, 18, 19, 24
"Splendid isolation" policy, 217
Sport, in late Victorian era, 195
Spring guns, made illegal, 15
Stanley, H. M., 187
   discovers Livingstone, 156
Stanley, Lord, 170
   Colonial Secretary, 103
   on trade with India, 111
Steam-power, introduced, 20
Steamships, introduction of, 134
Steel, conversion of iron into, 132, 145, 222
Stephen, Sir James, 36, 100
Stephens, James, 171
Stephenson, George, railway designs of, 95
Stock Exchange, 136
Strikes, Builders', of 1859, 202
   Dock-workers', 1889, 205
   Engineers', 207
   General, of 1926, 74, 272
   limitation of right of, 42, 272
   London Match Girls', 1888, 205
   Miners', 208, 215, 269
   of 1911 and 1912, 215
   Railway workers', 215, 269
   Sailors' and Firemen's Union, 1911, 215
   Shipwrights', 43
   Trades Union and, 73
   Transport workers', 215, 269
Submarine, warfare, 236, 242, 243
Sudan, conquest of, 188
   national revolt in, 162
Suez Canal, 150, 151, 280
Suffragettes, militant, 227
Sugar, 18, 52
Sunday Schools, 36
Surtees, Robert Smith, 23
Suttee, custom of, abolished, 107
Swimming pools, maintenance of, 290
Switzerland, recognized as independent State, 46

TAIPING REBELLION in China, 163
Talleyrand, Charles Maurice de, 46
Tamworth Manifesto of 1834, 88
Tanganyika, under British Mandate, 258, 282
   Lake, discovery of, 156
Tanks, in warfare, 236, 243
Tariff Reform, 53, 191, 192, 266
Tasmania, becomes self-governing, 105

Taxation, Cobbett on, 33
   in early 19th century, 29
Taxes, 29, 33, 51, 52, 289
Tea, import duty on, abolished, 138
Telegraph, introduced into India, 108
Telephone, introduced, 145
Telford, James, road building of, 22
Tennyson, Alfred, Poet Laureate, 145
Territorial Army, formed, 229
Thackeray, William Makepeace, 145
Theodore, Negus of Abyssinia, 156
Thierry, Baron de, 103
Thistlewood, Arthur, 41
Thomas, Gilchrist, 222
Thorne, Will, 205
Thrace, given to Greece, 255
Tillett, Ben, leads dock-workers' strike, 205
Timbuktu, search for, 155
Tobago, retained by England, 49
Togoland, under British and French Mandate, 258
Tollemache Bank, 30
Tolpuddle Martyrs, 74
Tone, Wolfe, 167
Town planning, 291, 292
Toynbee Hall, founded, 196
Tractarians, 79
Trade Cycle, 90
Trade Unions, Annual Congress of, 206, 208, 272
   development of, 200
   foundation of, 73
   given legal protection, 43, 202
   Government opposition to, 201
   origin of, 42
Trams, first electric, 195
Transport, by canal, 23
   by railway, 23
   services, 291
Trans-Siberian Railway, built, 160, 220
Transvaal, independence of, 100, 181
   Jameson Raid on, 185
Treaties, Adrianople, 60
   Anglo-French *Entente*, 1904, 225
   Berlin, 1878, 226
   Brest-Litovsk, 1917, 245
   commercial, with France, 139
   Franco-Russia *Entente*, 1894, 220
   French post-war, 262
   Lausanne, 1923, 255
   London, 1841, 116
   1915, 236
   Paris, 1856, 152
   Peace of Paris, 124
   St. Germain-en-Laye, 1919, 253

Treaties—*contd.*
  San Stefano, 154
  Sèvres, 1920, 255
  Trianon, 1920, 253
  Triple Alliance, 220
  Triple *Entente*, 1907, 226
  Unkiar-Skelessi, 1833, 116
  Versailles, 1919, 252
  Vienna, 1814, 45
    1815, 48
  Vienna Congress, 117
  Waitangi, 1840, 103
Trevithick, Robert, 95
Trianon, Treaty of, 253
Trinidad, retained by England, 49
Triple Alliance, 1882, 220
Triple *Entente*, 1907, 226
Trotsky, Communist leader, 244, 245
Truck, 86
Turkey, and the Treaty of London, 116
  attacked by Russia, 121
  Crete rebels against, 220
  defeats Greece, 255
  driven from Baghdad, 245
    from Palestine, 246
  fleet defeated at Sinope, 121
  Nationalism in, 57
  new treaty offered to, 255
  offensive against, in 1915, 237
  proposed partition of, 120
  repudiates Peace Treaty, 255
  Russia declares war on, 152
  Russian campaign against, 60
  signs Treaty of Sèvres, 255
  surrenders in 1918, 247
  Turkish atrocities in Bulgaria, 152
  Empire, territory of, 57
  massacre of archbishops, 59
    of Armenians, 220
Turnpikes, 22
Typhus, deaths from, 84

U-BOAT campaign, 236, 242, 243
Uganda, becomes part of British Empire, 218
Uitlanders in South Africa, 184, 195
Ulster, Civil War threatened in, 175
  not included in Irish Free State, 179
  Scotsmen settle in, 166
  tenant right in, 172
Unemployment, " dole," 268
  emigration to colonies as relief for, 101
  in 1815, 28
  insurance, 209, 213
    cost of, 289

Unemployment—*contd.*
  post-war, 265, 268, 273, 279
  relief, cuts in, 274, 275
  Speenhamland system of relief for, 70
Unionist Party, formed, 164
United Empire Loyalists, 99, 104
United States of America, 55
  at war with Spain, 218
  British emigration to, 114, 171
  Civil War in, 125
  dumping of goods in England, 192, 193
  enter the Great War, 243
  industrialization of, 182
  post-war wealth of, 262
  refuses to join League of Nations, 256
  trade with South America, 57
University College, founded, 69
University Colleges, in Ireland, 170
University, grants, provision of, 291
Universities, reforms in, 69
Unkiar-Skelessi, Treaty of, 116
Urban District Councils, 290
Utilitarians, aims of, 79

VAN DIEMEN'S LAND. *See* Tasmania
Venetia, annexed to Austria, 46
Venezuela, independence of, 54
Venizelos, M., 241
Verdun, battle of, 239
Versailles, Settlement a failure, 264
  compared with Vienna Settlement, 258
  ideals of, 279
  Treaty of, 252
Victor Emmanuel, King of Italy, 125
Victoria, Australia, becomes self-governing, 105
Victoria, Queen of England, 62, 77, 94
  and Palmerston's policy, 119
  and Peel, 86
  death of, 193
  Jubilees of, 194
  marriage of, 77
  on women's rights, 198
Victoria Nyanza, Lake, 156
Vienna, Congress, 45, 117
  Settlement, a bar to Nationalism, 50
  compared with Versailles Settlement, 258
Vincent, Harry, Chartist, 77
von Bülow, Prince, and the Morocco treaty, 225
von Kluck, General, 233
von Scheer, Admiral, 240
von Tirpitz, Admiral, 228

INDEX

Wafd in Egypt, 280
Wakefield, Edward Gibbon, 101 *et seq.*, 113
Wales, 77, 284
War, code for conduct of, 221
    Congress System to prevent, 48
    debts, payment of, 271
    Loan, reduction of interest on, 279
    Pensions, cost of, 289
    reparations, 253, 261
Wars, Afghanistan, 1839, 108
    against the Maoris, 103
    America and Spain, 1898, 218
    American Civil War, 126
    Balkan, 1913, 229
    Boer, 160, 185
    China and Japan, 1894, 218
    ending in 1815, 13
    Franco-Prussian, 128
    French Civil War, 129
    German Civil War, 251
    Great War, 217 *et seq.*, 232 *et seq.*
    Hundred Years, 221
    Italian independence, 124
    Italy and Abyssinia, 258, 266
    Napoleonic, 28
    Opium War of 1842, 112
    Prussian-Austrian, 127
    Russia and Japan, 226
    Russia and Turkey, 120
    South African, 1899, 185
    Turkey and Greece, 255
    Zulu, 158
Water-power, introduction of, 19
Water supply, 290
Watts, James, invents steam engine, 20
Wealth of Nations (Adam Smith), 52, 91
Weavers, Union of, 42
Weaving, machinery for, 18
Webb, Beatrice, 209
Webb, Sydney, and the Fabian Society, 209
Wedgwood Works, building of, 18
Wei-hai-wei, occupied by Britain, 218
Wellington, Duke of, 94
    and Catholic Emancipation, 88
    becomes Prime Minister and Foreign Secretary, 60
    mob smash windows of, 66
    on Peel, 86
    resignation of, 63
Wellington, N.Z., British Colony at, 103
West Indies, French possessions in, 46
    sugar from, 18
    trade of, 98

Westminster Bank, 57
Wheat, prices in 1815, 30
Wilberforce, William, 100
    and abolition of slavery, 67
    as reformer, 36
Wilde, Oscar, 196
Wilhelm II, Emperor of Germany, abdication of, 247
    and the Berlin-Baghdad railway, 225
    and the Suez Canal, 151
    goes to Tangier, 225
    strengthens German navy, 224
William IV, King of England, 38, 66, 77
Wilson, Woodrow, President, as mediator in the Great War, 241
    at Peace Conference, 251
    ideals of, 250, 279
Window tax, abolished, 52
Windsor Castle, rebuilt, 37
Wines, reduction of tax on, 52
Wolseley, Sir Garnet, 161, 164
Women, and the vote, 197, 228
    claim legal right to their property, 197
    emancipation of, 196
    professional careers of, 197
Wood, Matthew, Lord Mayor of London, 40
Wool, trade with the colonies, 113
Woollen goods, export of, 135
    industry, development of, 22
    in reign of George III, 18
    mills, erection of, 20
Wordsworth, William, Poet Laureate, 32, 145
Workhouse relief, 16, 70
Working class and the industrial revolution, 199
    and the Reform Bill, 65
    conditions, Engels on, 85
    Disraeli's reforms for, 150
    education for, 211
    eight-hour day for, 205
    improved conditions of, in mid-Victorian era, 142
    insurance against sickness, 209
    International Labour Office to protect interests of, 255
    man, enfranchisement of, 139
    Movement, 199—216
    organizations, origin of, 41
    Owen's views on, 36
    reforms for, 73
    rioting in reign of William IV, 39
    wages, in the nineties, 215
    Wilberforce's view on, 36

Working Men, London Association of, 75
Wren, Christopher, 84

YORKSHIRE, cloth manufacture in, 18
 machinery wrecking in, 39
 mining in, 21
 woollen industry, progress of, 52
Young English Group, 82, 149

Young Ireland Party formed, 170
Yugo-Slavia a republic, 259
 despotism in, 264
 post-war conditions in, 262
 treaty with France, 262
Yukon, gold discovered in, 89

ZAGLUL, 280

ST. CLEMENT DANES
GRAMMAR SCHOOL